SOVEREIGNTY
AND DOMINION

Volume 2

SOVEREIGNTY AND DOMINION

AN ECONOMIC COMMENTARY ON GENESIS

Volume 2

GARY NORTH

POINT FIVE PRESS
Dallas, Georgia

Sovereignty and Dominion: An Economic Commentary on Genesis
Volume 2
Previously title: *The Dominion Covenant: Genesis*

Copyright © 1982, 1987, 2012, 2020 by Gary North

Published by
Point Five Press
P.O. Box 2778
Dallas, Georgia 30132

Typesetting by Kyle Shepherd

TABLE OF CONTENTS

Volume 1

APPENDIX A

FROM COSMIC PURPOSELESSNESS
TO HUMANISTIC SOVEREIGNTY

Through billions of years of blind mutation, pressing against the shifting walls of their environment, microbes finally emerged as man. We are no longer blind; at least we are beginning to be conscious of what has happened and of what may happen. From now on, evolution is what we make it.

So wrote Hermann J. Muller, the 1946 Nobel Prize winner in physiology.[1] Muller stated his position quite clearly. His statement of faith is almost universally believed within scientific and intellectual circles today. The idea is commonplace, part of the "conventional wisdom" of the age. Man will henceforth direct the evolutionary process. But who will represent man in this cosmic endeavor? Who will direct the process? Answer: Darwinian scientists.

A. The Legacy of Hermann Muller

Muller's thesis regarding a new, man-directed evolution is worth considering in detail. It provides insight into the underlying vision and motivation of modern evolutionary science. The goal is the creation of a new humanity. Man, meaning scientific man, becomes the creator.

Muller was a disciple of Francis Galton, Darwin's cousin. Like Galton, he believed in eugenics: the scientific manipulation of human

---

1. Hermann J. Muller, "One Hundred Years Without Darwinism Are Enough," *The Humanist*, XIX (1959); reprinted in Philip Appleman (ed.), *Darwin: A Norton Critical Edition* (New York: Norton, 1970), p. 570. I first saw an incomplete version of this quotation in an article by Elisabeth Mann Borghese, "Human Nature Is Still Evolving," in *The Center Magazine* (March/April 1973), a publication of the now defunct Center for the Study of Democratic Institutions, a Santa Barbara humanist think-tank which was influential in the 1950s and 1960s. It was founded by Robert Maynard Hutchins. My point: this is a standard idea among liberals and humanists.

genetic inheritance. For decades, he was America's leading scientific theorist of eugenics. He won his Nobel Prize for his research on how radiation affects genes.

Unlike his peers, he was consistent in his proclamation of scientific planning of the species. He was also a dedicated Marxist. He fled the United States in 1932 because of his sponsorship of a college student Marxist group at the University of Texas. He went to work at the Rockefeller-funded eugenical Institute for Brain Research in Germany even after Hitler came to power in March of 1933. Muller was technically a Jew; his mother was Jewish, which, by Rabbinical law, made him a Jew. Still, he remained in Germany through 1933. In June of 1933, he wrote to the Rockefeller Foundation, which funded the Institute's work, asking it to pressure the Nazi government to keep the Institute's work going under its director, who was being threatened with dismissal. The Nazi government did decide to allow him remain in charge.[2] Muller continued to do research in Germany that advanced the cause of eugenics.

The Nazis soon passed eugenic laws mandating sterilization. Muller decided that it was no longer safe for him in Germany. He did not leave out of opposition to Nazi eugenics policies. He moved to the Soviet Union from 1934 until 1937, when Stalin found out that he did not follow Lysenko's theory of the inheritance of acquired characteristics.

1. A Genetic New World Order

His 1935 book, *Out of the Night*, detailed his vision of a new genetic world order.

> The child on the average stands half-way, in its inherited constitution, between its father and the average of the general population, and so it would be theoretically possible even now—were it not for the shackles upon human wills in our society—so to order our reproduction that a considerable part of the very next generation might average, in its hereditary physical and mental constitution, half-way between the average of the present population and that of our greatest living men of mind, body, or "spirit" (as we choose). At the same time, it can be reckoned, the number of men and women of great though not supreme ability would thereby be increased several hundred fold. It is easy to show that in the· course of a paltry century or two (paltry, considering the advance in question) it would be possible for the majority of the population to become of the innate qual-

---

2. Edwin Black, *War on the Weak: Eugenics and the American Campaign to Create a Master Race* (New York: Four Walls Eight Windows, 2003), pp. 302–3.

ity of such men as Lenin, Newton, Leonardo, Pasteur, Beethoven, Omar Khayyam, Pushkin, Sun Yat Sen, Marx.[3]

How can this be accomplished? By sperm banks. Through artificial insemination, "a vast number of children of the future generation should inherit the characteristics of some transcendentally estimable man...."[4] Dare we say it? A superman will lead to the creation of a master race: the universal human race.

His view of eugenics was messianic. He announced that "we should be able to raise virtually all mankind to or beyond levels heretofore attained only by the most remarkably gifted."[5] He assured his readers that this can be done voluntarily. This can be done, on the one hand, by furthering birth control, providing low-cost abortions on demand, and universal child care outside the home, "with more motherly mothers, and hence more brotherly brothers."[6] This will require the end of capitalism: "the change from the profit system to socialization...."[7] There will be some compulsion, of course. Science requires compulsion "in a negative role, as a potential force standing ready only to prevent exploitation of the enhanced possibilities of multiplication by unduly egoistic, aggressive, or paranoid individuals."[8] He did not use the words "forced sterilization." In 1935, there was no need. Forced sterilization laws had been on the books ever since 1907, when Indiana passed the first one.

Muller believed in government planning of the economy and the scientific elite's planning of the races. He is the consummate model of the scientist who used Darwinism to promote the sovereignty of the state. (He was among the most respected evolutionists of his generation.)

It might be objected that he was a lone wolf who was not representative of Darwinian geneticists in his era. With respect to his overt Marxism, this is correct. It is not correct with respect to his view of both genetic planning and economic planning.

2. The Geneticists' Manifesto

In August 1939, in the week before World War II began, a meeting of geneticists was held in Edinburgh: the Seventh International

---

3. Hermann Muller, *Out of the Night* (New York: Vanguard, 1935), pp. 112–13.
4. *Ibid.*, p. 111.
5. *Ibid.*, p. 113.
6. *Ibid.*, p. 106.
7. *Ibid.*, p. 107.
8. *Ibid.*, p. 118.

Congress of Genetics. World-famous geneticists from around the world attended. In response to a question cabled by a non-attendee, ("How can the world's population be improved most effectively genetically?")a group of the attendees produced a detailed report.[9] It became known as the Geneticists' Manifesto. The paper announced six principles.

> 1. There is no valid way to assess the "intrinsic worth of different individuals without economic and social conditions which provide approximately equal opportunities for all members of society instead of stratifying them from birth into classes with widely different privileges."[10] [This means: (1) there are valid, though unmentioned ways to do this; (2) civil governments must create the proper equal-opportunity society.–G.N.]

> 2. There must be no race prejudice. "This requires some effective sort of federation of the whole world, based on the common interests of all peoples."[11]

> 3. Children must be raised by parents who have "a very considerable economic security," including education and medical funding. This means a world in which "dwellings, towns and communities are reshaped with the good of children as one of their main objectives."[12]

> 4. There must be birth control, which requires a society in which "the superstitious attitude toward sex and reproduction now prevalent has been replaced by a scientific and social attitude."[13]

> 5. People and the state must recognize biological principles. Heredity and environment are both major factors—factors that "are under the potential control of man and admit of unlimited but interdependent progress."[14] This requires "some kind of conscious guidance of selection."[15]

> 6. To guide selection, there must be "an agreed direction for selection to take...." This cannot be accomplished "unless social motives predominate in society. This in turn implies its socialized organization."[16]

This will produce a new world order and a new humanity. Within "a comparatively small number of generations," we are assured, this new era could come into existence, a world in which "everyone might

---

9. On this background, see *Eugenical News* (June 1946), pp. 33–34. The full document was republished. This was the post-War era. The pre-War eugenics movement was fading in popularity, due to Hitler's use of forced sterilization, which gave the practice a bad press. But the laws remained on the books for two more decades.

10. "The 'Geneticists' Manifesto'," *Studies in Genetics: The Selected Papers of H. J. Muller* (Bloomington, Indiana: Indiana University Press, 1962), p. 545. He died in 1967.

11. *Ibid.*, pp. 545–46.

12. *Ibid.*, p. 546.

13. *Idem.*

14. *Idem.*

15. *Ibid.*, p. 547.

16. *Idem.*

look upon 'genius,' combined of course with stability, as his birthright. And, as the course of evolution shows, this would represent no final stage at all, but only an earnest of still further progress in the future."[17]

Who signed this manifesto? Muller, of course, and six others initially. More added their signatures later, for a total of 21, including Julian Huxley, J. B. S. Haldane, C. H. Waddington, and Theodosius Dobzhansky.[18]

B. Man Must Plan

Theodosius Dobzhansky's influence matched Muller's. He taught zoology at Columbia University and several other universities. He concluded his essay, "The Present Evolution of Man," which appeared in the widely read *Scientific American* (September 1960), with these words:

> Yet man is the only product of biological evolution who knows that he has evolved and is evolving farther. He should be able to replace the blind force of natural selection by conscious direction, based on his knowledge of his own nature and on his values. It is as certain that such direction will be needed as it is questionable whether man is ready to provide it. He is unready because his knowledge of his own nature and its evolution is insufficient; because a vast majority of people are unaware of the necessity of facing the problem; and because there is so wide a gap between the way people actually live and values and ideals to which they pay lip service.

Therefore, man must now direct the evolutionary process, but the majority of men will not face up to their responsibilities in this respect. He did not elaborate, but the implication is clear enough: *a minority of men*, who will face up to their responsibilities for directing the evolutionary process, must step in and provide the scientifically required leadership.

In a 1967 book, Dobzhansky discussed the role of the masses. They exist only in order to provide the raw numbers of humans out of whom will arise the elite. "Are the multitudes supererogatory? They may seem so, in view of the fact that the intellectual and spiritual advances are chiefly the works of elites. To a large extent, they are due to an even smaller minority of individuals of genius. The destiny of a vast majority of humans is death and oblivion. Does this majority play any role in the evolutionary advancement of humanity?"

---

17. *Idem.*
18. *Ibid.*, p. 548.

He admitted that the elites need the majority if they themselves are to survive. And the masses provide more than mere "manure in the soil in which are to grow the gorgeous flowers of the elite culture. Only a small fraction of those who try to scale the heights of human achievement arrive anywhere close to the summit. It is imperative that there be a multitude of climbers. Otherwise the summit may not be reached by anybody. The individually lost and forgotten multitudes have not lived in vain, provided they, too, made the effort to climb."[19] It is mankind, a collective whole, that was the focus of his concern, but it is obvious that the elite members are the directing geniuses of the progress of man, as mankind struggles to reach the summit, whatever that may be. "Man is able, or soon will be able, to control his environments successfully. Extinction of mankind could occur only through some suicidal madness, such as an atomic war, or through a cosmic catastrophe."[20] Man, the directing god of evolution, need fear only himself, the new cosmic sovereign, or else some totally impersonal event, such as a supernova. Insofar as personalism reigns, *man is sovereign.*

It should be clear by now that the evolutionist is not humble. He has never viewed man as a helpless, struggling product of chaos. *A cosmic leap of being has taken place.* Dobzhansky spoke of two events of transcendence in the history of natural processes: the origin of life and the origin of man. Man is the second great transcendence. "Only once before, when life originated out of inorganic matter, has there occurred a comparable event."[21] As he wrote, "The origin of life and the origin of man are, understandably, among the most challenging and also the most difficult problems in evolutionary history."[22] The continuity of slow evolutionary change is clearly not an applicable law when these tremendous "leaps in being" occur. In fact, these two remarkable discontinuities are notable only for their magnitude; there have been others, such as the appearance of terrestrial vertebrates from fish-like ancestors.[23]

Nevertheless, the appearance of man was a true revolution: "The biological evolution had transcended itself in the human 'revolution.' A new level of dimension has been reached. The light of the human

---

19. Theodosius Dobzhansky, *The Biology of Ultimate Concern* (New York: New American Library, 1967), p. 132.
20. *Ibid.*, p. 129.
21. Dobzhansky, *Scientific American* (Sept. 1960), p. 206.
22. Dobzhansky, *Biology of Ultimate Concern*, p. 45.
23. *Ibid.*, p. 50.

spirit has begun to shine. The *humanum* is born."[24] His language is unmistakably religious, as well it should be, given his presentation of a distinctly religious cosmology. The post-Darwin evolutionist is no less religious than the Christian creationist. *Evolutionists reverse God's order of creation.* The Christian affirms that a sovereign, autonomous, omnipotent personal God created the universe. The evolutionist insists that a sovereign, autonomous, omnipotent impersonal universe led to the creation (development) of a now-sovereign personal god, mankind.

[handwritten: Elimination of God — Extension of space & time (forward & backward)]

C. Making the Universe Bigger

Central to the task of eliminating God from the universe and time were two important intellectual developments. The first was the extension of space. The second was the extension of time, forward and backward.

1. The Copernican Revolution

The late-medieval and early modern world saw the shattering of the pre-modern world's conception of the size of the universe. One of the standard arguments found in textbook accounts of the history of science is that when Copernicus broke the spell of the older Ptolemaic universe, which had hypothesized the sun and heavenly bodies circling the earth, he somehow diminished the significance of man. Astronomer William Saslaw repeated this standard analysis in a 1972 essay. He wrote, "by diminishing the earth, Copernicus also diminished our own importance to the Universe."[25]

This kind of language goes back to the early years of the Darwinian controversy. Thomas H. Huxley, one of Darwin's earliest defenders, and the most influential promoter of Darwin's gospel in England in the nineteenth century, wrote these words:

> For, as the astronomers discover in the earth no centre of the universe, but an eccentric speck, so the naturalists find man to be no centre of the living world, but one amidst endless modifications of life; and as the astronomer observes the mark of practically endless time set upon the arrangements of the solar system so the student of life finds the records of ancient forms of existence peopling the world for ages, which, in relation to human experi-

---

24. *Ibid.*, p. 58.
25. William C. Saslaw, "An Introduction to the Emerging Universe," in Saslaw and Kenneth C. Jacobs, (eds.), *The Emerging Universe* (Charlottesville: University of Virginia Press, 1972), no page number, but introductory paragraph.

ence, are infinite. . . . Men have acquired the ideas of the practically infinite
extent of the universe and of its practical eternity; they are familiar with
the conception that our earth is but an infinitesimal fragment of that part
of the universe which can be seen; and that, nevertheless, its duration is,
as compared with our standards of time, infinite. . . . Whether these ideas
are well or ill founded is not the question. No one can deny that they exist,
and have been the inevitable outgrowth of the improvement of natural
knowledge. And if so, it cannot be doubted that they are changing the
form of men's most cherished and most important convictions.[26]

This supposed diminishing of man was accompanied by the rise of
humanism, and Copernicus' theory was in fact basic to humanism's
growth. A diminished view of man has somehow led to an elevated
view of man. How was this possible?

One lucid answer was provided by Arthur O. Lovejoy, the historian of ideas. He argued that the traditional account of the significance of Copernicus' theory has been erroneous. It has misunderstood the place of the earth in the medieval cosmology. For them, hell
was the center of the universe.

It has often been said that the older picture of the world in space was pe-
culiarly fitted to give man a high sense of his own importance and dignity;
and some modern writers have made much of this supposed implication of
pre-Copernican astronomy. Man occupied, we are told, the central place in
the universe, and round the planet of his habitation all the vast, unpeopled
spheres obsequiously revolved. But the actual tendency of the geocentric
system was, for the medieval mind, precisely the opposite. For the centre
of the world was not a position of honor; it was rather the place farthest removed from the Empyrean, the bottom of the creation, to which its dregs
and baser elements sank. The actual centre, indeed, was Hell; in the spatial
sense the medieval world was literally diabolocentric. And the whole sub-
lunary region was, of course, incomparably inferior to the resplendent and
incorruptible heavens above the moon. . . . It is sufficiently evident from
such passages that the geocentric cosmography served rather for man's
humiliation than for his exaltation, and that Copernicanism was opposed
partly on the ground that it assigned too dignified and lofty a position to
his dwelling-place.[27]

To break the intellectual hold of the older medieval conception of
the universe as well as man's place on a cursed earth, the humanists
found it convenient to promote Copernicus' cosmography. The basic

26. Huxley, "On Improving Knowledge" (1886), in Frederick Barry (ed.), *Essays*
(New York: Macmillan, 1929), pp. 227–29.
27. Arthur O. Lovejoy, *The Great Chain of Being: A Study of the History of an Idea* (New
York: Harper Torchbook, [1936] 1965), pp. 101–2.

step in creating a new, autonomous universe did not reduce the cosmological significance of man, for it was a key to establishing the centuries-long intellectual process of *shoving God out of the universe*. It was necessary to reduce God's significance in order to give to mankind the monopoly of cosmological significance. The infinite universe could be substituted for the once-central earth as the arena of man's drama. There is a problem, however. *An impersonal universe, however large, cannot provide meaning.* Man, therefore, can now become the source of meaning in (and for) the universe, by virtue of his exclusive claim to cosmic personalism[28]—the only source of personal purpose in this infinite universe. Even better from autonomous man's perspective, this modern universe does not relegate man to the pit of sin and spiritual warfare, as the medieval view of the universe had done.

2. *The Darwinian Revolution*

What the Copernican revolution did for man's sense of autonomy and monopoly of power within the spatial dimension, Darwin's revolution did for man's sense of temporal autonomy. An analogous error in the textbook accounts of the history of science and the history of modern thought is that Darwin made man the descendant of apes (or pre-apes).[29] This supposedly debased man's view of himself and his importance in history. The opposite is the case. What Darwin did was to rescue rebellious Western man from Christianity's theology of moral transgression and its doctrine of eternal doom.

A valuable analysis of the impact Darwinian thought had on late-nineteenth-century religious thought was presented by Rev. James Maurice Wilson, Canon of Worcester, in a 1925 essay, "The Religious Effect of the Idea of Evolution." Man became the focal point

---

28. Chapter 1.

29. Predictably, some overly sensitive evolutionist, upon reading this reference to man's ancestors, the apes, will be horrified. "Darwin never said that man descended from apes!" On this point, let me quote George Gaylord Simpson, Harvard's prestigious paleontologist: "No one doubts that man is a member of the order Primates along with lemurs, tarsiers, monkeys and apes. Few doubt that his closest living relatives are apes. On this subject, by the way, there has been too much pussyfooting. Apologists emphasize that man cannot be a descendant of any living ape—a statement that is obvious to the verge of imbecility—and go on to state or imply that man is not really descended from an ape or monkey at all, but from an earlier common ancestor. In fact, that common ancestor would certainly be called an ape or monkey in popular speech by anyone who saw it. Since the terms ape and monkey are defined by popular usage, man's ancestors were apes or monkeys (or successively both). It is pusillanimous if not dishonest for an informed investigator to say otherwise." Simpson, *This View of Life: The World of an Evolutionist* (New York: Harcourt, Brace & World, 1964), p. 12.

of religion, for "it is only in the study of man's nature that we can hope to find a clue to God's Purpose in Creation. Herein lies, as I think, the great service that the idea of evolution is rendering to theology."[30] Darwin freed man from the biblical God, concluded Rev. Wilson, and so did his contemporaries.

> The evolution of man from lower forms of life was in itself a new and startling fact, and one that broke up the old theology. I and my contemporaries, however, accepted it as fact. The first and obvious result of this acceptance was that we were compelled to regard the Biblical story of the Fall as not historic, as it had long been believed to be. We were compelled to regard that story as a primitive attempt to account for the presence of sin and evil in the world... But now, in the light of the fact of evolution, the Fall, as a historic event, already questioned on other grounds, was excluded and denied by science.[31]

Understandably, the rejection of the doctrine of the ethical rebellion of man against God, at a particular point in human history, necessarily transformed that generation's interpretation of Christianity.

> The abandonment of the belief in a historic "Fall" of a primeval pair of human beings has removed one of the great obstacles to the acceptance by our generation of the Christian Faith which had required that belief. Yet taken by itself it certainly tends to create, as well as to remove, a difficulty. For if there was no historic Fall, what becomes of the Redemption, the Salvation through Christ, which the universal experience of Christendom proves incontestably to be fact? How does Jesus save His people from their sins? *He makes men better.*[32]

Man now becomes a co-worker with a vague, undefinable God who does not judge. "It is the sins of the world and our sins that He who died on the Cross is taking away, by making us better. Salvation is not then thought of as an escape from hell; but as a lifting us all out from living lives unworthy of us. Religion so conceived is not the art of winning heaven, but the effort to become better and to work with God."[33]

Man now becomes part of God, who in turn is part of the universe. There is *a continuity of life* through evolution. There is therefore *a continuity of being.* Wilson concluded:

30. James Maurice Wilson, "The Religious Effect of the Idea of Evolution," in *Evolution in the Light of Modern Knowledge: A Collective work* (London: Blackie & Son, 1925), p. 492.

31. *Ibid.*, pp. 497–98.

32. *Ibid.* pp. 498–99.

33. *Ibid.*, p. 501.

The idea of evolution affects Christology because it assumes and implies continuity along with advance in creation. And it is this idea and fact of continuity, impressed on us from all quarters, that is now determining what men are able to believe concerning Divine action in every sphere. The evidence for continuity everywhere is overwhelming. The implicit or explicit recognition of it among educated people, and a general sense of it, are becoming universal and axiomatic. . . . What a chain it is! Begin anywhere: with your own intelligence as you read, or mine as I write. First go down the chain. Intelligence is not confined to those who can read and write. It is shared by every human being. It is shared by animals. It is not limited to animals. Plants cannot be denied a share of it. It is found in roots and leaves and flowers. Go down farther still; and farther. You cannot find the end of the chain. And then go up. . . . To us intelligence, mind, spirit, is now seen as one long continuous chain, of which we see neither beginning nor end. We are perhaps at least as far from the top of it as we are from the bottom.[34]

This is a modern version of the ancient religion known as *pantheism*. It is certainly one reasonable extension of Darwinism. This is another reason why a generation of public school graduates in the late 1960s could turn to pantheism and then to forms of animism. The best-selling book, *The Secret Life of Plants* (1974), was essentially a defense of the animist cosmology, where sprites and personal "forces" inhabit plants and special regions of the earth.

This doctrine of the continuity of being was basic to ancient paganism, most notably in Egypt's theology of the divine Pharaoh and his divine state. It is the oldest heresy of all, tempting man "to be as god" (Gen. 3:5). Rev. Wilson was being too modest. Man is not only closer to the top of the chain than to the bottom, he actually is the top. Dobzhansky made this point inescapably clear. He knew how erroneous the textbook account is; he knew that Darwin elevated mankind by making him the product of ape-like beings, which in turn were products of impersonal random forces governed only by the law of natural selection. He wrote:

It has become almost a commonplace that Darwin's discovery of biological evolution completed the downgrading and estrangement of man begun by Copernicus and Galileo. I can scarcely imagine a judgment more mistaken. Perhaps the central point to be argued in this book is that the opposite is true. Evolution is a source of hope for man. To be sure, modern evolution has not restored the earth to the position of the center of the universe. However, while the universe is surely not geocentric, it may con-

---

34. *Ibid.*, pp. 501–2.

ceivably be anthropocentric. Man, this mysterious product of the world's evolution, may also be its protagonist, and eventually its pilot. In any case, the world is not fixed, not finished, and not unchangeable. Everything in it is engaged in evolutionary flow and development.[35]

A changing, evolving world is at last free from the providence of God.

> Since the world is evolving it may in time become different from what it is. And if so, man may help to channel the changes in a direction which he deems desirable and good....In particular, it is not true that human nature does not change; this "nature" is not a status but a process. The potentialities of man's development are far from exhausted, either biologically or culturally. Man must develop as the bearer of spirit and of ultimate concern. Together with Nietzsche we must say: "Man is something that must be overcome."[36]

Man, in short, must transcend himself. He must evolve into the pilot of the universe. He can do this because he alone is fully self-conscious, fully self-aware. "Self-awareness is, then, one of the fundamental, possibly the most fundamental, characteristic of the human species. This characteristic is an evolutionary novelty....The evolutionary adaptive significance of self-awareness lies in that it serves to organize and to integrate man's physical and mental capacities by means of which man controls his environment."[37] Man must take control of man and the environment.

Understandably, Dobzhansky despised Protestant fundamentalism. Above all, he had to reject the idea of creationism. To accept such a creed would be to knock man from his pedestal, to drag him away from the pilot's wheel. In fact, scholarly fundamentalists enraged him.

> There are still many people who are happy and comfortable adhering to fundamentalist creeds. This should cause no surprise, since a large majority of these believers are as unfamiliar with scientific findings as were people who lived centuries ago. The really extraordinary phenomenon is the continued existence of a small minority of scientifically educated fundamentalists who know that their beliefs are in utter, flagrant, glaring contradiction with firmly established scientific findings....Discussions and debates with such persons is [sic] a waste of time; I suspect that they are unhappy people, envious of those who are helped to hold similar views by plain ignorance.[38]

---

35. Dobzhansky, *Biology of Ultimate Concern*, p. 7.
36. *Ibid.*, pp. 8–9.
37. *Ibid.*, pp. 68–69.
38. *Ibid.*, pp. 95–96.

What is the heart of the evolutionist's religion? Dobzhansky made his humanism clear: "One can study facts without bothering to inquire about their meaning. But there is one stupendous fact with which people were confronted at all stages of their factual enlightenment, the meaning of which they have ceaselessly tried to discover. This fact is Man."[39] This is the link among all of man's religions, he said. Man with a capital "M" is the heart of man's religions; so, on these terms, evolutionism must certainly be the humanistic world's foremost religion. It is not surprising that Dobzhansky's book was published as one of a series, edited by Ruth Nanda Anshen: "Perspectives in Humanism."

You need to understand from the beginning that *evolutionism's cosmology involves an intellectual sleight-of-hand operation*. It appears initially to denigrate man's position in a universe of infinite (or almost infinite) space and time, only subsequently to place man on the pinnacle of this non-created realm. Man becomes content to be a child of the meaningless slime, in order that he might claim his rightful sovereignty in the place once occupied by God. By default—the disappearance of God the Creator—man achieves his evolving divinity.

D. Uniformitarianism

Uniformitarianism is the deeply religious and inherently unprovable assumption that rates of astrophysical and geological change observed today have been the same since the beginning of time. Differently put, uniformitarianism teaches that the processes that acted in the evolution of the universe and the earth were the same as those that operate today. (Some evolutionary scientists have finally abandoned this straightforward version of uniformitarianism,[40] but it is the one

---

39. *Ibid.* p. 96.

40. See, for example, Simpson, *This View of Life*, p. 132. Simpson denied that rates of geological change observable today have always prevailed. "Some processes (those of vulcanism or glaciation, for example) have evidently acted in the past with scales and rates that cannot by any stretch be called 'the same' or even 'approximately the same' as those of today." However, he still clung to uniformitarianism as a principle, though unprovable, because it is scientifically necessary to assume its existence: "Gravity would be immanent (an inherent characteristic of matter now) even if the law of gravity had changed, and it is impossible to prove that it has not changed. Uniformity, in this sense, is an unprovable postulate justified, or indeed required, on two grounds. First, nothing in our incomplete but extensive knowledge of history disagrees with it. Second, only on this postulate is a rational interpretation of history possible, and we are justified in seeking—as scientists we must seek—such a rational interpretation" (p. 133). Cf. Stephen Jay Gould, "Evolution: Explosion, Not Ascent," *New York Times* (Jan. 22, 1978); *Ever Since Darwin* (1977), and *The Panda's Thumb* (1980), both published

Speed of light is not a reliable constant

Age of stars — an illusion   Not old

which has long been acceptable to most scientists, especially geologists, astronomers, and life scientists.)

Science needs a constant, even the science of Einstein's theory of relativity. That constant is the speed of light. By striking at the validity of such a constant, the Bible necessarily denies the doctrine of uniformitarianism in relation to origins of the universe. Either the transmission of light from the most distant stars began on the same day as the transmission of light from the moon, with the rays of light from all sources striking the earth on the day the heavenly bodies were created, or else the Genesis account of the creation is false. The Bible's account of the chronology of creation points to an illusion, one created by the modern doctrine of uniformitarianism. *The seeming age of the stars is an illusion.* The events that we seem to be observing, such as novas (exploding stars), did not take place billions of years ago. If they did take place, they took place recently. If so, the speed of light is not a reliable constant. If the speed of light has been a constant since the creation of the earth, then the flashes of light which we explain as exploding stars are in no way related to actual historical events like explosions, unless the universe is relatively small. Either the constancy of the speed of light is an illusion, or the size of the universe is an illusion, or else the physical events that we hypothesize to explain the visible changes in light or radiation are false inferences. The speed of light should not be used to estimate the age and size of the universe.[41]

---

by Norton, New York. Gould was a Harvard professor of paleontology, just as Simpson was. See also Steven N. Stanley, *The New Evolutionary Timetable* (New York: Basic Books, 1982).

41. A story written by Walter Sullivan in the *New York Times* (Dec. 20, 1978) reported on four quasars that appeared to be moving through space at speeds far in excess of the speed of light. Scientists were frantically trying to find some sort of explanation for this phenomenon, since it challenged the modern world's only accepted constant, namely, the speed of light. Nevertheless, John Kolena, Assistant Professor of Astronomy at Duke University in Durham, North Carolina, could write in total confidence in a letter to the Editor: "The earth's age is thus based neither on 'assumptions' nor on 'faith' but on a law of nature, experimentally verified literally millions of times without exception." He was referring to the radioactive decay of uranium atoms. He ended his letter with an appeal to the Deist's God of the eighteenth century: "Those of us who still need to believe in God should in fact, be even more impressed by his or her decision to make just a few natural laws and yet keep the universe running so well for so many billions of years without any necessity for active intervention." *Durham Morning Herald* (Nov. 1, 1979). It is inspiring to know that such a God (male or female) should be so smart as to create the world and then conveniently disappear for 13 billion years, in order to demonstrate His (or Her) majestic sovereignty. Meanwhile, the quasars went merrily along, at eight times the speed of light. Maybe.

E. Cosmic Purpose

Genesis 1:14–16 has implications outside the discipline of astronomy. These verses are uniquely important for the biological and social sciences. First, they teach us that *the origin of life was outside the cause-and-effect sequence of today's environment.* Plant life appeared before the creation of the sun. If biological processes were the same then as now, then chlorophyll preceded the appearance of the sun. Light did not "call forth the plant"—not solar light, anyway. The biological processes of plant life were in operation before the existence of the star that today sustains all plant life. *The sun, in this sense, was created for the present benefit of the plants.* The Bible's account of creation reverses modern biological science's interpretation of cause and effect. Plants had capacities for reproduction and survival before the present basis of plant life was created. Nothing could be further removed from the hypothesis of modern biology. Such a creationist view of reality indicates the future-orientation of cause and effect, as if the plants called forth the sun. God, of course, called forth both plants and sun, but from the point of view of chronology, the biblical account denies the past-orientation of secular theories of cause and effect. Science declares that every event has some set of prior causes. At least with respect to the creation of the world, the Bible denies that such causes were in any way environmentally determined by existing matter-energy.

A second implication of Genesis 1:14–16, which is related to the first, is significant in the social sciences as well as in the biological sciences. *The stars, sun, and moon were created in order to serve the needs of plants, animals, and men.* Modern science does not permit the use of the words "in order to" except when a human being or thinking animal is seeking to achieve some goal. *The concept of cosmic purpose is not allowed to exist in modern science except in relationship to man.* The processes of hypothetically autonomous nature are explained by modern science strictly in terms of purposeless prior events. The universe's origins were purely random and therefore completely without purpose. What all modern science denies absolutely is the old Christian doctrine of *teleology.*

"Teleology" is not a commonly used word any longer. It refers to *final causation*: ultimate ends. Modern science is concerned only with prior causation. Cosmic impersonalism necessarily has to exclude any concept of final causation, since there can be no personal, directing agent who has created our world in order to achieve certain ends. Without a directing agent—a conscious, powerful planner—the concept of purpose is meaningless. Modern science denies the doctrine of transcendent cosmic personalism, so it also has to deny teleology, except with reference to the goals of man or men. (It is man, and only man, who has brought purpose into the rationalist's universe.) *Causation had to be purposeless causation prior to man. Final causation implies a personal agent who is directing creation towards a goal which was chosen prior to the appearance of man.* This is precisely what the Bible affirms (Eph. 1). This is precisely what modern, rationalist science denies.

Teleology, the doctrine of final causation, was used by Aquinas as one of the five proofs of God. It became a popular apologetic device used by Protestants to defend the faith "rationally," especially after the appearance of William Paley's books, *A View of the Evidences of Christianity* (1794) and *Natural Theology* (1802). The signs of design in creation point to God's plan for the ages, Paley argued. He used the famous analogy of the clock and the universe: a designer must be postulated in both cases. (The radical Deist, whose universe is mechanistic, can use this analogy to prove God's neglect of man's affairs, thereby denying the doctrine of providence, which is why Paley also relied on the evidence of miracles—providential discontinuities—to state the case for Christianity.) Paley's *Evidences* was still assigned to Cambridge University students just prior to World War I, though it is doubtful that many of them took it seriously. Malcolm Muggeridge certainly was unimpressed.[42] Is the universe orderly because God has specific ends for it, and has therefore directed its operations? If the universe is orderly, can some other explanation be given besides conscious design?

It has been the goal of the modern evolutionist, ever since the days of Darwin, to find a suitable alternate explanation. Darwin's answer was evolution through natural selection. George Bernard Shaw confidently stated that Darwin had thrown Paley's watch into the ocean. Marjorie Greene added:

> It was not really, however, the watch he threw away, but the watchmaker. Darwinism is teleologically decapitated; everything in nature is explained in terms of its purpose, but an unplanned purpose in which the organism is tool, tool user, and beneficiary all in one. And the artifact analogy is as basic to Darwinism, both old and new, as it is to natural theology: not only is the concept of natural selection grounded on the analogy with the great

---

42. Malcolm Muggeridge, *Chronicles of Wasted Time: The Green Stick* (New York: William Morrow, 1973), p. 75.

livestock breeders, but the organisms themselves are conceived in Paleyan terms as contrivances, aggregates of characters and functions of good—for what? For survival, that is, for going on and being good for, going on and being good for—and so on ad infinitum.[43]

Instead of eternity, the Darwinist substitutes infinite extension, at least until all energy is dissipated in the final cold of entropy. Instead of immortality, he substitutes the survival of the species. Anyway, the old-fashioned, less consistent Darwinist did these things. The new ones are growing less confident about man's survival as they grow more consistent concerning man's autonomous power, e.g., nuclear war or biological warfare that uses microbes that are genetically engineered to be racially specific.

The great enemy of modern science is purpose apart from man's purposes. As the Medawars stated so clearly, "It is upon the notion of *randomness* that geneticists have based their case against a benevolent or malevolent deity and against there being any overall purpose or design in nature."[44] The old-fashioned version of Darwinism did include an element of purposefulness, at least in its language. The so-called "survival of the fittest" indicated that there was upward progress inherent in the processes of evolution. This phrase was coined by Herbert Spencer, the nineteenth-century sociologist, in his 1852 essay, "A Theory of Population, deduced from the General Law of Animal Fertility," and Darwin inserted the phrase into the fifth edition of *The Origin of Species*. Spencer's language was ethical and teleological: "From the beginning, pressure of population has been the proximate cause of progress." Again, "those left behind to continue the race, are those in whom the power of self-preservation is the greatest—are the select of their generation."[45] The words "progress" and "select" are giveaways. Mere biological change is equated with progress, with all the nuances associated with "progress," and the best are "selected" by nature, converting a random, impersonal process into something resembling purposeful action.

One reason why Darwinism swept through nineteenth-century thought was because of the seemingly teleological implications of the

---

43. Marjorie Greene, "The Faith of Darwinism," *Encounter* (Nov. 1959), p. 53.
44. Peter and Jean Medawar, "Revising the Facts of Life," *Harper's* (Feb. 1977), p. 41.
45. Cited by William Irvine, *Apes, Angels, and Victorians: The Story of Darwin, Huxley, and Evolution* (New York: McGraw-Hill, 1955), p. 30.

language of Darwinism. The public was not yet ready to abandon teleology as rapidly as the more consistent scientists were. Even today,
the language of evolutionists is still clouded by the language of final
causation and purpose. A. R. Manser wrote:

> Darwin's theory is generally claimed to be non-teleological. But the very
> criterion of success in the "struggle for existence," survival and/or expan-
> sion, seems to put a teleological notion back into the center of evolution-
> ary thought. This explains why it is generally assumed that evolution is
> in an "upward" direction, that new species are an improvement of the
> old....I am not claiming that this anthropomorphism is necessarily in-
> volved in Darwin's theory itself, or that Darwin must have thought in these
> terms; all I claim is that this was one of the elements that made the theory
> acceptable both to scientists and to laymen.... From a historical point of
> view, it seems likely that many of the nonscientific supporters of Darwin
> would have been less willing to accept the theory if this prop had not been
> available.[46]

Furthermore, he pointed out, "even now it is clear that many biologists have to make a conscious effort to prevent themselves from
lapsing into such a mode of thought or expression."

From the beginning, Darwin used the analogy of the professional
breeder in defending the idea of natural selection, and this led to
continuing confusion on the part of readers, both scientific and amateur, who had assimilated his explanation of the so-called mechanism
of evolution. Again and again, popularizers (including Harvard's
influential nineteenth-century biologist, Asa Gray) tried to combine
some version of Paley's *Natural Theology* with an activist version of natural selection. Darwin over and over had to explain that his language
was not to be taken literally, that Nature is not a planning, conscious
entity that selects one or another species to survive. Yet, in the first
edition of *Origin of Species*, he had written that "Natural Selection, as
we shall hereafter see, is a power incessantly ready for action, and is
as immeasurably superior to man's feeble efforts, as the works of Nature are to Art."[47] No wonder he had to keep revising each edition to
eliminate such language! The sixth edition was so far removed from
the first that something like 75% of the first was rewritten by the final
edition—rewritten as many as five times each, in the case of some sentences. The sixth edition was one-third longer than the first.[48]

46. A. R. Manser, "The Concept of Evolution," *Philosophy*, XL (1965), p. 22.
47. Cited by Robert M. Young, "Darwin's Metaphor: Does Nature Select?" *Monist*,
LV (1971), p. 462.
48. *Ibid.*, p. 496.

As a result of constant criticism, he steadily abandoned natural selection as the sole cause of evolution. He adopted elements of the idea of Jean Baptiste Lamarck: the "inheritance of acquired characteristics," an idea that has been repudiated by modern Darwinians. He referred back to an earlier statement in the first edition, in the conclusion of the sixth edition: "I am convinced that natural selection has been the main but not the exclusive means of modification."[49] Those who have seen the triumph of Darwinism forget that for half a century after the publication of *Origin of Species*, the ideas of evolution and uniformitarianism came to be accepted universally, but the idea of natural selection as the mechanism (explanation) went into decline. As Robert M. Young commented:

> As a result of successive theoretical and experimental developments in biology which seemed inconsistent with Darwin's mechanism of natural selection, this aspect of his theory went into increasing decline, so much so that Nordenskiold's standard *History of Biology* (written between 1920–24 and still in print [as of 1970—G.N.]) included long chapters chronicling the decline of Darwinism, in the same period as evolution was being increasingly accepted. "To raise the theory of selection, as had often been done, to the rank of a 'natural law' comparable in value with the law of gravity established by Newton is, of course, quite irrational, as time has already shown; Darwin's theory of the origin of the species was long ago abandoned." Within ten years, however, biologists were generally convinced that Darwin had been right in the first place....[50]

The phrase, "in the first place," refers to the first edition of *Origin*, before he had begun to compromise the theory of natural selection so severely. What Darwin had accomplished in 1859 was impressive: the presentation of a seeming mechanism which could explain evolution. But his book was tinged with teleological elements in its language, thereby making far easier the spread of the idea of evolution among people who still wanted to believe in a semi-providence-governed universe. The public did not understand the importance of natural selection, despite the fact that this was Darwin's hypothesis justifying belief in biological evolution. Even Darwin steadily abandoned the hypothesis as an all-encompassing explanation. He seems to have abandoned confidence in chance as a meaningful explanation of origins in his last years. In the last letter that he wrote to Alfred Russel Wallace,

---

49. Charles Darwin, *The Origin of Species*, 6th ed. (New York: Modern Library, [1871]), p. 367.
50. Young, *Monist* (1971), p. 497. Cf. Simpson, *This View of Life*, pp. 14ff.

the co-discoverer of "evolution through natural selection," Darwin commended a book by William Graham, *The Creed of Science*, which was straightforwardly teleological in approach. Graham had written: "We are compelled to interpret the course of evolution as being under guidance; to believe that the final results were aimed at; that Nature did not stumble on her best works by sheer accident,... Chance, as an explanation—and if design be denied, chance must be offered as the explanation—is a word expressing nothing, a word which, under pretence of explanation, affirms nothing whatever. It is this; but it is also much more serious; for it is the express denial of God and it is thus genuine atheism."[51] Darwin wrote to Graham that "you have expressed my inward conviction, though far more vividly and clearly than I could have done, that 'the universe is not the result of chance.'"[52]

But if not chance, then what? Modern science cannot accept explanations for events that are outside of nature itself. Modern science cannot accept final causation. Therefore, *modern science had to abandon Darwin in the name of Darwinian presuppositions.* Better the lawless laws of chance than God; better chaos than providence, says the secular scientist.

In biology, and especially genetics, the element of randomness enters at the very beginning of life. The scientist knows no way of predicting either chromosome combinations or genetic mutations. Furthermore, he does not know which environmental factors will prove conclusive in the development of the particular species in question. He may speak about the "survival of the fittest," yet the only way to test the fittest is to see, in retrospect, which species actually do survive. The so-called survival of the fittest is a tautology; it means simply *the survival of the survivors.* There is no mechanism today that geneticists can use that enables them to predict, in advance, which species will survive or which species will not. Darwin's theory is therefore a descriptive theory, not a theory useful in scientific prediction. The heart of the meaning of the "survival of the fittest," therefore, is not scientific but rather historical.[53] More to the point, it is more *religious* than anything. It is a statement about God and His relationship with the creation. As one philosopher has written:

---

51. Cited by Young, *ibid.*, pp. 486–87.

52. Cited by Young, *ibid.*, p. 486. One difficulty in attributing this passage as a late opinion of Darwin's is that he had questioned the purely random universe in earlier correspondence, such as his Nov. 26, 1860, letter to Asa Gray: *The Life and Letters of Charles Darwin*, 2 vols., ed. Francis Darwin (New York: Appleton, 1887), II, p. 146.

53. A. R. Manser, *Philosophy* (1965), pp. 24–25. Cf. Simpson, *This View of Life*, p. 96.

All that the statement "It is the fit that survive" can mean is that for any kind of organism in any circumstances there are some possible features whose possession is more conducive to survival than that of their alternatives. But the phrase "the survival of the fittest," though it is something of a catchphrase, does indicate something of importance. It indicates that according to the theory there is nothing mysterious in the fact of the survival of some forms in preference to others; there is no need to postulate the unfathomable designs of a divine will.[54]

God is eliminated from biological science. This is the very essence of all modern, anti-teleological science. This is why science must not be teleological, the secularist argues.

The secular scientist really does not want randomness all of the time. He wants *predictable randomness.* He wants the operation of the law of large numbers. He wants the laws of probability. He wants sufficient order to give him power, but he usually wants sufficient randomness to preserve him from the power of others, especially God. When the biologist speaks of randomness, he means man's limited ability to predict the future, yet no scientist clings to a theory of total randomness. As Barker wrote concerning randomness as it applies to Darwinism: "It is an essential presupposition of the theory that variation should occur at random with respect to any advantage or disadvantage it may confer on the organism, in its relations with factors in its internal or external environment."[55] As he emphatically stated, "any theory that did not postulate randomness of this kind, or at least which involved its denial, could not count as a scientific theory."[56] Here is the heart of the argument concerning teleology. Any trace of teleology must be scrapped by secular science. The secular scientists have *defined* science to exclude all forms of final, teleological causation. Darwin, however confused he may have been, or however attracted to the teleological arguments of William Graham he may have become at the end of his life, made it plain in the final edition of *Origin of Species* that he could not accept any trace of God-ordained benefits in the processes of nature. "The foregoing remarks lead me to say a few words on the protest lately made by some naturalists, against the utilitarian doctrine that every detail of structure has been produced for the good of its possessor. They believe that many structures have been created for the sake of beauty, to delight man or the

---

54. A. D. Barker, "An Approach to the Theory of Natural Selection," *Philosophy,* XLIV (Oct. 1969), p. 274.
55. *Ibid.*, p. 278.
56. *Ibid.*, p. 283.

Creator (but this latter point is beyond the scope of scientific discussion), or for the sake of mere variety, a view already discussed. Such doctrines, if true, would be absolutely fatal to my theory."[57] Indeed; they would be absolutely fatal for all forms of modern secular science. Or, should I say, would have been *up until now* fatal for modern secular science.

G. Man: The New Predestinator

There is an exception to the *a priori* denial of teleological causation in the universe. Man is this exception. The secularist has denied that there could be even a trace of final causation, meaning ends-dominated causation, anywhere in the origin of nature or in nature's products. But when we come to a consideration of man, now freed from God or any other form of conscious causation external to man, the position of the secularists changes. *Man is the new sovereign over nature.* Nature's otherwise mindless processes have now produced a thinking, acting creature, man. Man can learn the laws of nature, and he can then subdue nature to his ends. He can plan and execute his plans. *Man proposes and man disposes*, to quote Karl Marx's partner, Frederick Engels.[58] Nature has therefore transcended its own laws. A series of uncreated random developments has resulted in the creation of a planning being. *Teleology has come into the world.* Man, the new predestinator, can take over the directing of evolution, even as the selective breeders who so fascinated Darwin took over the breeding of animals and plants. What modern science has denied to God and nature, it now permits to man.

57. Darwin, *Origin of Species*, p. 146.
58. Frederick Engels, *Herr Eugen Dühring's Revolution in Science* (Anti-Dühring) (London: Lawrence & Wishart, [1877] 1934), p. 348. Engels wrote: "We have already seen, more than once, that in existing bourgeois society men are dominated by the economic conditions created by themselves, by the means of production which they themselves have produced, as if by an extraneous force. The actual basis of religious reflex action therefore continues to exist, and with it the religious reflex itself. . It is still true that man proposes and God (that is, the extraneous force of the capitalist mode of production) disposes. Mere knowledge, even if it went much further and deeper than that of bourgeois economic science, is not enough to bring social forces under the control of society. What is above all necessary for this, is a social act. And when this act has been accomplished, when society, by taking possession of all means of production and using them on a planned basis, has freed itself and all its members from the bondage in which they are at present held by these means of production but which now confront them as an irresistible extraneous force; when therefore man no longer merely proposes, but also disposes—only then will the last extraneous force which is still reflected in religion vanish; and with it will also vanish the religious reflection itself, for the simple reason that then there will be nothing left to reflect" (pp. 347–48).

The Bible affirms that the stars were created by God for the benefit of His creatures on earth. The Bible absolutely denies the first principle of all secular natural science, namely, that there can be no teleology in nature prior to man. But the Bible also subordinates man and the creation to God, the Creator. Modern secular science comes to a new conclusion: there is teleology, but man—generic, collective mankind—is the source of this final causation. The Bible denies this. The Bible affirms that God proposes and God disposes, and that man is responsible before God (Rom. 9). God's ends are sovereign over both man and nature.

The war between the first principles of the Bible's account of creation and secular science is absolute. No compromise is possible. Christians who happen to hold advanced degrees in biology and geology may think that some sort of working compromise is possible, but the humanists deny it. George Gaylord Simpson called teleology "the higher superstition." He wrote: "Another subtler and even more deeply warping concept of the higher superstition was that the world was created for man. Other organisms had no separate purpose in the scheme of creation. Whether noxious or useful, they were to be seriously considered only in their relationship to the supreme creation, the image of God."[59] Simpson was adamant: "There is no fact in the history of life that requires a postulate of purpose external to the organisms themselves."[60] *This is clearly a statement of religious faith.* Simpson then asked: "Does this mean that religion is simply invalid from a scientific point of view, that the conflict is insoluble and one must choose one side or the other? I do not think so. Science can and does invalidate some views held to be religious. Whatever else God may be held to be, He is surely consistent with the world of observed phenomena in which we live. A god whose means of creation is not evolution is a false god."[61] He thought that the world of observed phenomena—observed by us, today—automatically teaches historical evolution. It does, if you assume, *a priori*, that evolution is always true, and that every fact of the universe is in conformity with this dogma.

1. A Sleight-of-Hand Operation

Secular science has attempted a sleight-of-hand operation. Denying the existence of any transcendent conscious purpose, and denying

---

59. Simpson, *This View of Life*, p. 7.

60. *Ibid.*, p. 175.

61. *Ibid.*, p. 232.

even the scientific consideration of such a transcendent conscious purpose, secular scientists conclude that there is no authority above man to deflect man's conscious purposes. You cannot be a respectable scientist and assume transcendent purpose, since "postulating the transcendental always stultifies inquiry."[62] *Nature must first be depersonalized.*

> As astronomy made the universe immense, physics itself and related physical sciences made it lawful. Physical effects have physical causes, and the relationship is such that when causes are adequately known effects can be reliably predicted. We no longer live in a capricious world. We may expect the universe to deal consistently, even if not fairly, with us. If the unusual happens, we need no longer blame *kanaima* (or a whimsical god or devil) but may look confidently for an unusual or hitherto unknown physical cause. That is, perhaps, an act of faith, but it is not superstition. Unlike recourse to the supernatural, it is validated by thousands of successful searches for verifiable causes. This view depersonalizes the universe and makes it more austere, but it also makes it dependable.[63]

The depersonalization of nature was originally asserted in terms of a philosophy that proclaimed nature's autonomy. This autonomy for nature no longer will be permitted. Once man achieves his *freedom from undesigned nature* by means of his knowledge of nature's laws, he can then assert his *autonomous sovereignty over nature* (including, of course, other men). There are no conscious ends in the universe that can overcome the conscious purpose of the planning elite. There is no court of higher appeal. R. J. Rushdoony summarized this new cosmology very well:

> Humanistic law, moreover, is inescapably totalitarian law. Humanism, as a logical development of evolutionary theory, holds fundamentally to a concept of an evolving universe. This is held to be an "open universe," whereas Biblical Christianity, because of its faith in the triune God and His eternal decree, is said to be a faith in a "closed universe." This terminology not only intends to prejudice the case; it reverses reality. The universe of evolutionism and humanism is a closed universe. There is no law, no appeal, no higher order, beyond and above the universe. Instead of an open window upwards, there is a closed cosmos. There is thus no ultimate law and decree beyond man and the universe. Man's law is therefore beyond criticism except by man. In practice, this means that the positive law of the state is absolute law. The state is the most powerful and most highly organized expression of humanistic man, and the state is the form and expression of humanistic law. Because there is no higher law of God as judge

62. *Ibid.*, p. 170.
63. *Ibid.*, p. 5.

over the universe, over every human order, the law of the state is a closed system of law. There is no appeal beyond it. Man has no "right," no realm of justice, no source of law beyond the state, to which man can appeal against the state. Humanism therefore imprisons man within the closed world of the state and the closed universe of the evolutionary scheme.[64]

Simpson, one of the most prominent paleontologists of the mid-twentieth century, offered us this interpretation of man, the new sovereign: "Man is the highest animal. The fact that he alone is capable of making such a judgment is in itself part of the evidence that this decision is correct.... He is also a fundamentally new sort of animal and one in which, although organic evolution continues on its way, fundamentally a new sort of evolution has also appeared. The basis of this new sort of evolution is a new sort of heredity, the inheritance of learning."[65]

2. The New Evolution

Simpson contrasted *organic evolution*, nature's non-teleological, random development of nonhuman species, with the new *social evolution* of mankind. "Organic evolution rejects acquired characters in inheritance and adaptively orients the essentially random, non-environmental interplay of genetical systems. The new evolution peculiar to man operates directly by the inheritance of acquired characters, of knowledge and learned activities which arise in and are continuously a part of an organismic-environmental system, that of social organization."[66] A new Lamarckianism, with its inheritance of acquired characteristics, has arisen; it has brought with it *a legitimate teleology*. Man, the product of nature, can at last provide what autonomous nature could not: *conscious control*. "Through this very basic distinction between the old evolution and the new, the new evolution becomes subject to conscious control. Man, alone among all organisms, knows that he evolves and he alone is capable of directing his own evolution. For him evolution is no longer something that happens to the organism regardless but something in which the organism may and must take an active hand."[67]

---

64. Rushdoony, "Introduction" to E. L. Hebden Taylor, *The New Legality* (Nutley, New Jersey: Craig Press, 1967), pp. vi–vii. The text of this citation was incorrectly printed in Taylor's book and was later corrected by Mr. Rushdoony.

65. Simpson, *The Meaning of Evolution: A Study of the History of Life and of Its Significance for Man* (New Haven, Connecticut: Yale University Press, [1949] 1969), p. 286.

66. *Ibid.*, p. 187.

67. *Ibid.*, p. 291.

Man's control over future evolution is limited, of course. He cannot choose every direction of a new evolution, nor the rate of change. "In organic evolution he cannot decide what sort of mutation he would like to have,"[68] but he does have power, and therefore must make responsible decisions. "Conscious knowledge, purpose, choice, foresight, and values carry as an inevitable corollary responsibility."[69] Of course, we know that all ethics is relative, in fact, "highly relative."[70] "The search for an absolute ethic, either intuitive or naturalistic, has been a failure."[71] There are no fixed ethical principles. "They become ethical principles only if man chooses to make them such."[72] Man, the creative force behind today's evolution, becomes at the same time the creator and judge of his own ethics. "Man cannot evade the responsibility of choice."[73] Whatever the outcomes of our search for ethical principles, this much is certain: "The purposes and plans are ours, not those of the universe, which displays convincing evidence of their absence."[74] *We are the new predestinators, the source of the universe's new teleology.*

> Man was certainly not the goal of evolution, which evidently had no goal. He was not planned, in an operation wholly planless. . . . His rise was neither insignificant nor inevitable. Man did originate after a tremendously long sequence of events in which chance and orientation played a part. Not all the chance favored his appearance, none might have, but enough did. Not all the orientation was in his direction, it did not lead unerringly human-ward, but some of it came this way. The result is the most highly endowed organization of matter that has yet appeared on the earth—and we certainly have no good reason to believe there is any higher in the universe.[75]

Man proposes, and man, working with nature, also disposes.

H. Evolutionism's Sleight-of-Hand

The humanistic philosophy of Darwinism is an enormously successful sleight-of-hand operation. It has two primary steps. *First*, man must be defined as no more than an animal, the product of the same meaningless, impersonal, unplanned forces that produced all the forms of

---

68. *Idem.*
69. *Ibid.*, p. 310.
70. *Ibid.*, p. 297.
71. *Ibid.*, p. 311.
72. *Idem.*
73. *Idem.*
74. *Ibid.*, p. 293.
75. *Ibid.*, pp. 293–94.

life. This axiom is necessary in order to free man completely from the concept of final judgment. Man must not be understood as a created being, made in God's image, and therefore fully responsible before God. Man is no more unique, and therefore no more responsible, than an amoeba. *Second*, man, once freed from the idea of a Creator, is immediately redefined as the unique life form in the universe. In short, he is and is not special, depending on which stage of the argument you consider.

1. Simpson on Teleology

Simpson provided the argumentation for both steps. *First*, man is just another life form.

> This world into which Darwin led us is certainly very different from the world of the higher superstition. In the world of Darwin man has no special status other than his definition as a distinct species of animal. He is in the fullest sense a part of nature and not apart from it. He is akin, not figuratively but literally, to every living thing, be it an amoeba, a tapeworm, a flea, a seaweed, an oak tree, or a monkey—even though the degrees of relationship are different and we may feel less empathy for forty-second cousins like the tapeworms than for, comparatively speaking, brothers like the monkeys. This is togetherness and brotherhood with a vengeance, beyond the wildest dreams of copy writers or of theologians.[76]

Man has not been favored in any way by the impersonal and directionless process of evolution through natural selection. "Moreover, since man is one of many millions of species all produced by the same grand process, it is in the highest degree improbable that anything in the world exists specifically for his benefit or ill. . . . The rational world is not teleological in the old sense."[77]

Second, man is unquestionably teleological in the new sense—the post-Darwin sense. Nothing was designed by God to meet the needs of man, but because man is now the directing agent of evolution, he can take control over everything. Furthermore, he does not need to humble himself as a steward before God. All of the fruits of the meaningless universe are now man's, for he is the pinnacle, not of creation, but of evolution. Simpson moved to the second step of the argument a dozen pages later.

> Man is one of the millions of results of this material process. He is another species of animal but not just another animal. He is unique in peculiar and

---

76. Simpson, *This View of Life*, pp. 12–13.
77. *Ibid.*, p. 13.

extraordinarily significant ways. He is probably the most self-conscious of organisms, and quite surely the only one that is aware of his own origins, of his own biological nature. He has developed symbolization to a unique degree and is the only organism with true language. This makes him also the only animal who can store knowledge beyond individual capacity and pass it on beyond individual memory. He is by far the most adaptable of all organisms because he has developed culture as a biological adaptation. Now his culture evolves not distinct from and not in replacement of but in addition to biological evolution, which also continues.[78]

He elaborated: "The evolutionary process is not moral—the word is simply irrelevant in that connection—but it has finally produced a moral animal. Conspicuous among his moral attributes is a sense of responsibility. . . . In the post-Darwinian world another answer seems fairly clear: man is responsible to himself and for himself. 'Himself' here means the whole human species, not only the individual and certainly not just those of a certain color of hair or cast of features."[79] Man, meaning collective man or species man, is sovereign. Individuals are responsible to this collective entity. Simpson made his position crystal clear.

> Man is a glorious and unique species of animal. The species originated by evolution, it is still actively evolving, and it will continue to evolve. Future evolution could raise man to superb heights as yet hardly glimpsed, but it will not automatically do so. As far as can now be foreseen, evolutionary degeneration is at least as likely in our future as is further progress. The only way to ensure a progressive evolutionary future for mankind is for man himself to take a hand in the process. Although much further knowledge is needed, it is unquestionably possible for man to guide his own evolution (within limits) along desirable lines. But the great weight of the most widespread current beliefs and institutions is against even attempting such guidance. If there is any hope, it is this: that there may be an increasing number of people who face this dilemma squarely and honestly seek a way out.[80]

With these words, Simpson ended his book.

Are Simpson and Dobzhansky representative of post-Darwinian evolutionism? They are. It is difficult to find biologists who do not take this approach when they address themselves to these problems. Many, of course, remain silent, content to perform the most prosaic

---

78. *Ibid.*, p. 24.
79. *Ibid.*, p. 25.
80. *Ibid.*, p. 285.

tasks of what Thomas Kuhn has called "normal science."[81] When they speak out on the great questions of cosmology, however, their words are basically the same as Simpson's.

2. Thomas Huxley on Teleology

Thomas Huxley was one of those who began to make the case for step two. Darwin for the most part had been content to deal with step one, devoting himself to wrapping up the case for an anti-teleological universe, with its order-producing process of natural selection. Huxley, his contemporary and early defender, was ready to place man on the pinnacle of the evolutionary process. In his famous 1893 Romanes Lectures, "Evolution and Ethics," Huxley announced: "The history of civilization details the steps by which men have succeeded in building up an artificial world within the cosmos. Fragile reed as he may be, man, Pascal says, is a thinking reed: there lies within him a fund of energy, operating intelligently and so far akin to that which pervades the universe, that it is competent to influence and modify the cosmic process. In virtue of his intelligence, the dwarf bends the Titan to his will."[82] Huxley was no optimist. He was convinced that eventually, the law of entropy would triumph.

> If, for millions of years, our globe has taken the upward road, yet, some time, the summit will be reached and the downward route will be commenced. The most daring imagination will hardly venture upon the suggestion that the power and the intelligence of man can ever arrest the procession of the great year.... But, on the other hand, I see no limit to the extent to which intelligence and will, guided by sound principles of investigation and organized in common effort, may modify the conditions of existence, for a period longer than that now covered by history. And much may be done to change the nature of man himself.[83]

When Huxley spoke of man, he meant collective man:

> Further, the consummation is not reached in man, the mere animal; nor in man, the whole or half savage; but only in man, the member of an organized polity. And it is a necessary consequence of his attempt to live in this

81. Thomas Kuhn, *The Structure of Scientific Revolutions*, 2nd ed. (Chicago: University of Chicago Press, [1962] 1970), coined this phrase. For an extended discussion of Kuhn's important distinction between "normal science" and "revolutionary science," see Imre Lakatos [LakaTOSH] and A. E. Musgrave (eds.), *Criticism and the Growth of Knowledge* (New York: Cambridge University Press, 1970).
82. T. H. Huxley, "Evolution and Ethics," (1893), in *Collected Essays*, 9 vols. (London: Macmillan, 1893), IX, pp. 83–84.
83. *Ibid.*, p. 85.

way; that is, under those conditions which are essential to the full development of his noblest powers. Man, the animal, in fact, has worked his way to the headship of the sentient world, and has become the superb animal which he is, in virtue of his success in the struggle for existence. The conditions having been of a certain order, man's organization has adjusted itself to them better than that of his competitors in the cosmic strife.[84]

Huxley strongly opposed Social Darwinism, with its ethic of individualism and personal competition in a free market, which he referred to as "fanatical individualism."[85] He reminded his listeners of "the duties of the individual to the State...."[86] We cannot look, he said, to the competitive processes of nature (meaning other species) as a guide for human social ethics and social organization, since "the ethical progress of society depends, not on imitating the cosmic process, still less in running away from it, but in combatting it."[87]

I. The Theology of Self-Transcendence

Huxley's grandson, the biologist Sir Julian Huxley, delivered the Romanes lectures a half century after his grandfather had, in 1943. He attempted to reconcile the seeming dichotomy that his grandfather had presented, namely, the conflict between cosmic evolution and human ethics. He did so by focusing on the leap of being which man represents, a new evolutionary power that can direct the cosmic processes by means of his own science and values. In other words, he argued for *continuity of evolutionary processes*—a denial of any conflict between ethics and evolution—by stressing the *radical discontinuity represented by man*. The first great discontinuity was the appearance of life, which was Dobzhansky's assertion, too.[88] As life developed, "there increased also the possibilities of control, of independence, of inner harmony and self-regulation, of experience."[89] Animal brains made their advent. But then came nature's crowning glory, man, meaning *collective man*. As he wrote, "during the last half-million years or so a new and more comprehensive type of order of organization has arisen; and on

---

84. *Ibid.*, p. 92.
85. *Ibid.*, p. 92.
86. *Idem.*
87. *Idem.*
88. Theodosius Dobzhansky, "The Present Evolution of Man," *Scientific American* (Sept. 1960), p. 206.
89. Julian Huxley, "Evolutionary Ethics," (1943), in T. H. Huxley and Julian Huxley, *Touchstone for Ethics, 1893–1943* (New York: Harper & Bros., 1947), p. 13. Reprinted by Arno Press.

this new level, the world-stuff is once more introduced to altogether new possibilities, and has quite new methods of evolutionary operation at its disposal. Biological and organic evolution has at its upper end been merged into and largely succeeded by conscious social evolution."[90] This, of course, is the second great discontinuity in the history of evolution.

1. The Order of Creation

Earlier, I argued that evolutionists have reversed the order of creation. Instead of affirming that a sovereign, autonomous, omnipotent *personal* God created the universe, they argue that a sovereign, autonomous, omnipotent, and *impersonal* universe has created a now-sovereign personal god, mankind. Julian Huxley took this argument one step further. He also abandoned uniformitarianism, the device by which God was supposedly shoved out of the universe. The slow time scale of cosmic evolution now speeds up, for it now has a planning agent directing it. The new god, mankind, has the power to speed up evolutionary processes, even as Christians have argued that God demonstrated His power over time in creating the world in six days.

> With this, a new type of organization came into being—that of self-reproducing society. So long as man survives as a species (and there is no reason for thinking he will not) there seems to be no possibility for any other form of life to push up to this new organizational level. Indeed there are grounds for supposing that biological evolution has come to an end, so far as any sort of major advance is concerned. Thus further large-scale evolution has once again been immensely restricted in extent, being now it would seem confined to the single species man; but at the same time immensely accelerated in its speed, through the operation of the new mechanisms now available.[91]

Why should this be true? Because man has replaced genetic mutation (ordered by natural selection) with language, symbols, and writing. "The slow methods of variation and heredity are outstripped by the speedier processes of acquiring and transmitting experience."[92] Therefore, "in so far as the mechanism of evolution ceases to be blind and automatic and becomes conscious, ethics can be injected into the evolutionary process."[93]

90. *Ibid.*, pp. 133–34.
91. *Ibid.*, p. 134.
92. *Ibid.*, p. 135.
93. *Idem.*

2. Relativism and Statism

Huxley, predictably, argued for ethical relativism. There can be no "Absolute" ethics.[94] "The theologian and the moralist will be doing wrong so long as they cling to any absolute or unyielding certitude."[95] (We might ask the obvious questions: Would the "absolutizing" theologian or moralist *always* be wrong? Was Huxley *absolutely certain* of this?) In a later essay, Huxley criticized his grandfather's view of ethics as being too static.

> We can now say that T. H. Huxley's antithesis between ethics and evolution was false, because based on a limited definition of evolution and a static view of ethics.... More than that, we perceive that ethics itself is an organ of evolution, and itself evolves. And finally, by adopting this dynamic or evolutionary point of view of ethics as something with a time-dimension, a process rather than a system, we obtain light on one of the most difficult but also most central problems of ethics—the relation between individual and social ethics, and perceive that the antithesis between the individual and society can also be reconciled.[96]

Evolution means, above all, *process*—the ethics of historical relativism. How can these two forms of ethics be reconciled? In his 1943 lecture, Huxley argued for the supremacy of individualistic ethics, since "it is clear on evolutionary grounds that the individual is in a real sense higher than the State or the social organism.... All claims that the State has an intrinsically higher value than the individual are false. They turn out, on closer scrutiny, to be rationalizations or myths aimed at securing greater power or privilege for a limited group which controls the machinery of the State."[97] He delivered this speech during World War II, and he made certain that his audience knew where he stood. "Nazi ethics put the State above the individual."[98] The Nazi method is against evolutionism "on the grounds of efficiency alone."[99] All of a sudden, evolutionism's ethics of relativism grew rock-hard: "Furthermore, its principles run counter to those guaranteed by universalist evolutionary ethics."[100] The Nazis were doomed to fail, he concluded.

---

94. *Ibid.*, p. 129.

95. *Ibid.*, p. 138.

96. *Ibid.*, p. 217.

97. *Ibid.*, pp. 138–39.

98. *Ibid.*, p. 147.

99. *Ibid.*, p. 148.

100. *Idem.* Huxley could resist taking a swing at the Old Testament for its exaltation of the idea of a special chosen people. "In this the Nazis merely translate into modern

Four years later, in 1947, Huxley was calling for a one-world state. The atomic bomb had appeared, and civilization now had the possibility of destroying itself. (While the evolutionists never call thermonuclear holocaust "theocide," this is what they mean: god can now commit suicide.) In short, "the separate regions of the world have, for the first time in history, shrunk politically into a single unit, though so far not an orderly but a chaotic one: and now the atomic bomb hangs with equal grimness over all parts of this infant commonwealth of man.... The threat of the atomic bomb is simple—unite or perish."[101] He went on:

> So long as the human species is organized in a number of competing and sovereign nation-states, not only is it easy for a group to pick another group to serve as enemy, but it is in the group's narrow and short-term interest that it should do so.... The specific steps which will have to be taken before we can reach this next stage of ethical evolution are somewhat various. There is first the practical step of discovering how to transfer some of the sovereign power of several nation-states of the world to a central organization. This has its counterpart in the moral world: for one thing, any practical success in this task will make it easier for men to abandon the tribalist ethics (for tribalist they still are, however magnified in scale) associated with the co-existence of competing social groups.[102]

Even more strongly: "This is the major ethical problem of our time—to achieve global unity for man.... Present-day men and nations will be judged by history as moral or immoral according as to whether they have helped or hindered unification."[103]

3. A Unified God

Huxley provided documentation for Rushdoony's assessment that "humanity is the true god of the Enlightenment and of French Revolutionary thought. In all religious faiths one of the inevitable requirements of logical thought asserts itself in the demand for *the unity of the godhead*. Hence, since humanity is a god, there can be no division in this godhead, humanity. Mankind must therefore be forced to unite."[104] This is another reason why Rushdoony called the United

---

terms the ethics of tribes or peoples in an early barbarous phase of the world's history, such as the ancient Hebrews before the prophetic period" (p. 147).

101. *Ibid.*, p. 197.

102. *Ibid.*, pp. 247–49.

103. *Ibid.*, p. 255.

104. R. J. Rushdoony, *This Independent Republic: Studies in the Nature and Meaning of American History* (Vallecito, California: Ross House, [1964] 2001), p. 130.

Nations a religious dream.[105] Huxley confirmed this suspicion. Unity will advance mankind to the next stage of evolution. "I would suggest that the secondary critical point in human evolution will be marked by the union of all separate traditions in a single common pool, the orchestration of human diversity from competitive discord to harmonious symphony. Of what future possibilities beyond the human this may be the first foundation, who can say? But at least it will for the first time give full scope to man's distinctive method of evolution, and open the door to many human potentialities that are as yet scarcely dreamed of."[106] But who will lead the orchestra? He did not ask or say.

Huxley ended this book on evolutionary ethics with a statement quite similar to the one introducing this appendix: "Man the conscious microcosm has been thrown up by the blind and automatic forces of the unconscious macrocosm. But now his consciousness can begin to play an active part, and to influence the process of the macrocosm by guiding and acting as the growing-point of its evolution. Man's ethics and his moral aspirations have now become an integral part of any future evolutionary process."[107]

This theme became a familiar one in later books by Huxley. No statement is more forthright, however, than the opening chapter of his 1957 book, *Knowledge, Morality, and Destiny*, which he titled "Transhumanism." "As a result of a thousand million years of evolution, the universe is becoming conscious of itself, able to understand something of its past history and possible future. This cosmic self-awareness is being realized in one tiny fragment of the universe—in a few of us human beings."[108] Here is the combination of "Flyspeck Earth" and "man, the new predestinator." There is nothing humble about residing on a tiny bit of dust in an immense universe, whether one is a Christian or an evolutionist. Huxley repeated the now-familiar theme: man as a leap of being. "For do not let us forget that the human spe-

105. Rushdoony, "The United Nations: A Religious Dream," in *Politics of Guilt and Pity* (Vallecito, California: Ross House, [1970] 1995), pp. 184–99. He wrote two other essays on the religious quest of the United Nations: "The United Nations," in Rushdoony, *The Nature of the American System* (Vallecito, California: Ross House, [1965] 2001), ch. 7, and "Has the U.N. Replaced Christ as a World Religion?" in *Our Church: Their Target* (Arlington, Virginia: Better Books, 1966), ch. 10.

106. Huxley, "Conclusion," *Touchstone for Ethics*, p. 255. This is a quotation from an earlier book by Huxley, published by the United Nations' Educational, Scientific, and Cultural Organization (UNESCO): *The Prerequisites of Progress* (Paris: Editions Fontaine, 1947).

107. *Ibid.*, p. 257.

108. Julian Huxley, *Knowledge, Morality, and Destiny* (New York: Mentor Book, [1957] 1960), p. 13.

cies is as radically different from any of the microscopic single-celled animals that lived a thousand million years ago as they were from a fragment of stone or metal."[109] He, too, affirmed that the two great discontinuities in the uniformitarian universe were the appearance of life and the appearance of man. Evolutionists use uniformitarianism to push God back to the pre-life past or into the post-life future, and to deny the six-day creation. They do not use uniformitarianism to refute these two great discontinuities.

4. A New Evolution

We are supposedly now at another great period of evolutionary discontinuity. A new era is about to dawn. "The new understanding of the universe has come about through the new knowledge amassed in the last hundred years—by psychologists, biologists, and other scientists, by archaeologists, anthropologists, and historians. It has defined man's responsibility and destiny—to be an agent for the rest of the world in the job of realizing its inherent potentialities as fully as possible."[110] An amazing bit of luck for all of us, isn't it? It took ten billion years to get from the "big bang" to the advent of life in the solar system. Then it took another 3.497 (or possibly 3.498) billion years to get from life's origin (3.5 billion until about 300,000 years ago) to that second great cosmological discontinuity, man. And now, here we are, ready for stage three, the ascension of man to his position of universal power. If you had been born a Neanderthal man (let alone a brontosaurus), or even an eighteenth-century *Philosophe*, you would have missed it. Missed what? This:

> It is as if man had been suddenly appointed managing director of the biggest business of all, the business of evolution—appointed without being asked if he wanted it, and without proper warning or preparation. What is more, he can't refuse the job. Whether he wants to or not, whether he is conscious of what he is doing or not, he is in point of fact determining the future direction of evolution on this earth. That is his inescapable destiny, and the sooner he realizes it and starts believing in it, the better for all concerned.[111]

A new humanity is coming: "The human species can, if it wishes, transcend itself—not just sporadically, an individual here in one way, and an individual there in another way, but in its entirety, as human-

109. *Idem.*
110. *Idem.*
111. *Ibid.*, pp. 13–14.

ity. We need a name for this new belief. Perhaps transhumanism will serve: man remaining man, but transcending himself, by realizing new possibilities of and for his human nature."[112]

In case readers fail to recognize this ancient heresy, it is called gnosticism. This, in turn, was simply a variation of the original sin, the desire of man to be as God, to transcend man's own creaturely limitations by seeking special knowledge. Adam sought the knowledge of good and evil. The gnostics, in the second and third centuries A.D. in Asia Minor and North Africa, sought mystical illumination. In the Middle Ages, alchemists sought self-transcendence through repetitive chemical rituals—the quest for the so-called "philosopher's stone," which was not simply a means of converting lead into gold, but a means of enabling the alchemist to transcend his own limits as a creature. It is not surprising, then, that with the rise of secular humanism—in the late-medieval and early modern periods, as well as today—has come occultism, sorcery, demonism, and the quest for mystical utopia, especially through the techniques of Eastern religion, which has always been evolutionary in philosophy.[113] Humanism, whether Renaissance humanism or post-Darwinian humanism, is in league with occultism.[114]

5. Genetic Engineering

It would be unproductive to multiply citations of the evolutionists' sleight-of-hand operation. The Darwinists have used the dogma of cosmic purposelessness to free man from the constraints of biblical law and the threat of eternal judgment. Once freed from God, man is said to become the new predestinator. Dobzhansky, the Huxleys, Simpson, and others holding similar views have presented secular man with the humanists' version of the dominion covenant. Man is to conquer. With the discovery by Watson and Crick of the make-up of the DNA molecule, scientists are now in the process of creating new forms of life. The General Electric Company filed patents on one new life form, and an appeals court in 1979 upheld the firm's property right to this new species. The "gene splicers" are in our midst. Warn-

112. *Ibid.*, p. 17.
113. C. S. Lewis, *The Abolition of Man* (New York: Macmillan, [1947] 1967), pp. 87–89. Cf. Thomas Molnar, *God and the Knowledge of Reality* (New York: Basic Books, 1973); Frances Yates, *Giordano Bruno and the Hermetic Tradition* (New York: Vintage, [1964] 1969).
114. Gary North, *Unholy Spirits: Occultism and New Age Humanism* (Ft. Worth, Texas: Dominion Press, 1986), ch. 10.

ings are unlikely to stop the experimental mania of modern biological scientists. The technological imperative is too strong: "If it can be done, it must be done."[115] The hope of profits also lures research firms into the field. Financial success, which is likely over the short run at least, will bring in the competition. Recombinant DNA, the tool of the "gene splicers," discovered in 1973, has opened a true pandora's box of moral, intellectual, medical, and legal problems.[116] As one popular book on the subject warned: " 'Man the engineer' may soon become 'man the engineered.'"[117] The authors went on to cite recent statements by biological scientists that are in line with everything that has been said since the days of Thomas Huxley.

> Over these past three billion years, one hundred million species have existed on this planet. Of those, ninety-eight million are now extinct. Among the two million that remain today, only one, Homo sapiens ("wise man"), has evolved to the point of being able to harness and control its own evolutionary future. Many biologists welcome this possibility, seeing it as a great challenge that will ennoble and preserve our species. "Modern progress in microbiology and genetics suggests that man can outwit extinction through genetic engineering," argues Cal Tech biologist James Bonner. "Genetic change is not basically immoral. It takes place all the time, naturally. What man can do, however, is to make sure that these changes are no longer random in the gigantic lottery in nature. . . . Instead, he can control the changes to produce better individuals." Bonner's viewpoint is seconded by Dr. Joseph Fletcher, professor of Medical Ethics at the University of Virginia School of Medicine, who sees in genetic engineering the fulfillment of our cosmic role on earth. "To be men," he believes, "we must be in control. That is the first and last ethical word." Promises a third scientist, our newly developed eugenic potential will lead humanity to "a growth of social wisdom and glorious survival toward the evolution of a kind of superman."[118]

The book is well titled: *Who Should Play God?*

---

115. The idea of the technological imperative is the foundation of the critical book by Jacques Ellul, *The Technological Society* (New York: Vintage [1964] 1967).

116. John Lear, *Recombinant DNA: The Untold Story* (New York: Crown, 1978).

117. Jeremy Rifkin and Ted Howard, *Who Should Play God?* (New York: Dell, 1977), p. 14.

118. *Ibid.*, p. 21. See also Michael Rogers, *Biohazard* (New York: Knopf, 1977); June Goodfield, *Playing God: Genetic Engineering and the Manipulation of Life* (New York: Random House, 1977); Nicholas Wade, *The Ultimate Experiment: Man-Made Evolution* (New York: Walker & Walker, 1977).

J. Darwin's Intellectual Revolution

What a magnificent sleight-of-hand operation the defenders of evolution and humanism have accomplished! *First,* the universe was depersonalized. Darwin put it very forcefully: "It has been said that I speak of natural selection as an active power or Deity; but who objects to an author speaking of the attraction of gravity as ruling the movement of the planets? Everyone knows what is meant and implied by such metaphorical expressions; and they are almost necessary for brevity. So again it is difficult to avoid personifying the word Nature; but I mean by Nature, only the aggregate action and product of many natural laws, and bylaws the sequence of events as ascertained by us."[119] God was shoved out of the universe, leaving only humble man, whose power seems to be limited to "ascertaining laws," which are the sequence of events observed by us.

Second, man was reduced to being a mere cog in a mighty machine, not the representative of an infinite God, governing the earth as a subordinate in terms of the dominion covenant. A few paragraphs later, Darwin wrote: "How fleeting are the wishes and efforts of man! how short his time! and consequently how poor will be his results, compared with those accumulated by Nature during the whole geological periods! Can we wonder, then, that Nature's productions should be far 'truer' in character than man's productions; that they should be infinitely better adapted to the most complex conditions of life, and should plainly bear the stamp of higher workmanship?"[120] Not the higher workmanship of the God of the Bible or even the deistic god of Paley's *Natural Theology,* man is the "higher workmanship" of planless, meaningless, "random, yet cause-and-effect-governed" geological and biological process.

Third, evolutionists added a purposeful, meaning-providing conscious agent to this "random, yet cause-and-effect-governed," *previously* impersonal process. Darwin gave the intellectual game away in the concluding paragraph of *The Descent of Man* (second edition, 1874): "Man may be excused for feeling some pride at having risen, though not through his own exertions, to the very summit of the organic scale; and the fact of his having thus risen, instead of having been aboriginally placed there, may give him hope for a still higher

---

119. Charles Darwin, *Origin of Species,* ch. 4; in *The Origin of Species and the Descent of Man* (New York: Modern Library edition), p. 64.
120. *Ibid.,* p. 66.

destiny in the distant future."[121] But not so distant a future after all! In 1957, Sir Julian Huxley concluded: "Assuredly the concept of man as instrument and agent of the evolutionary process will become the dominant integrator of all ideas about human destiny, and will set the pattern of our general attitude to life. It will replace the idea of man as the Lord of Creation, as the puppet of blind fate, or as the willing or unwilling subject of a Divine Master."[122]

Man had lowly origins, but man is now the source of direction and meaning for the evolutionary process. This is Darwin's intellectual legacy. As he concluded *The Descent of Man*, "We must, however, acknowledge, as it seems to me, that man with all his noble qualities, with sympathy which feels for the most debased, with benevolence which extends not only to other men but to the humblest living creature, with his god-like intellect which has penetrated into the movements and constitution of the solar system—with all these exalted powers—Man still bears in his bodily frame the indelible stamp of his lowly origin."[123] Notice that Darwin chose to capitalize the word "man" in his final reference to this exalted being, as befits the name of one's deity. Man is no longer the image of God, but the image of apes, pre-apes, amoebae, and meaningless cosmic process. Still, he has this "god-like intellect," which shows sympathy and benevolence. He is therefore "exalted." But lowly, always the product of humble origins. In fact, *it is precisely man's humble, impersonal origins that provide him with his credentials of being the sole source of cosmic meaning.*

There is no one higher than man, for there is no one—no self-aware Creator—who preceded man. Anyone who is not familiar with this monumental sleight-of-hand operation may fail to grasp this, *the single most important intellectual transformation in the heart and soul of the religion of humanism.* Marxism was an important subordinate stream in this intellectual transformation, but by the late twentieth century, few people outside of a handful of Western intellectuals really believed in the tenets of original Marxism. They may well have believed in exercising power in the name of the Marxist intellectual heritage, but the priests, no less than the laymen, had lost faith in the old dogma. They had not abandoned faith in Darwin's dogma.

In 1959, Hermann J. Muller could write that *The Origin of Species* "was undoubtedly the greatest scientific book of all time... The result

---

121. *Ibid.*, p. 920.
122. Julian Huxley, *Knowledge, Morality, and Destiny*, p. 54.
123. Darwin, *op. cit.*, p. 920.

has been that this revolutionary view of life now stands as one of the most firmly established generalizations of science...."[124] It is a religion, as Muller's words indicate: "We dare not leave it to the Soviets alone to offer to their rising generation the inspiration that is to be gained from the wonderful world view opened up by Darwin and other Western biologists."[125] On both sides of the Iron Curtain, the priesthoods were enlisting the faithful, offering them salvation by means of evolution. This is a religion that supposedly will provide meaning, and the objections of anti-evolutionists must be stifled for the sake of the masses: "The history of living things, and its interpretation, can be made a fascinating story that will give our young people a strong sense of the meaning of life, not only for plants and animals in general, but for mankind in particular, and for them themselves.... We have no more right to starve the masses of our youth intellectually and emotionally because of the objections of the uninformed than we have a right to allow people to keep their children from being vaccinated and thus endanger the whole community physically."[126] Statement after statement like this one can be found in the extraordinarily revealing book, *Darwin: A Norton Critical Edition* (1970).

The humility of post-Darwin humanists is a myth—a myth fostered by them, and one which has its roots in Darwin's own sleight-of-hand operation. Anyone who thinks that man was anything but elevated by Darwinism has deluded himself. He has swallowed only the first bit of bait tossed to him by the Darwinians. There was more to come.

Thomas Huxley, Darwin's first great promoter and Sir Julian's grandfather, could write about earth, "the speck," or the supposed fact that man is not the "centre of the living world, but one amidst endless modifications of life,"[127] but this was (and is) part of an enormous deception. Consider the words of Philip Handler, who was the president of the National Academy of Sciences in 1976. He delivered this speech to the General Assembly of the International Council of Scientific Unions, so it was not intended to be too off-beat, too radical, or too embarrassing to its author. You will not find his view of man's role particularly long on humility.

124. Hermann J. Muller, "One Hundred Years Without Darwinism Are Enough," *The Humanist*, XIX (1959); reprinted in Philip Appleman (ed.), *Darwin: A Norton Critical Edition*, p. 545.
125. *Idem.*
126. *Ibid.*, p. 547.
127. Thomas H. Huxley, "On Improving Natural Knowledge" (1866), *Collected Works*, I, p. 39.

How very privileged we are—we who have lived through the last half-century of science, that historic few decades in which the mind of man first came really to understand the nature of the atomic nucleus; first learned the history of our planet and identified the forces that continue to refigure its surface, the habitat of our species; the time when man's mind first engaged the immense sweep and grandeur of the cosmos in what we believe to be its true dimensions; the time when our species commenced upon the physical exploration of the solar system. Ours is the fortunate generation that, for the first time, came to understand the essential aspects of the marvelous phenomenon which is life, a phenomenon describable only in the language of chemistry; came to understand the mechanisms that have operated over the eons of biological evolution. In short, ours may well be the first generation that knows what we are and where we are. That knowledge permitted the acquisition of new capabilities whereby we utilize an extraordinary assemblage of synthetic materials, each created for a specific purpose, whereby we manipulate our environment, communicate, move about, protect our health, avoid pain and even extend the power of our own intellects.... In a historic sense, the scientific endeavor began only yesterday, yet we have come a wondrous distance from our primeval ignorance in so short a time....[128]

This remarkable testimony of a prominent biologist's faith was published in *The Washington Post* (Dec. 22, 1976), the most widely read newspaper in the political capital of the United States.

Evolution is the religion of modern humanism. It was also the religion of ancient humanism. The explanation is different evolution by natural selection—but the religion's really important dogma has not been changed significantly since the primary version was presented to mankind by Satan: We shall be as gods (Gen. 3:5).

K. Fictional Science, Science Fiction

One of occultism's universal themes is the appearance of a new creation, some sort of positive human mutation.[129] But do serious scientists take this vision very seriously? Some do, as indicated by their explicit statements concerning recombinant DNA and genetic engineering. Another bit of evidence appeared in *The Wall Street Journal* (Sept. 10, 1979), on the back page. An expensive advertisement was run by Pertec Computer Corporation, apparently some sort of "public service" advertisement. It featured a photograph of America's most

---

128. Philip Handler, "Science and Hope," *Science: A Resource for Mankind*, Proceedings of the National Academy of Science, Bicentennial Symposium (Oct. 10–14, 1976), pp. 12–13.

129. Cf. Gary North, *Unholy Spirits*, ch. 10.

prolific author, Dr. Isaac Asimov, who had written over 200 books at the time the ad appeared.[130] He held a Ph.D. in biochemistry, but he was more famous for his science fiction stories and his popularizations of modern natural science. During one period of 100 months, Asimov turned out 100 books. He did all his own typing (90 words a minute), almost every day, for most of the day. He has at least one book in nine of the ten Dewey decimal classification categories. He did not write a book on philosophy. In short, he was no raving lunatic. The advertisement read: "Will computers take over?"

Asimov addressed the question of computer intelligence. Could computers ever become more intelligent than men? Asimov's answer: the knowledge stored by a computer is not the same as man's knowledge. They are two separate developments. "The human brain evolved by hit-and-miss, by random mutations, making use of subtle chemical changes, and with a forward drive powered by natural selection and by the need to survive in a particular world of given qualities and dangers. The computer brain is evolving by deliberate design as the result of careful human thought, making use of subtle electrical charges, and with a forward drive powered by technological advancement and the need to serve particular human requirements." From the "hit-and-miss" random evolution of man's brain, to man the battling and planning survivor, to the forward-driven computer (impersonal, purposeless mechanism, to purposeful organic agent, to personalized mechanism): here is the standard, post-Darwin account. But Asimov blazed new trails. The two forms of intelligence are too different to be compared on the same scale. We cannot make such comparisons. We must keep the systems distinct. Each should specialize. "This would be particularly true if genetic engineering was deliberately used to improve the human brain in precisely those directions in which the computer is weak." We must avoid wasteful duplication he said.

> Consequently the question of "taking over" need never arise. What we might see, instead, would be symbiosis or complementation, human brain and computer working together, each supplying what the other lacks, forming an intelligence pair that would be greater than either could be alone, an intelligence pair that would open new horizons, not now imaginable, and make it possible to achieve new heights, not now dreamed of. In fact, the union of brains, human and human-made, might serve as the doorway through which human beings could emerge from their isolated childhood into their combination adulthood.

---

130. *Time* (Feb. 26, 1979).

The advertisement sold no product and did not instruct the reader to clip a coupon or take any sort of action. It simply offered a message—a message of a new evolution.

The same theme is found in the first *Star Trek* movie, released in December of 1979. The movie's science advisor was Asimov. The movie is about a future space ship crew that confronts an unimaginably powerful intelligence. This intelligence turns out to be an enormous machine, one which had been built by a civilization run entirely by machines. It literally knows everything in the universe, yet it is travelling back to earth to seek the "Creator" and to join with the "Creator" in a metaphysical union (Eastern mysticism). The machine is perfectly rational, totally devoid of feeling, and is a "child" at the very beginning of its evolution. It turns out that the center of the machine's guidance system is a centuries-old United States space probe, the Voyager, which had been sent into space to seek knowledge and send back that knowledge to earth. Hence, the "Creator" was man. The movie ends when an officer of the crew joins in metaphysical union with the machine, along with a mechanical robot built by the machine—a robot that duplicated his ex-lover. The officer, the female robot, and the enormous machine then disappear. Science officer Spock, a human-Vulcan genius—a mutant product of two races—announces that a new being has just evolved from the fusion of man, man-made machinery, machinery-made machinery, and a machine-made robot that is "almost human" (actually, Deltan, whatever the planet Delta produces; the lady had a shaved head to match her vow of chastity). Spock, a cult figure from the mid-1960s through the next 45 years, who had been seeking total rationalism (his Vulcan side) to the exclusion of feeling (his human side), now is content to remain with the humans on board the Starship *Enterprise*, apparently satisfied with his somewhat schizophrenic mind-emotion dualism. And why not? He had seen the perfectly rational (the huge machine), and it had been lonely, seeking its "Creator." To make the next evolutionary step, it required fusion with mankind. Spock, with his pointed ears and his computer-like brain, is as close to that next evolution as any Vulcan-human could ever hope for. The movie, based on a popular television series of the late 1960s, immediately attracted ticket buyers among the millions of "trekkies," their cult-like fans.

If Asimov's vision does not border on the occult, what does? If the message of that computer company's advertisement and the *Star Trek* movie does not represent a religious position, what else should we call such a message? Science? Science fiction? "Mere" entertainment? Or a combination of all three, which in addition is also a religion?

L. Christian Orthodoxy vs. Process Philosophy

Readers may think that I am belaboring a point, but this point is crucial for understanding the confessional foundation of modern humanism. Charles Darwin created an intellectual revolution. That intellectual revolution still affects us. He did not simply provide interesting new evidence concerning historical geology or biological reproduction; he created a new world-and-life view. It was this new perspective on man's origins, not the factual data, that made Darwin's *Origin of Species* an instant best-seller. The clergy in Darwin's day recognized the threat to the biblical world-and-life view which was posed by the *Origin*. As Philip Appleman observed:

> Theologians worried because they saw, perhaps more clearly than others, the philosophical implications of post-Darwinian thought. It was not just that Darwin had complicated the reading of Genesis, or even that he had furnished impressive scientific authority for the nineteenth-century habit of thinking in terms of wholes and continuities rather than in discrete parts and rigidities; or that the evolutionary orientation stressed context and complexity—though all of these influences could be bothersome when used by "materialists." The worst threat of all was that Darwin's universe operated not by Design but by natural selection, a self-regulating mechanism.... Natural selection pictured the world in a constant process of change, but without any prior intention of going anywhere in particular or of becoming anything in particular. This was a devastating proposition to the conventional theologian—more so, perhaps, than the Copernican theory had been, because it struck so close to home. Natural selection therefore seemed, to many, hopelessly negative, fraught with blasphemy and conducive of despair.[131]

This despair was initially covered over by optimism concerning the power of man to take over the direction of the evolutionary process, an optimism that still survives, though not without fear and foreboding on the part of some scientists and philosophers.

> So it *made a difference* to philosophers and theologians that man not only evolved, but evolved by natural selection rather than by a vital force or cosmic urge of some sort. Darwinism seemed uncompromisingly non-teleological, non-vitalist, and non-finalist, and that basic fact could not help

---

131. Philip Appleman, "Darwin: On Changing the Mind," Epilogue in Appleman (ed.), *Darwin*, pp. 636–37.

but affect the work of philosophers. "Once man was swept into the evolutionary orbit," Bert James Lowenberg has written, "a revolution in Western thought was initiated. Man was seen to be a part of nature, and nature was seen to be a part of man. The Darwinian revolution was not a revolution in science alone; it was a revolution in man's conception of himself and in man's conception of all his works."[132]

Appleman chronicled the decline in the opposition to Darwinism on the part of Roman Catholics and other theologians. "The activities of science, relentlessly pushing back the margins of the unknown, have in effect been forcing the concept of 'God' into a perpetual retreat into the still-unknown, and it is in this condition that 'God' has frequently come to have meaning for modern man."[133] The modern evolutionist is a defender of a concept of process that removes God and His control from the universe, so that man and man's sovereignty can be substituted for the supposedly nonexistent God. Meaningless process is the evolutionist's god of origins. Only when a meaningful God who created the universe in terms of His *eternal, unchanging decree* is finally removed from our thought processes, can our thought processes take control of all other processes, the modern evolutionist argues. *Evolutionary process is the humanist's god of origins*, a god whose crucial purpose for man is to remove from the question of origins any concept of purpose. Man's monopoly of cosmic purpose is supposedly assured as a direct result of the non-purposeful origins of the universe. This is why Rushdoony took such pains to contrast process philosophy and creationism.[134]

---

132. *Ibid.*, p. 637.

133. *Ibid.*, pp. 638–39.

134. R. J. Rushdoony, *The Mythology of Science* (Vallecito, California: Ross House, [1967] 2001), pp. 53–54, 85. Process philosophy, which is basic to all evolutionary systems, leads inescapably into relativism. The implicit relativism of evolutionism cannot be reconciled with the implicit authoritarianism of the biblical doctrine of creation. Rushdoony's discussion of evolutionism is fundamental: "In this concept, being is evolving and is in process. Because being is in process, and being is seen as one and undivided, truth itself is tentative, evolving, and without finality. Since being has not yet assumed a final form, since the universe is in process and not yet a finished product, truth itself is in process and is continually changing. A new movement or 'leap of being' can give a man a new truth and render yesterday's truth a lie. But, in an order created by a perfect, omnipotent, and totally self-conscious Being, God, truth is both final, specific, and authoritative. God's word can then be, and is inevitably, infallible, because there is nothing tentative about God himself. Moreover, truth is ultimately personal, because the source, God, is personal, and truth becomes incarnate in the person of Jesus Christ and is communicated to those who believe in Him. Jesus Christ as Lord and Savior, as the way, the truth, and the life, is also the Christian principle of continuity. The Christian doctrine, therefore, involved a radical break with the pagan

It is revealing to read the attempted refutation of Rushdoony written by a self-proclaimed orthodox Christian geologist (who argued for a 4.6 billion-year-old earth).[135] He had no understanding of what process philosophy is and how Darwinism promotes it. "Rushdoony's fears are unfounded. An affirmation of process in itself certainly does not constitute an attack on the sovereignty of God. Scripture reveals in [sic] the sovereignty of God in history, in day-to-day affairs, in the ordinary rising and setting of the sun. Process is going on all about us now, and God is every whit as sovereign as He was in the creation."[136]

Exactly what kind of creation did Dr. Young have in mind? A creation in which the sun, moon, and stars were created after the earth? Not necessarily.[137] The six-day creation? No, because *we have no human interpretation of Genesis 1 that is infallible.*"[138] A view of Genesis 1 which says that Adam and Eve were created on the sixth day? No, because the genealogies in the Bible do not tell us enough to say that man is only a few thousand years old.[139] "On the basis of these considerations it is probably virtually impossible for the Christian to identify, from the fossil record, the time when special creation occurred."[140] In short, he asserted, everything the Bible says is indeterminate with respect to chronological time. Therefore, he continued to use the 4.6 billion-year-old date as his operating presupposition, thereby providing himself with full acceptability within the state university faculty of secular humanists where he was employed. If he believed otherwise, he would have had to give up that work which he has chosen as his profession, namely, providing explanations for the hypothetically one-billion-year-old rocks. He said as much: "If Scripture really does teach unequivocally that the universe was miraculously created in 144 hours a few thousands of years ago, then I, as a Christian geologist, will be willing to stop scientific interpreta-

doctrine of continuity of being and with the doctrine of chaos. It also involved a break with the other aspect of the dialectic, the pagan, rationalistic concept of order. Order is not the work of autonomous and developing gods and men but rather the sovereign decree of the omnipotent God. This faith freed man from the sterile autonomy which made him the helpless prisoner of Fate, or the relentless workings of a blind order." Rushdoony, *The One and the Many: Studies in the Philosophy of Order and Ultimacy* (Vallecito, California: Ross House, [1971] 2007), pp. 151–52.

135. Davis A. Young, *Creation and the Flood: An Alternative to Flood Geology and Theistic Evolution* (Grand Rapids, Michigan: Baker Book House, 1977), p. 87.

136. *Ibid.*, p. 49.

137. *Ibid.*, pp. 128–29.

138. *Ibid.*, p. 133.

139. *Ibid.*, p. 151.

140. *Ibid.*, p. 155.

tion of the supposedly one-billion-year-old rocks of northern New Jersey which I have been studying for the past several years. Obviously my only task now is to describe those rocks and to find valuable resources in them. If the mature creationist interpretation of Genesis 1 is correct, I am wasting my time talking about magmas and metamorphism inasmuch as these rocks were created instantaneously in place."[141]

Those of us who, like myself, believe in the Bible's narrative of a six-day creation, must conclude that Dr. Young did indeed waste his time by studying those rocks in terms of a uniformitarian presupposition. He also used money confiscated from me by the state of North Carolina, where Dr. Young taught when I lived there. The state used my money to hire Dr. Young to indoctrinate students with uniformitarianism. Dr. Young then wrote an intellectual defense of his uniformitarian faith, so that other Christians might be convinced! Confiscated tax dollars were promoting Dr. Young's professional religion, uniformitarianism. (His professed religion has been compromised by his professional, academic religion. He later taught at Calvin College.)

We must not be naive. *The uniformitarian interpretation of geological processes is a religion.* It has led to a more consistent religion, that of evolution through natural selection. The god of uniformitarian, meaningless, directionless process was created by nineteenth-century humanists and compromising Christian geologists—whose intellectual and spiritual heirs are still publishing books—in order to provide an explanation of this world which did not require full allegiance to the plain teaching of Genesis 1. The god of uniformitarian geology, whose high priest was Charles Lyell, metamorphosed (evolved?) into a far stronger deity, the god of evolution through natural selection. Charles Darwin became the founder and high priest of this new god, whose kingdom is the whole academic and scientific world. Finally, Darwin's god of meaningless process has developed into the modern god, mankind, who will take over the operations of evolutionary process.

Anyone who fails to recognize the satanic nature of uniformitarianism's process divinity is hopelessly naive, for it is this divinity who has torn the eternal decree of God from the presuppositions of modern man, leaving man with only random process, or man-directed tyrannical process, to comfort him. Christians cannot afford to be

141. *Ibid.*, p. 82.

hopelessly naive, even if this self-imposed naiveté is their justification for remaining on the faculties of state university geology or biology departments. The price of such naiveté is still too high, for them and for their equally naive Christian readers, who do not recognize a theological battle when they see it.

M. Social Darwinism: Phase I

The social philosophers of the late nineteenth century grappled with the same fundamental intellectual problems that faced the biologists. What is the nature of evolution? Is the species *Homo sapiens* governed by the same laws as those governing other species? Is "survival of the fittest" a law applying to mankind? If so, in what ways? Is competition primarily individualistic—man vs. man, man vs. environment—or primarily collectivist, with mankind as a united species seeking to conquer all other opponents for the domination of the external world?

There is no question concerning the existence of purpose. The economists and sociologists of the late nineteenth century, no less than those of the twenty-first, accepted the reality of human purpose. Like today's professional social thinkers, the leading defenders of the "new evolutionism" were often atheists and agnostics, in their methodology certainly, and usually also in their private beliefs. They did not rely on grandiose concepts of cosmic purpose. Man's purpose was sufficient to explain human cause and effect. But the word "man" posed a major problem: Was collective man, meaning mankind, the proper focus of concern, or was the individual man the source of purpose? Are we to speak of some sort of overarching purpose of man the species, or should we be content to explain the workings of political economy in terms of multiple individualistic purposes? Is our methodology to be holistic or individualistic? Are we to proclaim the sovereignty of "man, the purposeful, planning individual" or "man, the purposeful, planning species"? Are we talking about the survival of the fittest species, or about the survival of the fittest individuals *within* a particular species? Can we speak of the survival of the fittest species without stating the conditions for the survival of the most fit individuals within the species? What, in other words, is meant by "fit"?

1. Right-Wing Social Darwinism

The handful of Social Darwinists of the late nineteenth century, led by the British sociologist-philosopher Herbert Spencer and Yale

University's sociologist William Graham Sumner, focused on the individual. Individual action is primary, they said. Individuals have purposes; collective wholes do not. Sumner stated the case for individual rights in his book, *What Social Classes Owe to Each Other* (1883):

> The notion of civil liberty which we have inherited is that of *a status created for the individual by laws and institutions, the effect of which is that each man is guaranteed the use of all his own powers exclusively for his own welfare.* It is not at all a matter of elections, or universal suffrage, or democracy. All institutions are to be tested by the degree to which they guarantee liberty. It is not to be admitted for a moment that liberty is a means to social ends, and that it may be impaired for major considerations. Anyone who so argues has lost his bearing and relation of all the facts and factors in a free state. A human being has a life to live, a career to run. He is a centre of powers to work, and of capacities to suffer.[142]

His conclusion was straightforward: "It is not at all the function of the state to make men happy. They must make themselves happy in their own way, and at their own risk."[143]

As a Darwinist, Sumner believed in the survival of the fittest. (Spencer had coined the phrase in 1852.) Sumner criticized social reformers who believed that the civil government should intervene to help the weak and defenseless members of society. "They do not perceive, furthermore, that if we do not like the survival of the fittest, we have only one possible alternative, and that is the survival of the unfittest. The former is the law of civilization; the latter is the law of anti-civilization. We have our choice between the two, or we can go on, as in the past, vacillating between the two, but a third plan—the socialist desideratum—a plan for nourishing the unfittest and yet advancing in civilization, no man will ever find."[144]

Spencer was so worried about the survival of the least fit that he questioned even private charity, although he accepted the legitimacy of such charity, because its alternative—allowing the poor to reproduce their kind without guidance from those giving the charity—frightened him. As he said, "the problem seems insoluble."[145] There is only one possible answer: *suffering*. We cannot alleviate the misery

---

142. William Graham Sumner, *What Social Classes Owe to Each Other* (Caldwell, Idaho: Caxton, [1883] 1952), p. 30.

143. *Ibid.*, p. 31.

144. Sumner, cited by Richard Hofstadter, *Social Darwinism in American Thought*, rev. ed. (New York: George Braziller, 1959), p. 57.

145. Herbert Spencer, *The Principles of Ethics* (Indianapolis, Indiana: Liberty Classics, [1897] 1978), II, p. 409.

of the poor in general. "Each new effort to mitigate the penalties on improvidence, has the inevitable effect of adding to the number of the improvident."[146] Charity leads to more mouths to feed.

> Having, by unwise institutions, brought into existence large numbers who are unadapted to the requirements of social life, and are consequently sources of misery to themselves and others, we cannot repress and gradually diminish this body of relatively worthless people without inflicting much pain. Evil has been done and the penalty must be paid. Cure can come only through affliction. The artificial assuaging of distress by state appliances, is a kind of social opium eating, yielding temporary mitigation at the eventual cost of intenser misery.[147]

Ultimately, it would be best even to eliminate private charity. "If left to operate in all its sternness, the principle of the survival of the fittest, which, as ethically considered, we have seen to imply that each individual shall be left to experience the effects of his own nature and consequent conduct, would quickly clear away the degraded."[148]

Through the competition of individuals in a free market, the greatest possible output will be achieved, and this leads to greater wealth for those who survive, as well as greater strength for the species as a whole. Social Darwinism did not argue that there is not purpose in the universe, or that individuals do not belong to a species. Through voluntary cooperation in production, the division of labor increases each participant's wealth. Yet the higher a species, the more an individual member must live in terms of his own production and skills.[149] Man cannot escape this law of nature, Spencer wrote.

> Of man, as of all inferior creatures, the law by conformity to which the species is preserved, is that among adults the individuals best adapted to the conditions of their existence shall prosper most, and that the individuals least adapted to the conditions of their existence shall prosper least—a law which, if uninterfered with, entails the survival of the fittest, and the spread of the most adapted varieties. And as before so here, we see that, ethically considered, this law implies that each individual ought to receive the benefits and the evils of his own nature and consequent conduct: neither being prevented from having whatever good his actions normally bring to him, nor allowed to shoulder off on to other persons whatever ill is brought to him by his actions.[150]

---

146. *Ibid.*, II, p. 408.
147. *Ibid.*, II, p. 409.
148. *Ibid.*, II, p. 408.
149. *Ibid.*, II, p. 278.
150. *Ibid.*, II, p. 33.

This is the methodological individualism of right-wing Social Darwinism.

Right-wing Social Darwinists had to assume that there is a relationship between the prosperity of the productive individual and the prosperity of the species. In other words, the prosperity of the effective competitor leads to an increase of strength for the species. One obvious and troublesome exception seems to be success at offensive warfare, where the most courageous and dedicated men wind up killing each other, leaving the cowards and weaklings to return home to reproduce. Spencer realized this and specifically denied that offensive wars are a productive form of intra-species competition.[151] On the whole, though, individuals who compete successfully will be able to take the society along with them. The human race therefore ensures its survival by permitting the full competition of all its members. The *one* (society) is strengthened by the continual competition of its *parts* (individuals). This is the message of Darwin, which the Social Darwinists asked late nineteenth-century readers to believe.

This faith involved confidence in the integrating capacity of the free market. The "cut-throat" competition of individuals leads to social progress. Men need capital to equip them for the battle against nature, Sumner said. Capital is man's great tool of survival.

> Undoubtedly the man who possesses capital has a great advantage over the man who has no capital, in the struggle for existence.... This does not mean that the one man has an advantage against the other, but that, when they are rivals in the effort to get the means of subsistence from Nature, the one who has capital has immeasurable advantages over the other. If it were not so, capital would not be formed. Capital is only formed by self-denial, and if the possession of it did not secure advantages and superiorities of a high order, men would never submit to what is necessary to get it.[152]

This sounds plausible, until you realize that the disadvantaged man is, in fact, in direct competition for scarce resources, and if one man gets more of nature's goods out of the earth, then in some circumstances, his neighbor may be harmed (e.g., in a drought, when only one man can buy water, or in a famine, when only one of them can buy food). Since the neighbor is also a part of impersonal nature, then one aspect of man's struggle with nature is the defeat of his neighbor in the struggle for limited resources. Why, then, should we be so confident in the law of the survival of the fittest? Can we say

---

151. *Ibid.*, II, pp. 37–39.
152. Sumner, *Social Classes*, p. 66–67.

for sure that the inheritors of the rich man's capital will use it for the survival of the species, in the same way that evolutionists argue that the heirs of a successful mutant amoeba will have a better chance of surviving? Even here, is it really the original species that survives, or is the mutant a stepping stone in a new development which will not benefit the non-mutant original species? May not the mutant subspecies wipe out the original species in the competition for survival? Isn't that precisely what the survival of the fittest is all about—not the survival of species, but survival of mutant or genetically better equipped members of a particular species?

2. Deceiving the Victims

Let us consider an impossibility. What if the members of some lower species a billion years ago recognized the advent of a mutant member? The original members see that the newcomer possesses certain genetic advantages which will enable it to compete more successfully for the limited supply of food, shelter, and space. It will pick off the most desirable females (if it is male). Its progeny will survive, while the progeny of the original members of the older "about-to-be-superseded" population will be less likely to survive. The new tribe member, with its mutant genes, is the first representative of a somewhat different future species. After all, that is what evolution is all about.

The members of the older species recognize that whatever comes out of the "loins" of the mutant a million years or billion years down the evolutionary road, the heirs will not be the same species. In fact, if such an heir walked down the path right now, it would be regarded by everyone in the community as an enemy, dangerously different, and fit to be killed in the competition. In short, what would be the most rational response of the original members of the species? Wouldn't the smart thing be the immediate execution of the mutant, that herald of a conquering alien race, that emissary of future foreign conquerors?

The modern evolutionist would say that such a hypothetical scenario is preposterous. Why? Because lower species are ignorant. They do not understand evolution. They do not recognize mutants. Quite true, but man does. Men do know these supposed laws of evolution. How, then, do we convince today's species, *Homo sapiens*, not to kill off the mutants? If the primary form of evolution is now cultural and intellectual—a familiar theme among all evolutionists—then how does the average man protect himself against the "mutant" intellectual? How does the average man defend himself against the gene-splicing experts who proclaim themselves to be capable of altering the course of evolution, who say that some time in the future, they will be able to create a new race of supermen? How do the average members escape Aldous Huxley's brave new world? And if the right-wing Social Darwinists are correct, how does the poor man without capital guarantee the survival of his progeny, if he sees that the success of his rich neighbor is a threat to his family's success? *If we recognize the mutants, will we kill them?* If we do kill them, will the race survive without them? But if we don't, will some mutant heirs win out?

The answer of modern social evolutionists and non-Social Darwinists is not all that clear. Generally, they have countered the right-wing Social Darwinists in the name of a higher reason, a collective human reason. Man is the capstone of an unplanned evolutionary process. He has transcended this undirected process, or at least may be about to transcend it. Through conscious planning, elite members of the race will be able to integrate the plans of all the members into an overarching whole, and this overarching whole will guarantee the survival of all, including the "least fit," who might otherwise be prepared to kill off the "mutants."

What other approach would be better? If you believed that you are a "mutant"—an expert, a rich man, the member of the planning elite—wouldn't you come to the "about-to-be-superseded" masses and tell them that you are "just one of the boys," and "we're all in this together," and that we all need to buckle down "for the sake of humanity"? In other words, wouldn't you devise a social philosophy which would promise to the masses sufficient benefits to guarantee their survival in the competition? Or would you continue to shout them down as members of an about-to-be-superseded species, telling them that it is their responsibility to play the game by your ferocious rules or else get off the playing field, when getting off the field means death?

If you were really a mutant, then the one thing you would not have is numerical superiority. The one thing you could not risk would be a head-on collision with the massive numbers of "about-to-be-superseded" voters, troops, or whatever. You would make your sales pitch in terms of the greatest good for the greatest number. You would tell the masses that the greatest good for the greatest number involves playing the game by your rules, which on the surface seem to be democratic, but which in fact are radically elitist. You would deny that blood lines count, or that the feudal principle is valid. You would offer them democracy, bureaucracy, universal free education, welfare redistribution, and so forth. Then you would select only those members of the masses who showed themselves willing and able to compete in terms of the elitist system. You would give a few of them scholarships to the best universities, and you would recruit them into what they believe (and you may even believe) is "the inner circle." You would expand the power of the government, and then you would open high-level positions in that government only to those specially chosen by the ruling power.

What you would do, in short, is to construct precisely the statist system which exists today in every major industrial nation—a system that in the 1930s was called fascism, but which can also be called socialism, communism, the corporate state, the business-industrial complex, the new federalism, the Programming, Planning and Budgeting System (PPBS), or just to make your real goals explicit, the New World Order. What you would construct, in the name of man-controlled evolution, is a new Tower of Babel.

3. American Progressivism

The logic of the right-wing Social Darwinists was bound to fail. The "robber barons" (an unfortunate term) of the late nineteenth century may have appreciated the ruthless logic of right-wing Social Darwinism during the period of their upward mobility, but once they were established as the dominant forces in the market, they abandoned the market's competition in the name of "economic stability." In short, they preferred monopoly to competition. By 1900, the large American conglomerates began to look to government intervention, all in the name of protecting the consumer, for protection against newer, innovative, "cut-throat" firms.[153]

Almost at the same time, the Progressive movement in the United States began to make itself felt in politics. This political-intellectual movement was run by elitists for elitists, and it proclaimed a philosophy of economic interventionism. The state was now to replace the free market as the engine of evolution. The market was too free, too uncontrolled, too individualistic for the Progressives. They wanted to direct market forces for national, and later international, ends. They

---

153. Gabriel Kolko, *The Triumph of Conservatism: A Reinterpretation of American History* (New York: Free Press, 1963); Frederic C. Howe, *Confessions of a Monopolist* (Dearborn, Michigan: Alpine, [1906] 1977).

lost faith in the progress-producing automatic forces of market competition. The free market was too much like the hypothetical competition of evolutionary change. There was no way to guarantee the survival of humanity if humanity proved to be less fit. *The external environment had to be manipulated to conform to the needs of mankind, thereby reversing the purposeless, anti-teleological processes of natural selection.* Man, the new source of direction and meaning, must assert his dominance by means other than random competition. Random competition was fine for pre-human, pre-teleological evolution, but it will no longer suffice. The "survival of the fittest" henceforth would mean "the survival of the *fitters*." Planning man (collective man) would fit the environment (including other men) to fit his needs, aspirations, and skills.

With the Progressive movement came a new version of social Darwinism: left-wing social Darwinism. Within two decades, 1885–1905, it replaced right-wing social Darwininism. One intellectual, perhaps more than any other, was responsible for shifting American evolutionists' outlook from right-wing social Darwinism's free market competition to modern statism's central planning and interference with market forces. It was not Karl Marx. It was a long-forgotten government bureaucrat, one of the founders of American sociology, Lester Frank Ward.

N. Social Darwinism: Phase II

Lester Frank Ward wrote *Dynamic Sociology* (1883), the first comprehensive sociological treatise written in the United States.[154] He has been described as the father of the American concept of the planned society.[155] He was born in Illinois in 1841. His father was an itinerant mechanic and his mother the daughter of a clergyman. He was poor as a youth, but he still found time to teach himself Latin, French, German, biology, and physiology. He was self-disciplined. He joined the U. S. Treasury Department in 1865. He continued his studies at night school, and within five years he had earned degrees in medicine, law, and the arts. In the mid-1870s he worked for the Bureau of Statistics, and it was at this time that he concluded that a study of statistics could lead to the formulation of laws of society, which in turn could be used in a program of social planning. He continued his self-ed-

---

154. Hofstadter, *Social Darwinism*, p. 69.

155. Clarence J. Karier, *Shaping the American Educational State: 1900 to the Present* (New York: Free Press, 1975), p. 139. Cf. Sidney Fine, *Laissez-Faire and the General Welfare State* (Ann Arbor: University of Michigan Press, 1956), pp. 253–64.

ucation in the field of paleontology, and in 1883, the year *Dynamic Sociology* appeared, he was appointed chief paleontologist of the U.S. Geological Survey. Finally, after publishing five books in sociology, he was appointed to the chair of sociology in 1906 at Brown University, the same year that he was elected the first president of the newly formed American Sociological Association.[156]

Ward's *Dynamic Sociology* was ignored for a decade after its publication, selling only 500 copies.[157] In 1897, a second edition was issued, and within three years he was considered one of the leaders in the field. After his death in 1913, his reputation faded rapidly. He had laid the groundwork for American collectivism in the name of progressive evolution, but he was forgotten by the next and subsequent generations.

Ward broke radically with Spencer and Sumner. He had two great enemies, intellectually speaking: the social Darwinist movement and all supernatural religion. It is difficult to say which he hated more, although religion received the more vitriolic attacks. *Dynamic Sociology* stands as the first and perhaps the most comprehensive defense of government planning in American intellectual history. It was published about 15 years too early, but when his ideas caught on, they spread like wildfire. In fact, they became the "coin of the realm" in planning circles so rapidly that the source of these ideas was forgotten. Because the book is almost unknown today, and because Ward's concepts and language are so graphic, I am providing an extended summary and analysis of his thought.

In *Dynamic Sociology*, we have the heart and soul of modern, post-Darwin social evolutionist philosophy. Ward did not pull any punches. He did not try to evade the full implications of his position. Modern thinkers may not be so blatant and forthright, but if they hold to the modern version of evolution—man-directed evolution—then they are unlikely to reject the basic ideas that Ward set forth. If you want to follow through the logic of man-directed evolution, you must start with Ward's *Dynamic Sociology*.

1. Supernaturally Revealed Religion

Ward was forthright. He made it clear that the enemy is revealed religion, which in the United States in the early 1880s, meant Christianity. In the 82-page introduction to the book, in which he outlined his thesis, Ward announced that those people claiming to have re-

---

156. Ward's biography is supplied by Hofstadter, *Social Darwinism*, pp. 68–71.
157. *Ibid.*, p. 70.

ceived divine inspiration, and those who have founded religious systems, have been found by modern medicine to be not only "pathological" but to be burdened by "an actually deranged condition of their minds."[158] Because of the power these religious leaders have wielded historically, "we can only deplore the vast waste of energy which their failure to accomplish their end shows them to have made."[159] (Waste, above all, was what Ward said his system of social planning would avoid.) There is no evidence, he wrote in volume II, that religion provides any moral sanctions whatever. As a matter of fact, we find in the advanced countries that individuals who avow no religion are the true moral leaders. "The greater part of them are found among the devotees of the exact sciences. Yet there is no more exemplary class of citizens in society than scientific men..."[160] Furthermore, the "criminals and the dangerous classes of society are generally believers in the prevailing faith of the country which they infest...."[161] In any case, morals precede religion. "It is morality which has saved religion, and not religion which has saved morality."[162] Prayer is a social evil, because it is "inconsistent with that independence and originality of mind which accompany all progressive movements."[163] It deters effective action. He then devoted several pages to a demonstration of the anti-progressive influences of all religion, but he provided examples primarily from paganism and animism.[164] He said religion leads to a retreat from this world and a divorce between man and nature.[165] There are two methods for modifying the external world to make it conform to man's needs: science and religion. There is a perpetual conflict between these two methods, and religion will lose this war.[166]

2. Right-Wing Social Darwinism

Ward's second intellectual enemy was right-wing Social Darwinism. They misunderstood evolution, he argued. Nature's ways are not man's way. The progress of nature is too slow, and it is so inefficient

---

158. Lester Frank Ward, *Dynamic Sociology; or Applied Social Science, as Based Upon Statistical Sociology and the Less Complex Sciences*, 2 vols. (New York: Appleton, 1883), I, p. 12.
159. *Ibid.*, I, p. 17.
160. *Ibid.*, II, pp. 281–82.
161. *Ibid.*, II, p. 282.
162. *Ibid.*, II, p. 283.
163. *Ibid.*, II, p. 286.
164. *Ibid.*, II, pp. 287ff.
165. *Ibid.*, II, p. 298.
166. *Ibid.*, II, p. 305.

that earth's resources will not be able to support such slow progress forever. What is needed is "something swifter and more certain than natural selection," and this means man.[167] We need a new teleology, he argued—the crucial argument of all post-Darwin social and even biological evolutionists. The evolutionary process needs a sure hand to guide it. We must adopt, he said at the end of the second volume, "the teleological method."[168] We must reject Social Darwinism (although he never used this phrase to designate his opponents). Here is the familiar and central argument of modern evolution, predictably formulated first by a social scientist rather than a natural scientist:

> Again, it becomes necessary to combat the views of those scientists who, having probed deep enough to perceive how nature works, think they have found the key to the way man should work, thus ignoring the great distinguishing characteristic of intellectual labor. Having found the claims of those who believe that nature is a product of design and outside contrivance to be unsound, they conclude that there is no design or contrivance, and having seen that results in the organic world are produced through rhythmic differentiations, they infer that results in the superorganic world should be left to the same influences. Nothing could be more false or more pernicious. Scientists of this school, from the weight which their opinions must have, are really doing more to counteract the true tendencies of social progress than those who openly oppose them. All social progress is artificial. It is the consequence of teleological foresight, design, and intellectual labor, which are processes diametrically opposed in principle to the processes of nature. If in learning the law of evolution we must apply it to society, it would have been better to have remained ignorant of that law.[169]

Because the chief opponents of Social Darwinism were orthodox Christians, this statement indicates that Ward hated the right-wing social Darwinists' ideas more than he hated Christian orthodoxy.

Who was he challenging? Spencer and Sumner. He was attacking Sumner's whole methodology of investigating the conflicts found in nature and then transferring this conflict principle to human society. After all, it was Sumner who wrote in *What Social Classes Owe to Each Other* that "We cannot get a revision of the laws of human life. We are absolutely shut up to the need and duty, if we would learn how to live happily, of investigating the laws of Nature, and deducing the rules of right living in the world as it is."[170] Not so, announced Ward. "Civi-

---

167. *Ibid.*, I, p. 16.
168. *Ibid.*, II, p. 627.
169. *Ibid.*, II, p. 627–8.
170. Sumner, *Social Classes*, p. 14.

lization consists in the wholesale and ruthless trampling down of natural laws, the complete subordination of the cosmical point of view to the human point of view. Man revolutionizes the universe. . . . The essential function of Knowledge is to aid him in accomplishing this revolution."[171] *Man must exercise dominion.*

Ward set forth the basic conflict between the two forms of evolutionary thought. It is a question of properly interpreting the concept of *adaptation*, the central idea in Darwinian evolution. No one has made the issues any clearer.

> All progress is brought about by adaptation. Whatever view we may take of the cause of progress, it must be the result of correspondence between the organism and the changed environment. This, in its widest sense, is adaptation. But adaptation is of two kinds: One form of adaptation is passive or consensual, the other form is active or provisional. The former represents natural progress, the latter artificial progress. The former results in a growth, the latter in a manufacture. The one is the genetic process, the other a teleological process.[172]

Ward was clearly a proponent of activism.

3. Reducing Waste by Central Planning

How did Ward refute the "passive" evolutionists (Social Darwinists) in the name of Darwin? Ward came up with this fundamental idea: *Nature's processes are wasteful.*[173] This is completely in accord with Darwin and Wallace. It was their recognition of the enormous pressure of multiplying populations—a multiplication which pressed upon the limits of the environment—which leads to the survival of certain genetically advantaged members of any given species. The failure to survive caught their attention: the millions of extinct species that did not gain the advantage of random genetic changes that would have enabled them to compete successfully in the slowly changing environment, as well as the enormous number of non-survivors in each generation. The idea began with Malthus: the assertion that populations multiply far more rapidly than the food supply necessary to ensure the survival of all members of the multiplying species. Darwin cited Malthus' observation in the first paragraph of Darwin's 1858 essay, which appeared in the Linnean Society's *Journal.*[174]

---

171. Ward, *Dynamic Sociology*, II, p. 473.

172. *Ibid.*, I, p. 72.

173. *Ibid.*, II, p. 494.

174. Charles Darwin, "The Linnean Society Papers," in Appleman (ed.), *Darwin*, p. 83.

Waste is nature's way, and waste was Ward's sworn enemy. "The prodigality of nature is now a well-understood truth in biology, and one that every sociologist and every statesman should not only understand but be able to apply to society, which is still under the complete dominion of these same wasteful laws. No true economy is ever attained until intellectual foresight is brought to bear upon social phenomena. Teleological adaptation is the only economical adaptation."[175] Here was Ward's battle cry against right-wing social Darwinism: The civil government alone is capable of stamping out unplanned, natural, non-teleological waste.

Where do we find waste? In natural processes and in the free market. Free trade is enormously wasteful. "Free trade is the impersonation of the genetic or developmental process in nature."[176] He also understood that free trade is the archetype of all free market processes, and that defenders of the free market, from David Hume and Adam Smith to Spencer and Sumner, had used free trade to defend the idea of market freedom. Therefore, Ward concluded, market freedom is a great social evil. Do people establish private schools to educate children? Stop this waste of educational resources; the state alone should educate children, for the state alone is teleological, truly teleological. Better no education than private education, because "no system of education not exclusively intrusted to the highest social authority is worthy of the name."[177] Here is a key phrase: *the highest social authority*. If true foresight, true design, and true planning are to be brought into the wasteful world of nature and free markets, then the state, as the highest social authority, must bring them. Therefore, "education must be exclusively intrusted to the state...."[178] The state is the highest social authority in Ward's system.

There are other forms of economic waste. Take the example of the railroads. "That unrestricted private enterprise can not be trusted to conduct the railroad system of a rapidly growing country, may now be safely said to be demonstrated."[179] The state should operate them, as is done in Europe. Ward was America's first sociologist—though hardly the last—who called for the total sovereignty of the state in economic affairs. Here is his reasoning. His reasoning is shared, to one extent or another, by modern evolutionists. "While the railroad

---

175. Ward, *Dynamic Sociology*, I, pp. 74–75.
176. *Ibid.*, I, p. 74; II, p. 398.
177. *Ibid.*, II, p. 572.
178. *Idem.*
179. *Ibid.*, II, p. 576.

problem is just now the most prominent before the world, and best exemplifies both the incapacity of private individuals to undertake vast enterprises like this, and the superior aggregate wisdom of the state in such matters, it is by no means the only one that could be held up in a similar manner and made to conform to the same truth."[180] Ward's next paragraph presents his basic conclusion: "Competition is to industry what 'free trade' is to commerce. They both represent the wasteful genetic method, destroying a large proportion of what is produced, and progressing only by rhythmic waves whose ebb is but just less extensive than their flow."[181]

The question arises: Is the state truly economical? Ward's answer: Unquestionably! "Now, of all the enterprises which the state has thus appropriated to itself, there is not one which it has not managed better and more wisely than it had been managed before by private parties."[182] These include transportation, communications, and education. The greater the profitability of any private enterprise, the more need there is for state control, he concluded.[183] In fact, the legitimate purpose of state interference is to make business unprofitable! For instance, the state-operated railroads offer lower rates than private firms did, "which, from the standpoint of the public, is the kernel of the whole matter. The people should look with suspicion upon extremely lucrative industries, since their very sound financial condition proves that they are conducted too much in the interests of the directors and stockholders and too little in that of the public."[184] Ward then set forth the guiding principle of government bureaucrats and state-operated businesses, from his day to ours: *Losses testify to efficiency*. "The failure of the state to make them lucrative should also be construed as an evidence of the integrity and proper sense of duty of the officers of the state."[185] (Yes, he really wrote this. I am not quoting it out of context. It is the end of the paragraph, and he stated in the next paragraph that it is a fact "that whatever the state does is usually better, if not more economically, done than what is done by individuals." Then, to make sure his readers got the picture, he wrote on the same page: "It might similarly be shown that all the functions of government are usually performed with far greater

---

180. *Ibid.*, II, p. 578.
181. *Idem.*
182. *Ibid.*, II, p. 579.
183. *Ibid.*, II, p. 580.
184. *Ibid.*, II, pp. 581–82.
185. *Ibid.*, II, p. 582.

thoroughness and fidelity than similar functions intrusted to private individuals.")

Despite his praise of the state, he admitted that, in his day, the state had not advanced sufficiently to become truly scientific. In the introduction to his book, he freely admitted that governments have always avowed that they were working for the benefit of mankind, but government "has almost without exception failed to realize the results claimed...."[186] In fact, Ward went so far as to write this amazing paragraph: "Let us admit, however, as candor dictates, that almost everything that has been said by the advocates of laissez faire about the evils of government is true, and there is much more that has not been said which should be said on the same subject. Let us only take care not to admit the principle in its abstract essence, which is the only hope there is for the ultimate establishment of a teleological progress in society."[187]

Why this failure in practice (in volume I, anyway)? Answer: the failure of legislators to understand the laws of society, which are "so deep and occult that the present political rulers have only the vaguest conception of them...."[188] The practical answer is to train legislators in the laws of sociological science. "Before progressive legislation can become a success, every legislature must become, as it were, a polytechnic school,[189] a laboratory of philosophical research into the laws of society and of human nature.[190] (vol. II, p. 249). No legislator is qualified to propose or vote on measures designed to affect the destinies of millions of social units until he masters all that is known of the science of society. Every true legislator must be a sociologist, and have his knowledge of that most intricate of all sciences founded upon organic and inorganic science."[191] Not the philosopher-king, as Plato had hoped for, but *the sociologist-legislator*, will bring true teleology into the affairs of man.

4. The Elite vs. the Masses

This brings us to the question of elites. Ward's conception of teleology requires scientific planning and scientific legislation. There must be experts who provide the necessary teleological leadership. We find

---

186. *Ibid.*, I, p. 31.
187. *Ibid.*, I, pp. 54–55.
188. *Ibid.*, I, p. 55.
189. *Ibid.*, II, p. 252.
190. *Ibid.*, II, p. 249.
191. *Ibid.*, I, p. 37.

in Ward's book a characteristic dualism between the capacities of the elite and the capacities of the masses. The elite are unquestionably superior. Ward did not say that they are genetically superior, but they are nevertheless superior. Yet the masses outnumber the elite. What the elite must do, then, to gain the confidence of the masses, whose lives will be directed by the elite, is to proclaim their devotion to the needs of the masses. What statists of all shades of opinion have proclaimed as their ultimate goal, Ward set forth in *Dynamic Sociology*. Ward's commitment to the elite as a class is also their commitment.

The first step is to assert *the beneficence of the elite*. They are working for us all. They are the true altruists. "It is only within a few centuries that such [altruistic] sentiments can be said to have had an existence in the world. They now exist in the breasts of a comparatively few, but it is remarkable how much power these few have been able to wield."[192] You see, "The normal condition of the great mass of mankind, even in the most enlightened states, is one of complete indifference to the sufferings of all beyond the circle of their own immediate experience. In moral progress, almost as much as in material progress, it is a relatively insignificant number of minds that must be credited with the accomplishment of all the results attained."[193] This is the grim reality: "A very few minds have furnished the world with all its knowledge, the general mass contributing nothing at all."[194] However, we need not worry about this problem today. Public education is overcoming this uneven distribution of knowledge.[195] In fact, public education is making this distribution of knowledge far easier, since this process is "a comparatively simple and easy one."[196] In other words, *the elitist planners*, best represented by scientists and teachers, are raising the level of knowledge and consciousness possessed by the masses. The elite planners are really working to produce *a new evolution*, and the masses will be allowed to participate in this elevation of humanity. They will not perish in a non-teleological, natural evolutionary leap. There are two ways of elevating man: (1) scientific propagation of human beings (artificial selection) and (2) rational change of environment, which means an increase of human knowledge.[197] "The amount of useful knowledge possessed by the average mind is

---

192. *Ibid.*, II, p. 448.
193. *Idem.*
194. *Ibid.*, II, p. 485.
195. *Ibid.*, II, pp. 597–98.
196. *Ibid.*, II, p. 486.
197. *Ibid.*, II, p. 487.

far below its intellectual capacity. . . ."[198] This is a key to evolutionary advance: "That the actual amount of such knowledge originated by man, though doubtless still below his ability to utilize it, is sufficient, if equally distributed, to elevate him to a relatively high position, and to awaken society to complete consciousness."[199]

5. State-Run Education

The public schools are therefore fundamental in the teleological evolutionary process. They are the change agents of the new evolution.

Competitive private schools are evil.[200] The state must have an educational monopoly. "The system of private education, all things considered, is not only a very bad one, but, properly viewed, it is absolutely worse than none, since it tends still further to increase the inequality in the existing intelligence, which is a worse evil than a general state of intelligence would be."[201] Fortunately for society, he argued, private education has no academic standards, since parents control or at least heavily influence private education. Therefore, with respect to private education, "The less society has of it the better, and therefore its very inefficiency must be set down as a blessing."[202] The radical elitism here should be obvious, but Ward was kind enough to spell out the implications (something later elitist evolutionists have not always been willing to do).

> Lastly, public education is immeasurably better for society. It is so because it accomplishes the object of education, which private education does not. What society most needs is the distribution of the knowledge in its possession. This is a work which can not be trusted to individuals. It can neither be left to the discretion of children, of parents, nor of teachers. It is not for any of these to say what knowledge is most useful to society. No tribunal short of that which society in its own sovereign capacity shall appoint is competent to decide this question.[203]

Are there to be teachers? Yes, but very special kinds of teachers, namely, teachers totally independent from "parents, guardians, and pupils. Of the latter he is happily independent. This independence renders him practically free. His own ideas of method naturally har-

---

198. *Idem.*
199. *Idem.*
200. *Ibid.*, II, p. 584.
201. *Ibid.*, II, p. 588.
202. *Idem.*
203. *Ibid.*, II, p. 591.

monize more or less completely with those of the state."[204] True freedom, true independence, is defined as being in harmony with the
state. This, of course, is the definition of freedom that Christianity
uses with respect to a man's relation to God.

Was Ward a true egalitarian, a true democrat? Did he really believe
that the masses would at long last reach the pinnacle of knowledge,
to become equal with the scientific elite? Of course not. Here is the
perennial ambivalence of the modern evolutionists' social theory. Society needs planning and direction, and "society" is mostly made up
of individuals, or "the masses." So, they need direction. They need
guidance. They cannot effectively make their own plans and execute
them on a free market. *Teleology is too important to be left to the incom-
petent masses, acting as individuals on a free market.* The masses simply
are not intelligent enough. "Mediocrity is the normal state of the
human intellect; brilliancy of genius and weight of talent are exceptional.... This mass can not be expected to reach the excessive standards of excellence which society sets up. The real need is to devise
the means necessary to render mediocrity, such as it is, more comfortable."[205] (Aldous Huxley, brother of Sir Julian Huxley, and grandson
of Thomas Huxley, saw this clearly. He wrote *Brave New World* to describe the techniques usable by some future state to "render mediocrity, such as it is, more comfortable": drugs, orgiastic religion, and
total central control.)

The goal of total educational equality is really a myth. Then why
such emphasis on public education? *Control!* Teachers are to serve as
the new predestinators. "One of the most important objects of education, thus systematically conducted, should be to determine the
natural characteristics of individual minds. The real work of human
progress should be doubled with the same outlay of energy if every
member of society could be assigned with certainty to the duty for
whose performance he is best adapted.... Most men are out of place
because there has been no systematic direction to the inherent intellectual energies, and the force of circumstances and time-honored
custom have arbitrarily chalked out the field of labor for each."[206]
Ward's next paragraph tells us how we can overcome this lack of external directions. "The system of education here described affords

---

204. *Ibid.*, II, p. 590. Cf. Ward, "Education," (1871–73), in Karier (ed.), *Shaping the
American Educational State*, pp. 145–59.
205. *Ibid.*, II, p. 600.
206. *Ibid.*, II, pp. 623–24.

a means of regulating this important condition on strictly natural principles. . . . A school should be conducted on scientific principles." Teachers can discover "the true character of any particular mind," and then a safe conclusion can be drawn "as to what mode of life will be most successful, from the point of view of the interest both of the individual and of society."[207]

6. Education as Censorship

There is another important function of public education and all other tax-funded information services: *the total control over information and its distribution.* We cannot make progress compulsory, Ward said. "No law, no physical coercion, from whichever code or from whatever source, can compel the mind to discover principles or invent machines. . . . To influence such action, other means must be employed."[208] Men act in terms of their opinions, "and without changing those opinions it is wholly impossible perceptibly to change such conduct."[209] Here is the planner's task: "Instill progressive principles, no matter how, into the mind, and progressive actions will result."[210]

There are political pitfalls to overcome. "The attempt to change opinions by direct efforts has frequently been made. No one will now deny that coercion applied to this end has been a signal failure."[211] Is there some answer to this dilemma? Can the planner find a way to alter men's opinions without using coercion? Yes. *The planner must restrict access to competing ideas*—another form of evil competition. "There is one way, however, in which force may and does secure, not a change of existing opinion, but the acceptance of approved beliefs; but this, so far from weakening the position here taken, affords a capital defense of it. The forcible suppression of the utterance or publication in any form of unwelcome opinions is equivalent to withholding from all undetermined minds the evidence upon which such views rest; and, since opinions are rigidly the products of the data previously furnished the mind, such opinions cannot exist, because no data for them have ever been received."[212] In short, *another crucial key to social progress is systematic censorship.* He called this the "method of exclusion." He wrote:

---

207. *Ibid.*, II, p. 624.
208. *Ibid.*, II, p. 547.
209. *Idem.*
210. *Idem.*
211. *Idem.*
212. *Idem.*

It is simply that true views may as easily be created by this method of exclusion as false ones, which latter is the point of view from which the fact is usually regarded. The more or less arbitrary exclusion of error, i. e., of false data, is to a great degree justifiable, especially where the true data supplied consist of verified experiences, and all the means of reverifying them are left free. But the same end is practically attained by the intentional supply, on a large scale and systematically carried out, of true data without effort to exclude the false. This, however, is the essence of what is here meant by education, which may be regarded as a systematic process for the manufacture of correct opinions. As such, it is of course highly inventive in its character, and the same may be said of all modes of producing desired belief by the method of exclusion.[213]

The government's schools guarantee that competing data are excluded. "Assume an adequate system of education to be in force, and the question of the quantity and quality of knowledge in society is no longer an open one."[214] What about the freedom of the teacher? Basically, there is none. "To the teacher duly trained for his work may be left certain questions of method, especially of detail; but even the method must be in its main features unified with a view to the greatest economy in its application. This must necessarily also be the duty of the supreme authority."[215] As Ward said, "The state education implied in the foregoing remarks is, of course, the ideal state education."[216] Of course it is, if you are a teleological evolutionist.

The elites who control the government's education system are the agents of social change and progress. "The knowledge which enables a very few to introduce all the progressive agencies into civilization tends not in the least to render the mass of mankind, though possessing equal average capacity for such service, capable of contributing any thing to that result."[217] Then what are the masses, really?

> In contrast to this small, earnest class, we behold the great swarming mass of thoughtless humanity, filled with highly derivative ideas vaguely and confusedly held together; eagerly devouring the light gossip, current rumor, and daily events of society which are intensely dwelt upon, each in itself, and wholly disconnected from all others; entertaining the most positive opinions on the most doubtful questions; never looking down upon a pebble, a flower, or a butterfly, or up at a star, a planet, or a cloud; wholly unacquainted with any of the direct manifestations of nature,... passing

213. *Ibid.*, II, p. 548.
214. *Ibid.*, II, p. 549.
215. *Ibid.*, II, p. 591.
216. *Idem.*
217. *Ibid.*, II, p. 535.

through a half-unconscious existence with which they keep no account, and leaving the world in all respects the same as they found it.[218]

Ward understood quite well that the self-proclaimed scientist and change agent would anger the masses—at least the masses in 1883— and they would ridicule his pretensions. "The unscientific man looks upon the scientific man as a sort of anomaly or curiosity. . . . The man of science is deemed whimsical or eccentric. The advanced views which he always holds are apt to be imputed to internal depravity, though his conduct is generally confessed to be exemplary."[219] How does the man of science, the elite determiner of the next evolutionary social advance, rid himself of guilt about his feelings? Perhaps even more important, *how should he deflect the suspicion concerning his intentions* among these masses of emotional incompetents? One very good way is to tell them that the elite is on their side! Ward did. "It will be a long time before the world will recognize the fundamental truth that it is not to apotheosize a few exceptional intellects, but to render the great proletariat comfortable, that true civilization should aim."[220] It was the self-imposed task of the believers in statist planning by elites to buy off the proletariat by making proletarians comfortable, or at least by promising to make them comfortable soon, just as soon as the evolutionary leap of social being takes place.

7. Salvation by Knowledge

Ward, as with all evolutionists, believed in the dominion covenant, or rather *a* dominion covenant. This covenant rests on elite knowledge. Man elevates himself through knowledge. Man is therefore saved by knowledge. This is Satan's temptation: Ye shall be as gods, if ye eat of the tree of the knowledge of good and evil. Ward wrote: "We see in this brief sketch what a dominion man exercises over all departments of nature, and we may safely conclude that he has not yet reached the maximum limit of his power in this direction. But that power is wholly due to his intellectual faculty, which has guided his act in devising indirect means of accomplishing ends otherwise unattainable."[221] Men are not innately evil. "Mankind, as a whole, are honest."[222] *Man's problem is not sin; it is ignorance.* "If all the people knew

---

218. *Ibid.*, II, p. 505.
219. *Ibid.*, II, p. 503.
220. *Ibid.*, II, p. 368.
221. *Ibid.*, II, p. 385.
222. *Ibid.*, II, p. 508.

what course of action was for their best interest, they would certainly pursue that course."[223] It would be possible, through education, to eliminate crime. "The inmates of our prisons are but the victims of untoward circumstances. The murderer has but acted out his education. Would you change his conduct, change his education."[224]

What we must do, then, is *to raise society's consciousness*. Consciousness, not conscience, is the problem.

> After dynamic opinions of the universe, of life, and of man have been formed, it is easy to rise to the position from which society can be contemplated as progressive and subject to a central control. The duties of society toward itself are manifest enough so soon as its true character can be understood.... The great problem remains how to bring society to consciousness. Assuming it to have been brought to consciousness, the dynamic truths with which it must deal are comparatively plain. The mouthpiece of a conscious society is the legislature.[225]

In short, *the visible symbol of a fully conscious society is the self-conscious divinity of the state*. Society must agree about any particular course of action, but once unanimity of opinion is reached—and it is the function of public education to promote it—then debate ends. "Let there be no excuse for anyone to debate a question which has at any time or place, or in any manner, been once definitively answered."[226] Like the laws of the Medes and the Persians, once the divine ruler has made a law, it must not be broken (Dan. 6:8, 12).

Does this mean that democracy will allow all men to have a veto power over the decisions of the rulers? Of course not. The elite must continue to rule.

> Deliberative bodies rarely enact any measures which involve the indirect method. If individual members who have worked such schemes out by themselves propose them in such bodies, the confusion of discordant minds, coupled with the usual preponderance of inferior ones, almost always defeats their adoption. Such bodies, miscalled deliberative, afford the most ineffective means possible of reaching the maximum wisdom of their individual members. A radical change should be inaugurated in the entire method of legislation. By the present system, not even an average expression of the intelligence of the body is obtainable. The uniform product of such deliberations falls far below this average. True deliberation can never be reached until all partisanship is laid aside, and each member is

---

223. *Ibid.*, II, p. 238.
224. *Ibid.*, II, p. 241.
225. *Ibid.*, II, p. 467.
226. *Ibid.*, II, p. 407.

enabled to work out every problem on strictly scientific principles and by
scientific methods, and until the sum total of truth actually obtained is embodied in the enactment. The real work can not be done in open session.
The confusion of such assemblies is fatal to all mental application. There
need be no open sessions. The labor and thought should be performed
in private seclusion, the results reached by others should in this way be
calmly compared by each with those reached by himself, and in a general
and voluntary acquiescence by at least a majority in that which really con-
forms with the truth in each case should be deliberately embodied as law.
The nature of political bodies should be made to conform as nearly as
possible with that of scientific bodies....[227]

What, then, becomes of unanimity, of open covenants openly arrived at (to cite President Woodrow Wilson's unheeded principle of
diplomacy)? It should be obvious. When Ward said that he wanted
unanimity, he really meant *scientific planning without opposition.* "The
legislature must, therefore, as before maintained, be compared with
the workshop of the inventor."[228] There is no opposition to the inventor in his workshop, it should be pointed out.

Scientists must lead the legislators. Men of informed opinion must
tell them what needs to be done. Then the legislators can pass laws
that will compel the masses to follow the lead of the scientists into a
new realm of "comfort." Ward was quite explicit about this.

The problem is a difficult and complicated one. While legislators as a class
are far behind the few progressive individuals by whose dynamic actions
social progress is secured, it is also true that, as a general rule, they are
somewhat in advance of the average constituent, sometimes considerably
so. This is seen in many quasi-scientific enterprises that they quietly continue, which their constituents, could they know of them, would promptly
condemn. The question, therefore, arises whether the legislators may not
find means, as a work of supererogation, to place their constituents upon
the highway to a condition of intelligence which, when attained, will in
turn work out the problem of inaugurating a scientific legislature and a
system of scientific legislation.[229]

With these words, he ended chapter XI, "Action." The *Oxford
English Dictionary* defines "supererogation" as "The performance of
good works beyond what God commands or requires, which are held
to constitute a state of merit which the Church may dispense to others to make up for their deficiencies." Ward may have known what he

227. *Ibid.*, II, p. 395.
228. *Ibid.*, II, p. 396.
229. *Ibid.*, II, p. 399.

was writing; the state, as the dispenser of salvation, needs saints to build up merit to pass along to the proletariat, who can do nothing by themselves. Scientists and legislators are the saints.

8. *The State as Society*

When Ward wrote "society," he meant the state. "When we speak of society, therefore, we must, for all practical purposes, confine the conception to some single automatic nation or state or, at the widest, to those few leading nations whose commercial relations have to a considerable extent cemented their material interests and unified their habits of thought and modes of life." Yet even this is too loose a definition, he wrote. "Only where actual legislation is conducted can there be said to exist a complete social organism. Wherever any such complete social organism exists, it is possible to conceive of true scientific legislation."[230] *Where there is no scientific legislation, therefore, there is no true society.*

There was one, and only one, area of life where laissez faire was said to be legitimate. That was the area we call morality. Morality "is a code which enforces itself, and therefore requires no priesthood and no manual. And strangely enough, here, where alone laissez-faire is sound doctrine, we find the laissez faire school calling loudly for 'regulation.'"[231] For example (we could easily have predicted this example), "It is a remarkable fact that loose conduct between the sexes, which is commonly regarded as the worst form of immorality, seems to have no influence whatever upon the essential moral condition of those races among whom it prevails."[232] (When J. D. Unwin's studies showing the conflict between polygamy and cultural progress were published in the 1920s and 1930s, they were systematically ignored. The fornicators and adulterers who are the self-proclaimed scientific elite prefer not to have this dogma of the irrelevance of adultery shattered by historical research.[233])

Ward rejected the non-teleological (personal and individual teleology) Darwinism of the right-wing Social Darwinists. He rejected entirely their thesis that social progress must involve personal misery and competition. That is the way of nature, not mankind, Ward ar-

---

230. *Ibid.*, II, p. 397.

231. *Ibid.*, II, p. 373.

232. *Ibid.*, II, p. 455.

233. J. D. Unwin, "Monogamy as a Condition of Social Energy," *The Hibbert Journal*, XXV (Winter 1927); reprinted in *The Journal of Christian Reconstruction*, IV (1977–78); Unwin, *Sex and Culture* (Oxford University Press, 1934).

gued. A proper society, meaning state, "aims to create conditions under which no suffering can exist." This may involve the coercive redistribution of wealth by the state, for a good social order "is ready even to sacrifice temporary enjoyment for greater future enjoyment—the pleasure of a few for that of the masses."[234] Sumner was correct when he described this sort of social policy: "The agents who are to direct the State action are, of course, the reformers and philanthropists. Their schemes, therefore, may always be reduced to this type—that A and B decide what C shall do for D.... I call C the Forgotten Man, because I have never seen that any notice was taken of him in any of the discussions."[235] Ward called citizen C "the rich," and let it go at that. His intellectual heirs have not improved much on this strategy, especially when they run for public office.

We must understand precisely what Ward was trying to create: a totalitarian state. As he wrote, "the present empirical, anti-progressive institution, miscalled the art of government, must be transformed into a central academy of social science, which shall stand in the same relation to the control of men in which a polytechnic institute stands to the control of nature."[236] He was a defender of despotism.

9. Population Control

There is one final feature of his system which bears mentioning. The basis of Darwin's analysis of evolution through natural selection was Malthus' observation that species reproduce too fast for their environments. Then only a few will survive, concluded Darwin and Wallace. Ward accepted this as it pertained to nature. But man is a new evolutionary life form, and man's ways are not nature's ways. Man's successful heirs are not supposed to be those individuals who by special genetic advantages or inherited wealth will be able to multiply their numbers. Man, unlike the animals, advances by means of state planning. If society is to prevent suffering, as Ward said is necessary, then the multiplication of those who receive charity must be prohibited. (This was the same problem that baffled Spencer.) "This fact points to the importance of all means which tend to prevent this result."[237] Three children are probably the maximum allowable number. "In an ignorant community this could not be enforced, but

---

234. Ward, *Dynamic Sociology*, II, p. 468.
235. Sumner, *Social Classes*, p. 22.
236. Ward, *Dynamic Sociology*, II, pp. 251–52.
237. *Ibid.*, II, p. 307.

in a sufficiently enlightened one it could and would be."[238] In short, "What society needs is restriction of population, especially among the classes and at the points where it now increases most rapidly."[239] But who are these classes? The masses, of course, since the present moral code (1883) of having large families "is tacitly violated by intelligent people, but enforced by the ignorant and the poor, a state of things which powerfully counteracts all efforts to enlighten the masses."[240] The state needs to provide universal education to the masses to uplift them, but there are so many that the state's resources are strained to the limit. The answer: *population control*. In short, in Ward's version of the dominion covenant, "be fruitful and multiply" must be abolished, and the state, not individuals acting in voluntary cooperation, is to exercise dominion over nature. The rise of the family planning movement in Ward's era, and the appearance of zero population growth advocates in the mid-1960s, can be explained by means of the same arguments used in understanding Ward's humanistic version of the dominion covenant.

10. The Society of Satan

Ward proclaimed in the name of man-directed evolution that which Rushdoony described as the society of Satan. Rushdoony's four points apply quite well to the outline of the society sketched by Ward.

> First, it is held that man is not guilty of his sin, not responsible for his lawlessness, for the sources of his guilt are not personal but social and natural. . . . Second, a society is demanded in which it is unnecessary for man to be good. Everything is to be provided so that man may attain true blessedness, a problem-free life. . . . Third, a society is demanded in which it is impossible for men to be bad. This is a logical concomitant of the second demand. It is a demand that there be no testing. . . . Fourth, a society is demanded in which it is impossible for men to fail. There must be no failure in heaven or on earth. All men must be saved, all students must pass, all men are employable, all men are entitled to rights. As Satan stated it baldly in the wilderness, giving in short form the program for the "good" State, "If thou be the Son of God, command that these stones be made bread." Make it unnecessary for man to work, unnecessary for man to be good, impossible for man to be bad. Provide man with such a cushion of social planning, the temptations asserted, that man might neither hunger nor thirst, work or suffer, believe or disbelieve, succeed or fail, be good or evil. Let his every need be met and his world ordered in terms of his wishes. Let

238. *Ibid.*, II, p. 465.
239. *Ibid.*, II, p. 466.
240. *Ibid.*, II, p. 465.

it be a trouble-free world, cradle-to-grave security; let there be no failure. No failure is tolerable, and none recognized, save one, God's, for having dared to create a world in which we can suffer for our sins, in which we can be tried and tested, in which we can be good or evil, in which we can and must be men. Let us through communism, socialism or our welfare state construct a world better than God's, a world in which failure is impossible and man is beyond good and evil.[241]

What are some of the basic themes of the society of Satan, the evolutionist's new paradise, as described by Ward? What are the principles—cosmological principles—by which such a society is deduced? Here is a brief summary:

No teleology (purpose) in the natural realm (I, 57; II, 32).

Human consciousness is teleological (II, 9).

Human teleology is opposed to laissez faire (1, 55).

Man now directs nature and evolution (I, 29; II, 89).

The state directs social evolution (1, 37).

The state is society (II, 397).

Science is the basis of progress (II, 497, 507).

A scientific elite directs progress (II, 504, 535).

The masses are thoughtless (II, 506, 600).

The masses can be taught (II, 598, 602).

The state must monopolize education (II, 572, 589, 602).

Censorship is mandatory (II, 547).

Nature wastes; man should not (II, 494).

Competition is wasteful (1, 74; II, 576, 584).

Competition is laissez faire (I, 74).

Mankind is honest (II, 508).

Man's problem is lack of knowledge (II, 238).

Ignorance produces crime (II, 241).

Dominion is by means of the intellect (II, 385).

---

241. R.J. Rushdoony, "The Society of Satan," *Christian Economics* (1964); reprinted in *Biblical Economics Today*, II (Oct./Nov. 1979), p. [2].

Government is to be founded on secrecy (II, 395).

Dissent can be illegitimate (II, 407).

Morality is strictly an individual matter (II, 373).

Scientists are selfless (II, 583).

Believers in God's teleology are immoral (II, 508).

State administration is almost always better (II, 579).

Profitless management is honest management (II, 582).

Population control is mandatory (II, 307, 465).

The masses must be made comfortable (II, 368).

The social goal is zero suffering (II, 468).

The society of Satan is the kingdom of autonomous man. This is the continuing theme of post-Darwin evolutionists. Again, let us see what Ward had to say.

> In his pursuit of information with regard to the nature of the universe and his position in it, he must be deterred by no fears. If he can evade the action of natural laws, he has no other source of apprehension. Nature has neither feeling nor will, neither consciousness nor intelligence. He can lay open her bowels and study her most delicate tissues with entire impunity. Except as the great creative mother of all things, she is absolutely passive toward all sentient beings. Man's right to probe and penetrate the deepest secrets of the universe is absolute and unchallenged. It is only he himself who has ever ventured to question it.... He has been the servant of Nature too long. All true progress has been measured by his growing mastery over her, which has in turn been strictly proportional to his knowledge of her truths.[242]

Man is autonomous, the rightful master over nature. Here is autonomous man's self-assigned dominion covenant: "This is why, in the second place, man should assume toward Nature the attitude of a master, or ruler."[243] Man can seek *exhaustive knowledge* and therefore *total power*. He can claim the right to attain the attributes of God.

Here is evolutionist's creed. The universe was not created by God. It was not designed for man. Man must be thrown into the mud of insignificance only for a moment—to sever him from the idea of a personal God—and then he can become master of the earth. Satan also tempted Jesus along these same lines: Worship me, and all this

---

242. Ward, *Dynamic Sociology*, II, pp. 12–13.
243. *Ibid.*, II, p. 13.

world shall be yours (Luke 4:7).[244] Ward allowed man only one brief paragraph to grovel in the mud of insignificance:

> Anthropocentric ideas are essentially immoral. They puff their holders with conceit and arrogance, and lead to base, selfish abuses of power, warped by interest and passion. The old geocentric theory had the same tendency. All narrow views about nature not only contract in the mind, but dwarf and disfigure the moral nature of man. It is only when the eyes commence to open to the true vastness of the universe and the relative insignificance of human achievements, that it begins to be thought not worth while to boast, to oppress, or to persecute.[245]

Once freed of God and meaning—personal significance that is established in terms of the decree of God and man's status as God's image-bearer—then it is up, out of the mud, and on to the stars.[246]

O. Darwinian Economic Theory

Man cannot escape the dominion covenant. It is inherent to his being. He can only modify it. The evolutionists also operate in terms of Genesis 1:28.[247] Let us reread the words: "And God blessed them, and God said unto them, Be fruitful, and multiply, and replenish the earth, and subdue it: and have dominion over the fish of the sea, and over the fowl of the air, and over every living thing that moveth upon the earth." The entire scheme of modern post-Darwin evolution is built upon the premise that animals do, in fact, multiply to the limits of their environments.

Post-Darwin scientists also argue that by means of mastering the scientific laws of evolution, man can have dominion over the creation, including other men. When men start talking about "Man taking control of man," as the C. S. Lewis character warned in *That Hideous Strength*,[248] watch out: some men are planning to take control of others. But now that man has achieved mastery, or is about to, he must

---

244. Gary North, *Treasure and Dominion: An Economic Commentary on Luke* (Dallas, Georgia: Point Five Press, [2000] 2012), ch. 4.

245. Ward, *Dynamic Sociology*, II, p. 508.

246. It is a familiar theme in science fiction to speculate that man, through technology, will overcome the last remaining barrier of nature, the speed of light, to guarantee his dominion of the entire universe, and not just the solar system and those stars close enough to make sub-speed-of-light travel conceivable. Man will conquer the last remaining uniformitarian limit, since it has achieved its goal: shoving God out of the universe of time and space. Man will direct the processes of time.

247. Chapter 4.

248. C. S. Lewis, *That Hideous Strength: A Modern Fairy-Tale for Grown-Ups* (New York: Macmillan, 1946), p. 42.

stop reproducing so fast, stop multiplying, so that he can demonstrate to himself that he is no longer governed, as the animals are, by the Malthusian law of population growth. Man must not fulfill this part of the dominion covenant, for a process of compound population growth points inevitably to the limits of the environment, which is finite. It means that man will face either the limits to population growth—a sign of his own finitude—or else the limit of time, namely, the day of judgment. Both limits thwart autonomous, evolution-directing man. Man must thereby voluntarily limit his population, meaning that some men—the elite—will have to pass laws limiting the population growth of the stubborn, traditional, uneducated masses. Man must exercise dominion through genetic engineering, power politics, centralized economic planning, public education, and other techniques of control. He must act as God does, not multiplying but directing, not pressing against the limits of a finite environment, but mastering it for his own ends. And, to paraphrase Lewis, when you hear men speak about mastering the environment for the benefit of man, watch out: it will be the confiscation of the productivity of the environment for the uses of the elitist planners.

The overwhelming intellectual success of the philosophy of interventionism has been due, in large part, to the greater consistency the logic of interventionism has with post-Darwin evolutionism. Free market economists who cling to evolutionism have suffered an academic fate similar to that suffered by the right-wing Social Darwinists, namely, their case for the reliability of spontaneous market forces cannot compete with the case for man's directing hand through state power. Men want meaning, purpose, and confidence in their own survival. While Mises and Hayek rejected the old "dog eat dog, man eat man" philosophy of right-wing Social Darwinism, they did not succeed in convincing the modern evolutionists of the validity of the competitive, unhampered market. That sort of institutional arrangement does not seem to be in synchronization with the modern evolutionists' vision of man-directed, elite-directed, teleological evolution.

Israel Kirzner, Mises' disciple, wrote his theory of capital in terms of teleology. He said that "The principal point to be emphasized is that capital goods, thus defined, are distinguished in that they fall neatly into place in a *teleological* framework."[249] He was speaking of individuals' teleological frameworks, however, not Man's teleological framework.

---

249. Israel Kirzner, *An Essay on Capital* (New York: Augustus Kelley, 1966), p. 38.

Modern economists want the luxury of using statistical aggregates in their work. Kirzner demonstrated that the methodological presupposition undergirding all economic aggregates is the premise, stated or unstated, that there exists a single planning agent, with a single integrated plan. The quest for that single planning agent, with his single integrated plan, is enhanced when we operate in terms of the assumption, stated or unstated, that this planning mind does, in fact, have to exist. Couple this quest, whether implicit or explicit, with modern evolutionism's longing for a new evolution—the emergence of a new personal sovereign who can offer this impersonal, meaningless universe a comprehensive plan with comprehensive meaning—and you have created serious problems for the defenders of the free market.

The case for the free market as an impersonal, spontaneous, unplanned institution that can nevertheless successfully integrate the multitudinous plans of acting men is generally at odds with the intellectual spirit of the twenty-first century. Men are seeking cosmic purpose, having been told that collective mankind is capable of imposing such purpose by means of scientific planning and even genetic engineering. They are less likely to abandon this quest in exchange for the free market's decentralized planning mechanism, its freely fluctuating price system, and its system of economic calculation for private individuals. The price that post-Darwin evolutionists are asked to pay, religiously speaking, is simply too high. In short, *the defenders of the free market have priced themselves out of secular humanism's marketplace of ideas.*

This is not to say that every modern economist is self-consciously a defender of the kind of planning outlined by Lester Frank Ward. Not very many economists are *that* confident about centralized economic planning. This is also not to say that the majority of men, or even a majority of trained social scientists, understand fully the sleight-of-hand operation of modern evolutionism, with its shift from purposeless origins to man-directed evolutionary process. Nevertheless, the climate of opinion in the twenty-first century is strongly influenced by this sleight-of-hand operation, and its conclusions regarding the sovereignty of planning over collective mankind have permeated the thinking of those who probably do not fully understand the epistemological and metaphysical presuppositions of these conclusions. The fact is, *autonomous men want their godhead unified,* and the hydra-headed, impersonal, spontaneous institution we call the free market is not sufficiently conscious and purposeful to satisfy the longings of modern men for cosmic personalism, meaning humanism's version of cosmic personalism, meaning deified Man.

Conclusion

We should not hope to succeed in making a successful case for the free market by using the logic of Kant, the logic of Darwin, or the logic of Mises, Hayek, Friedman, and other Kantian Darwinists. We should not hope to convert modern evolutionists to the free market ideology if we ground that defense in terms of a less consistent version of evolutionism. The older Darwinist heritage simply does not gain large numbers of adherents, precisely because *modern evolutionists are involved in a religious quest for man-directed cosmic evolution*, and this quest is at odds with the logic of decentralized markets.

If the case for the free market is to be successful in the long run, it must be made in terms of a fully consistent philosophy of creationism and theocentric cosmic personalism. The case for the free market must be made in terms of the doctrines of divine providence, biblical revelation, the image of God in man, and the dominion covenant. While this intellectual defense may not impress today's humanistic evolutionists, including Christian scholars whose methodology is still grounded in humanistic evolutionism, it will enable Christians to have a foundation that will survive the predictable disruptions of the economic, political, intellectual, and social universe of the modern evolutionists. We must not try to establish the intellectual foundations of the kingdom of God in terms of the presuppositions of a doomed evolutionist religion. We may be able to use the conclusions of selected secular economists, when these conclusions are in conformity with biblical premises, but it is we who must pick and choose in terms of the Bible, not they. We must abandon evolutionary presuppositions in every area of human thought, including economics.

APPENDIX B

THE EVOLUTIONISTS' DEFENSE OF THE MARKET

The Book of Genesis cannot be reconciled with the books of Darwin. This is the leading presupposition of this book. Those who prefer to compromise Christian orthodoxy for the sake of academic respectability, or for the sake of their own commitment to the claims of modern science, have made various attempts to mix the two systems. Without exception, Christian orthodoxy is sacrificed on the altar of Darwinism. The Darwinists will accept no compromises with the creationism of Genesis 1. Far too many Christians have been less adamant about the intellectual claims of their religion's premises.

Throughout this book, I have been arguing in terms of a framework that is radically opposed to modern economics' epistemology. Modern schools of economics rest on the presuppositions of Darwinism: Marxism, socialism, free enterprise, and the various mixtures. They begin with the mind of man. They assume that the laws of nature and the laws of thought have evolved over countless eons, with the mind of man being able where necessary to grasp and use the regularities of nature. Not that the human mind can grasp everything; but it can grasp enough to create a science of economics. All systems officially accept some version of *process philosophy*: as conditions change, and the process of evolution continues, the *laws of thought* could conceivably change. Ludwig von Mises put it quite well:

> Human knowledge is conditioned by the power of the human mind and by the extent of the sphere in which objects evoke human sensations. Perhaps there are in the universe things that our senses cannot perceive and relations that our minds cannot comprehend. There may also exist outside of the orbit we call the universe other systems of things about which we cannot learn anything because, fr the time being, no traces of their existence penetrate into our sphere in a way that can modify our sensations. It may

403

also be that the regularity in the conjunction of natural phenomena we are observing is not eternal but only passing, that it prevails only in the present stage (which may last millions of years) of the history of the universe and may one day be replaced by another arrangement.[1]

At least as an official position, *the mind of man may become something different in the future*. Mises wrote: "Man—up to now, at least—has always gone lamentably amiss in his attempts to bridge the gulf that he sees yawning between mind and matter, between the rider and the horse, between the mason and the stone. It would be preposterous to view this failure as a sufficient demonstration of the soundness of a dualistic philosophy. All that we can infer from it is that science— at least for the time being—must adopt a dualistic approach, less as a philosophical explanation than as a methodological device."[2] This logical dualism is *post-Kantian dualism*: the split between thought and matter, and between the phenomena of science (scientific regularity) and the noumena of ethics (beyond rational categories). Somehow the two realms are connected (if man is to retain *power*), yet unconnected (if man is to retain *freedom*). This *nature-freedom dualism* is basic to all modern philosophy.[3] Secular economics cannot escape this dualism.[4]

As I have begun to demonstrate in this book, and as I demonstrate more thoroughly in the commentaries that follow, the Bible establishes as a social norm a system of civil government and personal responsibility that leads to the formation of a free market economy. I have drawn heavily from the writings of economists who favor the free market in order to explain certain relationships and consequences of such a market system. Predictably, those who argue that the Bible does not establish moral and judicial foundations that lead to capitalism tend also to reject the logic of free market economics. They wind up citing secular economists who favor Keynesian intervention by the civil government into economic affairs, or they cite even more radical secular economists. But both sides rely heavily on the conclusions of the warring camps of humanistic economists.

1. Ludwig von Mises, *Theory and History: An Interpretation of Social and Economic Evolution* (Auburn Alabama: Mises Institute, 2007), p. 8. This book was first published by Yale University Press in 1957.

2. *Ibid.*, p. 1.

3. Herman Dooyeweerd, *In the Twilight of Western Thought: Studies in the Pretended Autonomy of Philosophical Thought* (Philadelphia: Presbyterian & Reformed, 1960), pp. 46–52.

4. Gary North, "Economics: From Reason to Intuition," in North (ed.), *Foundations of Christian Scholarship: Essays in the Van Til Perspective* (Vallecito, California: Ross House, 1976).

If I have rejected environmental determinism, evolutionism, and humanism in general, how can I legitimately use the arguments of environmental determinists, evolutionists, and humanists to support my case for a free market social order? Can I evade the accusation of the "Christian socialists" and "liberation theologians" that what I propose is simply a disguised version of secular capitalism, a baptized version of Adam Smith's *Wealth of Nations*?

The best way that I can legitimately counter this criticism is to show that I do not accept Darwinian evolution as the scientific foundation of Christian economics, and then demonstrate that, to the extent that the defenders of the free market accept such a foundation, they wind up without a logical position to defend. I also have tried to show in Appendix A on Social Darwinism that the demise of nineteenthcentury Classical liberal economics was assured from the start, precisely because Darwinism really does not believe in the "survival of the fittest" and "evolution through natural selection," once *man, the rational planner* appears in history. In other words, to paraphrase Cornelius Van Til, the humanistic economists have borrowed their accurate conclusions from Christianity. They cannot tell us why human minds agree, or why such minds can interpret the universe, or why the universe is coherent (since it has its origins in randomness or chaos), or why there is human freedom in a deterministic universe, or why the noumenal realm of ethics (outside of the determined realm of scientific law) can determine affairs in the external, cause-determined world of matter. Yet they say they can make all kinds of statements about economic events. How can they do this? They do not say.

The Christian economist *can* say. He points to a sovereign God who is the Creator. He points to a record of the creation in Genesis, chapter 1. He points to man, who is made in the image of God. He points to God's assignment to man in Genesis 1:28 to subdue the earth. He points to man's ability to name the animals. All of these facts of the Genesis account provide the foundation of Christian thought in general and Christian economics in particular. *The orderly creation reflects an orderly, sovereign God.* Man is made in God's image, so he can understand the external world, for which he is responsible before God as a steward. Nature and man are not chance-determined, for *how can anything be determined in a chance universe?* Nor are nature and man determined by a law-chained system of impersonal, freedom-denying cause and effect. God is sovereign, man is responsible to God, and nature is orderly. The Christian announces this in confidence. The humanistic economists deny the first two assertions, so they have found no logical, universally acceptable arguments to affirm the third. They are intellectually defenseless.

A. Hayek's Evolutionism

F. A. Hayek won the Nobel Prize in economics in 1974, sharing the award with the Swedish socialist, Gunnar Myrdal. (It was widely rumored that Hayek never expected to win it, and Myrdal never expected to share it.) Hayek's award was made specifically for his early work in economics, which lent a degree of irony to the award, since so much of Hayek's early writings on trade cycles and capital theory was dependent upon the pioneering work of Ludwig von Mises.[5] Mises had died in relative obscurity in 1973, ignored by the economics profession, an outcast who had never been given a full professorship in the United States, even at New York University, which was not one of the more prestigious universities in America. He had remained a pariah in his own department, subsidized by outside funds, and officially a "visiting professor"—whose visit lasted from the mid-1940s until his retirement in the late 1960s.[6] Yet by 1912, Mises had established himself as one of the world's most eloquent defenders of free market economics.[7] He was a neo-Kantian rationalist who was unwilling to adopt the modern Darwinian view of Man, the sovereign central planner.

Hayek devoted a decade of his academic career to the construction of monetary and capital theory based on Mises' "Austrian" premises. The second phase of Hayek's career was more deeply social and philosophical, and it began in the 1940s. He is far more famous for the books and essays that he produced during this later period, especially *The Road to Serfdom* (1944). Hayek offered the finest statement of late-nineteenth-century classical social theory in his later books. They are erudite, heavily footnoted, eloquent defenses of Darwinian, Kantian social philosophy. They all rest on an explicit foundation of evolutionism.

5. F. A. Hayek, *Prices and Production* (London: Routledge & Kegan Paul, [1931] 1960); *Monetary Theory and the Trade Cycle* (New York: Augustus Kelley, [1933] 1966); *Profits, Interest, and Investment* (London: Routledge & Kegan Paul, 1937); *The Pure Theory of Capital* (London: Routledge & Kegan Paul, [1941] 1962). All are available as free downloads from the Mises Institute.

6. Margit von Mises, *My Years with Ludwig von Mises* (New Rochelle, New York: Arlington House, 1976), ch. 10.

7. Ludwig von Mises, *The Theory of Money and Credit* (Indianapolis, Indiana: Liberty Press, [1912] 1981). The first American edition was published in 1953 by Yale University Press.

1. The Two Rationalisms

One of the recurring themes in Hayek's writings is this one: There have been *two forms of rationalism* in the West. The *first form is best repre*-sented by the writings of the Scottish social theorists of the eighteenth century, most notably Adam Ferguson, who wrote: "Nations stumble upon establishments, which are indeed the result of human action, but not the execution of any human design."[8] Hayek used this phrase repeatedly, most notably in an essay "The Results of Human Action but not of Human Design" (1967). The *second* form of rationalism is the rationalism of the central planner. Human action is seen as being rational only when it is the result of human design, namely, the design of a sovereign, rational, scientific planning agency. The origin of this second position, as far as the history of the modern West is concerned, was the French Revolution. Hayek's book, *The Counter-Revolution of Science* (1952), is an historical study of the origin and development of "designing rationalism" in social theory.[9] He called this "constructivist rationalism." Men rationally construct social institutions.

If we use Darwinian categories, we can better understand the two rationalisms. The *first* form, which Hayek favored, is that propounded by Adam Ferguson, Adam Smith, Edmund Burke, and other eighteenth-century mainly Scottish social theorists. Their view was that human institutions are the product of long years of unregulated development. Legal, economic, and other institutional arrangements were not consciously designed by any human planning agency. Nevertheless, they are coherent, rational, and productive.

This argument impressed the early evolutionists, who took the paradigm and transferred it to geology and biology. A process of undesigned competition produced the biological world in which man finds himself, they argued. Eighteenth-century social theory influenced the development of nineteenth-century scientific evolutionary thought, not the other way around. Hayek made this explicit. The goal of the Scottish social theorists was to find the source of institutional regularity in man rather than God. The same motivation—*eliminating God from theory*—was basic to nineteenth-century scientific evolutionism. Hayek wrote:

---

8. Adam Ferguson, *An Essay on the History of Civil Society* (1797), p. 187; cited by Hayek, "The Results of Human Action but not of Human Design" (1967), in his book, *Studies in Philosophy, Politics and Economics* (Chicago: University of Chicago Press, 1967), p. 96n.

9. F. A. Hayek, *The Counter-Revolution of Science: Studies on the Abuse of Reason* (Indianapolis, Indiana: Liberty Press, [1952] 1979).

From these conceptions gradually grew a body of social theory that showed how, in the relations among men complex and orderly and, in a very definite sense, purposive institutions might grow up which owed little to design, which were not invented but arose from the separate actions of many men who did not know what they were doing. This demonstration that something greater than man's individual mind may grow from men's fumbling efforts represented in some ways an even greater challenge to all design theories than even the later theory of biological evolution. For the first time it was shown that an evident order which was not the product of a designing human intelligence need not therefore be ascribed to the design of a higher, supernatural intelligence, but that there was a third possibility—the emergence of order as the result of adaptive evolution.

Since the emphasis we shall have to place on the role that selection plays in this process of social evolution today is likely to create the impression that we are borrowing the idea from biology, it is worth stressing that it was, in fact, the other way around: there can be little doubt that it was from the theories of social evolution that Darwin and his contemporaries derived the suggestion for their theories.[10]

Man becomes the sovereign acting and planning agent in such a framework, but not man, the central planner. The Scottish philosophers were seeking for the origins of purposeful institutions outside of purposeful and comprehensive designs, either by men or God. Few of them were willing to abandon the concept of God entirely, but they did want to eliminate a continuing series of miracles from the record of man's institutions. They did not want to eliminate the idea of providence, but they also did not want to base their historical accounts of man's progress on miracles or other kinds of divine intervention. They were headed in the direction of *cosmic impersonalism*, and the scientific evolutionists a century later finally arrived, briefly, at their destination, only to substitute man as the new source of cosmic personalism.

The *second* form of rationalism also can be seen in the writings of the scientific evolutionists. Darwin was impressed with the skills of horticulturalists and animal breeders in breeding new variations of plants and animals.[11] He recognized that there is a role for conscious

---

10. F. A. Hayek, *The Constitution of Liberty* (Chicago: University of Chicago Press, 1960), pp. 58–59. (2011 ed.: ch. 4:3)

11. "We cannot suppose that all the breeds were suddenly produced as perfect and as useful as we now see them; indeed, in many cases, we know that this has not been their history. The key is man's power of accumulative selection: nature gives successive variations; man adds them up in certain directions useful to him. In this sense he may be said to have make for himself useful species." Darwin, *The Origin of Species* (New York: Modern Library edition), p. 29. This statement is taken from the first chapter of the book, "Variation Under Domestication."

planning. Natural selection's co-discoverer, Alfred Russel Wallace, was aware of the anomaly in the theory of natural selection, namely, the power of man's mind, which did not come from a slow, steady, continuous interaction with his environment, but which must have been the result of *a discontinuous leap in being*—a violation of the very heart of the theory of evolution through natural selection.[12] Man, the thinker, can begin to replace the purposeless, impersonal processes of nature. This same sort of transformation of the theory—from purposelessness to man's sovereignty—took place in biological theory as well as social theory. *This is the heart of modern humanism.*[13]

Hayek recognized the error of the late-nineteenth-century right-wing Social Darwinists.

> It is unfortunate that at a later date the social sciences, instead of building on their beginnings in their own field, reimported some of these ideas from biology and with them brought in such conceptions as "natural selection," "struggle for existence," and "survival of the fittest," which are not appropriate in their field; for in social evolution, the decisive factor is not the selection of the physical and inheritable properties of the individuals but the selection by imitation of successful institutions and habits. Though this operates also through the success of individuals and groups, what emerges is not an inheritable attribute of individuals, but ideas and skills—in short, the whole cultural inheritance which is passed on by learning and imitation.[14]

It should be obvious what Hayek was trying to do. He was trying to return social theory to the Scottish evolutionism of the eighteenth century. He was trying to get the model of impersonal, physical competition in biology out of economic theory. He wanted to return to eighteenth-century social evolutionism. But he was unsuccessful in his attempt. The modern version of evolutionistic social theory moves forward, not backward; its promoters want to bring to the forefront Man, the purposeful central planner—a source of coherence and design in an otherwise impersonal universe. Man, the decentralized actor is not sufficiently powerful to assure the species of survival, let alone domination and Godless dominion. Modern socialists want the dominion covenant, but they do not want God, except insofar as man as a species is God. Men want design. They just refuse to believe in a sovereign, supernatural Designer.

12. Cf. Loren Eiseley, *Darwin's Century: Evolution and the Men Who Discovered It* (Garden City, New York: Doubleday Anchor, [1958] 1961), ch. 11: "Wallace and the Brain."
13. Appendix A.
14. Hayek, *Constitution of Liberty*, p. 59. (2011 ed.: ch. 14:3)

2. Decentralized Knowledge

Hayek's defense of the free market social order rests on his concept of human knowledge. He argued for the division of labor in knowledge.[15] Men are not omniscient. Each individual knows his own talents and weaknesses, challenges and successes, better than anyone else. What is needed is an *integrating system* to call forth the most accurate and relevant knowledge that each man possesses to deal with the economic problems of a universe of scarce resources. This system needs a *feedback process*, so that erroneous information and inapplicable approaches are not funded endlessly, thereby wasting resources. Men need to learn from their mistakes. They also need to imitate successful strategies. Only by *decentralizing the decision-making process*, Hayek argued, can mankind call forth its greatest reserves in order to achieve...what? Each individual's highest personal goals. Hayek was an individualist. He believed that we must begin our social analysis with the individual decision-maker. By allowing each person to achieve his goals by whatever voluntary and non-coercive approach he decides is best-fitted to his skills and capital, we allow the spontaneous development of a social order that allows each of us to prosper. Conclusion: *what is best for a majority of economic actors is best for the society as a whole.* Out of individual competition comes collective prosperity. This is the essence of Adam Smith's *Wealth of Nations*, and it is still the essence of modern free market social theory. Hayek defended the idea.

This social philosophy requires great faith to sustain it. Its system of social causation is not self-evident. Men must believe that the voluntaristic exchange system is, in fact, a system. They must believe that beneficial social results stem from individual decisions to truck and barter. Out of the voluntary, self-centered decisions of the *many* will come a social order beneficial to the *one* of human society. This is the religion which Hayek offers to us. Very few post-Darwin intellectuals believe in this eighteenth-century religion.

"It is through the mutually adjusted efforts of many people that more knowledge is utilized than anyone individual possesses," Hayek wrote, "or than it is possible to synthesize intellectually; and it is through such utilization of dispersed knowledge that achievements are made possible greater than any single mind can foresee. It is be-

---

15. F. A. Hayek, "The Use of Knowledge in Society" (1945); reprinted in Hayek, *Individualism and Economic Order* (Chicago: University of Chicago Press, 1948), ch. 4. This was a seminal essay in economic theory.

cause freedom means the renunciation of direct control of individual efforts that a free society can make use of so much more knowledge than the mind of the wisest ruler can comprehend."[16] *This is the heart of Hayek's defense of human freedom: the better use of that most precious of scarce resources, knowledge.* "It is therefore no argument against individual freedom that it is frequently abused. Freedom necessarily means that many things will be done which we do not like. Our faith in freedom does not rest on the foreseeable results in particular circumstances but on the belief that it will, on balance, release more forces for the good than for the bad."[17]

Here is an undefendable faith indeed. "Our faith in freedom" rests on our "belief" that freedom will "on balance" produce more good than bad. Yet, as I have surveyed at some length in Chapter 5, the secular economist cannot possibly assess either good or bad in a social order, since it is not possible to make interpersonal comparisons of subjective utility—assuming that we are speaking about what rational, autonomous, scientific economics can logically proclaim. The same problem faces the ethicist. It is the old problem of aggregates: Is the total pleasure I get from sticking pins into you greater than the total pain you receive? How can we add and subtract good and bad? Modern subjectivist economics cannot possibly permit such aggregation, yet it must make such judgments in order to defend the validity of the free market's social order. "The benefits of this system, *on balance*, are greater than the costs." On what balance? Evaluated by whom? Hayek appealed to something that he knew is irrational and inconsistent with the very foundations of modern subjectivist economics. *He appealed to an aggregate that by definition cannot possibly exist, if we accept the logic of subjectivism.* In short, he could not logically defend the free market's benefits.

3. A Balanced Social Order

Socialists and interventionists do not take Hayek's faith seriously. They see it as irrational. How can we possibly believe that an unplanned, undesigned, individualistic economic system is beneficial, when we know some participants get hurt, or lose money? Why not allow the greater vision of central planners to intervene and remove the evils, while leaving the benefits? Not possible, said Hayek: to call forth men's best knowledge and best efforts, they must know that

16. Hayek, *Constitution of Liberty*, pp. 30–31. (2011 ed.: ch. 2:5)
17. *Ibid.*, p. 31. (2011 ed.: ch. 2:5)

the civil government will not intervene and redistribute the gains any man makes. Nonsense, say the interventionists. People want to live in a "fair" regime, in which nobody is faced with total disaster. We can "clean up" the market's failures. We can "balance" its inequities. Hayek's unnamed and undefined balance undergirds his system; the concept of the equitable nature of the civil government undergirds the socialists' system. Each side appeals to logic in order to convince us that such a balance exists. Yet neither side can show how such a balance can be perceived and achieved in a world devoid of a method of adding and subtracting individual assessments of utility.

Hayek's system rests on the idea that undesigned human institutional arrangements are reliable. The socialist wants us to believe that man-designed, centrally administered human institutions are reliable. Hayek wanted *species man*, the purposeful planners. The socialists want *scientific elites* who plan for the benefit of species man. The implicit and even explicit humanism of both camps should be obvious. Neither side is willing to appeal to *fixed standards* of ethics, economics, or civil government in the Bible. Neither side wants to consider the balance as being in the hand of an omniscient God. Men or Man, individuals or planning elites, must be understood to possess the balance. Economists insist that they can see good or evil in the aggregate. God is an irrelevant hypothesis for both camps. They both agree: *man is the starting point for economic and political analysis*. But man is both individual and corporate. Which man is fundamental to economic analysis?

The socialist wants to pass laws against sticking pins into people, so to speak—laws against "excessive" or "obscene" profits, laws against price competition, and so forth. The free market defender says that such "pins" are a lot better than the "pins" of unemployment (minimum wage laws), gluts (price floors), shortages (price ceilings), weak competition (restricted profits), and so forth. Which are the real "pins"? The two sides cannot agree. They cannot appeal to a reliable, eternal definition of pins, coercion, and immoral activity. They cannot define pin-sticking, let alone tally up pleasure and pain from pin-sticking.

4. Hayek's Historicism

In a perceptive essay by one of Hayek's former students, Eugene Miller, he pointed to an important contradiction in Hayek's thought. He did not point out that this same contradiction is basic to every humanist system, but the point is nonetheless well taken. Hayek rejected *historicism*: the theory that the mind of man changes with the stages of history. Yet he also rejected the idea of *fixed categories* of thought or sensory perception in the human mind. Hayek used the idea of fixed ideas in order to refute those who went too far for him in this area of historical change and its effects on human perception, thought, and action. Yet he was dependent on some variation of "mild" historicism in order to defend himself against the charge of static idealism. Miller summarized Hayek's dualism:

> On the one hand, Hayek wants to retain the idea that science can give a reliable explanation of regularities in the objective physical world. Indeed, his account of human cognition presupposes the validity of his physiological explanation of the principles that underlie the cognitive processes. On the other hand, his general conclusions about the character of human cognition seem to undermine the very possibility of objective knowledge and to concede the basic premises of extreme historicism. He argues that all perception and reasoning are predetermined by a classificatory system or "map" that varies from one individual and group to another and changes over time.[18]

Hayek's epistemology is therefore dualistic.

Hayek argued explicitly that *all values are evolutionary*. They are determined by the interaction of the changing environment and our civilization. He explicitly rejected radical historicism—the doctrine that each stage of history has its own values, laws, and perceptions— yet he implicitly adopted precisely this outlook. He wrote, "the basic conclusion that the whole of our civilization and all human values are the result of a long process of evolution in the course of which values, as the aims of human activity appeared, continue to change, seems inescapable in the light of our present knowledge. We are probably also entitled to conclude that our present values exist only as the elements of a particular cultural tradition and are significant only for some more or less long phase of evolution—whether this phase includes some of our pre-human ancestors or is confined to certain periods of human civilization. We have no more ground to ascribe to them eternal existence than to the human race itself."[19] Hayek believed in morals, since morality is the foundation of the free market order, but he wanted *morals derived from tradition*—the products of human ac-

---

18. Eugene F. Miller, "Hayek's Critique of Reason," *Modern Age* (Fall 1976), p. 390.

19. F. A. Hayek, "The Theory of Complex Phenomena" (1964); reprinted in Hayek, *Studies*, p. 38.

tion but not human design. In fact, he excoriated the "rationalism" of Descartes and the French Revolutionaries for having insisted that morality be subject to logical proof. He wrote:

> This moral system on which the formation of a worldwide market rested increasingly lacked credence and was partly destroyed, with the assistance of a new philosophy. In the seventeenth century, Hobbes, and particularly Descartes, at first in the intellectual, and then in the moral, field stated that one must not believe anything which cannot be proved. This view gradually spread, especially in the eighteenth century, and in the nineteenth century this philosophical doubt about traditional morals suddenly became practically effective. The loss of the moral beliefs which had been essential for the maintenance of the existing market system was suddenly given a sort of intellectual foundation. It came to be believed that the ruling moral beliefs were unfounded, were pretenses contrary to instinct and reason, and were invented for the protection of those who would profit by them. The young decided that since nobody could explain why they should obey these morals rather than others, they were going to make their own morals. Only morals which had been deliberately designed for a recognized common good purpose could really be accepted as worthy of a fully adult human race. And the purpose would have to be the satisfaction of the innate natural instincts of man.[20]

How could he defend himself against the accusation that his morality is irrational or relative? What if the socialist argues that we are entering into a new era? The old laws of capitalism, including bourgeois morality, are now being superseded by a new era of proletarian production, proletarian morality, and proletarian economics! This is precisely what Marx and his followers argued, beginning in the 1840s. It is the argument of all historicist systems: eras change, and morals change with them. How could Hayek, as an evolutionist, deal with historicism? He stated his preference for the traditionalism of Ferguson and Burke, which "is based on an evolutionary interpretation of all phenomena of culture and mind and on an insight into the limits of the powers of the human reason."[21] Miller commented:

> The fact is, however, that "tradition" is not a single, unified phenomenon. What we call "Western civilization" is but one of many traditions of mankind; and internal to it are many divergent and conflicting strands. Hayek himself acknowledges that the tradition of constructivist [designing] rationalism is as old and as strong within Western civilization as the tradition

---

20. *A Conversation with Friedrich A. von Hayek: Science and Socialism* (Feb. 9, 1978) (Washington, D.C.: American Enterprise Institute, 1979), p. 11.
21. Hayek, *Studies*, p. 161.

of critical [evolutionary] rationalism. What are we to do in the face of this conflict among and within traditions? Hayek leaves us only with the options of submitting humbly to the tradition which makes the most forceful claim upon us or else of choosing boldly but blindly among competing traditions. He eliminates the possibility that we can make a rational choice among traditions on the basis of what is true or good by nature. Reason cannot judge among traditions, because it can function only within such a matrix as tradition itself supplies; and this matrix is nonrational and devoid of meaning. Moreover, there are no permanent values by reference to which reason could make this judgment. All human values are the result of a long process of evolution, and they continue to change in the course of this process.[22]

Hayek's system, like all other modern systems of economics, is epistemologically committed to *process philosophy*, better known as *historicism*. It leaves his defense of the market intellectually defenseless against those more self-consistent historicists who boldly proclaim a change in eras, the arrival of a new world order.

5. Moral Structure and Change

Hayek, for all his immense erudition, was caught in a familiar bind of all humanistic scholarship: *the problem of structure and change.*[23] He wanted a moral order, but he did not want it imposed by a sovereign God who is outside the processes of history. He wanted a moral order that provides stability, so that the free market possesses widely recognized "rules of the game." His later career was marked by a series of studies relating to the way in which such rules are established, and how a society can enforce them without changing them unrealistically, or tampering with them too much, or converting them into arbitrary pieces of legislation. Without structure, there can be no orderly social and economic progress. Without a moral standard, it is not possible to determine whether any given social change is progressive. If everything is flux, then whirl is king, and Hayek never argued for whirl. But he did argue that all morality is, ultimately, the product of an interaction between decentralized acting men and a changing environment.[24]

---

22. Miller, "Hayek's Critique," *op. cit.*, pp. 392–93.

23. This dualism goes back to the pre-Socratics: Parmenides (logical structure) vs. Heraclitus (historical change).

24. "Every change in conditions will make necessary some change in the use of resources, in the direction and kind of human activities, in habits and practices. And each change in the actions of those affected in the first instance will require further adjustments that will gradually extend throughout the whole of society." Hayek, *Constitution of Liberty*, p. 28 (2011 ed.; ch. 2:3).

What kind of foundation is this? What kind of stable moral and legal order can result from such a concept of morality? How can any variety of process philosophy (evolutionism) produce a reliable, universally recognized, widely accepted moral framework? Hayek wound up calling for men to believe in the morality of selfishness, the benefits of which "we cannot see."

> There is, ultimately, a moral justification for selfishness, if you care to call it that, for just obeying the commands of the market system. If we can make people understand this, we may revive the kinds of general rules of behavior which, a hundred years ago, governed the Western world and which have become largely discredited, but without which our capacity to benefit others will decline. We can tell people that the rules which we are rapidly discarding do serve the benefit of mankind, although we cannot see it; we must not imagine that we can choose what to do in order to serve the benefit of mankind. All we can do is to obey the rules which have established themselves and produce the worldwide division of labor and perhaps gradually try to improve these rules.[25]

Why did Hayek expect to win the battle for men's minds with this kind of a defense of the market? It is initially repulsive morally (selfishness), until we consider the sophisticated arguments that undergird it. Yet even these arguments ultimately fail, for he could not demonstrate the benefits scientifically (no interpersonal comparisons of subjective utility),[26] and he could not demonstrate that the moral and legal rules of the game should not be changed in some future social order—or even in today's social order, which is no longer the environment of the late nineteenth century, let alone Scotland in the mid-eighteenth century.

Evolutionism is another variety of historicism, and historicism offers man no fixed, reliable, universal, and perpetually binding principles of law, legislation, and liberty (to use the title of Hayek's trilogy). How can any decentralist version of evolution win men's minds in an era in which the second stage of evolutionism, the infamous "sleight of hand"—elitist planners as the source of future evolution for the benefit of species man—has become the reigning faith?

Men must believe in some authority. They must obey that authority if they are to survive. It may be the market economy, or the civil government, or the Bible, but men need a source of reliable authority to commit themselves to. There can be no division of labor without

---

25. *Conversation*, pp. 14–15.
26. Chapter 5.

such subordination. *Men necessarily obey someone.* Hayek fully understood this principle of human action. He called on men to obey the laws and conventions of the undesigned free market order. Men are to exercise faith in the benefits and reliability of this order. They are to believe that it is, in fact, a true order, and not a capricious, random, and destructive anti-system. Hayek did not minimize the individual's obligation to obey: "...the individual, in participating in the social processes, must be ready and willing to adjust himself to changes and to submit to conventions which are not the result of intelligent design, whose justification in the particular instance may not be recognizable, and which to him will often appear unintelligible and irrational."[27] Men must, in short, exercise *blind faith.* They must subordinate themselves faithfully to social processes that they do not understand, processes that even appear irrational to them. They must do this if the free market order is to survive.

If survival is the criterion of success, then the free market order in the twentieth century began to resemble a social dodo bird, headed for extinction. If success in the open marketplace of ideas is the proper criterion, then the free market's undesigned structure has not produced the intellectual defenses that might insure its survival. Perhaps someday people will believe in the market as fervently as Hayek wanted men to believe—a blind faith in an undesigned order—but throughout the twentieth century, such faith shrank. Men are far more ready to believe in a designed social order as a way to secure man's place in the cosmos as the provider of cosmic personalism. This is a social order that in conformity to the second stage of the *Darwinian sleight of hand,* with scientific planners taking control of the impersonal forces of evolution. Hayek's decentralized rationalism runs against the grain of the dominant schools of post-Darwin social philosophy. Hayek's arguments, one could say, are not rationally designed to be successful in an era that wants to believe in rational designs.

6. Human Action

The great intellectual contribution of the Austrian School of economics is the focus on *purposeful human action.* Austrian School economists have again and again called attention to the individual decision-making of acting men. They have argued that a system of

---

27. F. A. Hayek, "Individualism: True and False" (1945); reprinted in Hayek, *Individualism and Economic Order*, p. 22.

voluntary exchange enables men to call forth the productivity of others, as well as to evaluate the economic value of their own contributions. The free market order has produced more wealth and more freedom, as well as more personal responsibility in economic affairs, than any other economic system in man's history. But the Austrians, being humanists, evolutionists, and radical subjectivists, cannot logically prove any of this.

The "designing rationalists," who want the power of the civil government to direct human actions, can point to the obvious coherence of the idea of national economic planning. They seldom find people who understand that the imposed rationalism of socialism creates what Mises has called "planned chaos," while the seemingly uncoordinated efforts of men voluntarily exchanging goods and services on a free market produce an integrated, growth-oriented production system. The "top-down" rationalism produces just the opposite of what the intellectual defenders of central planning have promised. It produces an uncoordinated, fragmented system of disrupted production. The "bottom-up" system of decentralized planning is alone capable of producing social order, for it places greater responsibility for decision-making in the hands of the individual. But without a concept of *a fixed moral order with its source outside of man*, imposed as an ideal for man by a sovereign Creator, Hayek and the other humanist economists cannot prove that a decentralized economic order can produce a just, productive, and desirable social order. Without standards of performance, men cannot make wise decisions.

7. Shifting Standards

Mises argued eloquently that without a market economy, men cannot make accurate economic calculations.[28] A Christian social philosopher points out that, without a system of *permanent, universal morality*, there is also no way to make accurate economic calculations, for there is *no constant* that survives over time—from the beginning of acting man's plan to its conclusion—by which any man can evaluate the success of his efforts. As the Bible says, what does it profit a man if he gains the whole world and loses his soul (Mark 8:36)?[29] Here is the most crucial of all economic decisions—the question of profitable stewardship before God—and secular man cannot make this decision

---

28. Ludwig von Mises, *Economic Calculation in the Socialist Commonwealth* (1920).

29. Gary North, *Trust and Dominion: An Economic Commentary on Mark and John* (Dallas, Georgia: Point Five Press, 2012), ch. 11.

accurately. He has no fixed moral or aesthetic standards by which to evaluate his success. *Process philosophy cannot provide permanent standards*, for no man can be sure that he has not entered into a new world order between the time when he began to plan and the time he believes he has brought his plan to completion. *Continuity over time*—moral, epistemological, social, economic—cannot be logically affirmed by means of any evolutionary philosophy.

How do we know that the market order still works? How do we avoid Marx's argument that capitalism was far more productive than feudal production methods, but its day has come at last, now that proletarians are about to bring in a new world order? Hayek could not tell us. How do we know that our capitalist tools still are performing better than socialist tools? Hayek wrote:

> . . . we command many tools—in the widest sense of that word—which the human race has evolved and which enable us to deal with our environment. These are the results of the experience of successive generations which are handed down. And, once a more efficient tool is available, it will be used without our knowing why it is better, or even what the alternatives are.
>
> These "tools" which man has evolved and which constitute such an important part of his adaptation to his environment include much more than material implements. They consist in a large measure of forms of conduct which he habitually follows without knowing why; they consist of what we call "traditions" and "institutions," which he uses because they are available to him as a product of cumulative growth without ever having been designed by anyone mind. Man is generally ignorant not only of why he uses implements of one shape rather than of another but also of how much is dependent on his actions taking one form rather than another. . . . Every change in conditions will make necessary some change in the use of resources, in the direction and kind of human activities, in habits and practices. And each change in the actions of those affected in the first instance will require further adjustments that will gradually extend throughout the whole of society. Thus every change in a sense creates a "problem" for society, even though no single individual perceives it as such; and it is gradually "solved" by the establishment of a new over-all adjustment. . . . Who will prove to possess the right combination of aptitudes and opportunities to find the better way is just as little predictable as by what manner or process different kinds of knowledge and skill will combine to bring about a solution of the problem.[30]

To use the same kind of reasoning, what if we are today at one of those periods in which new intellectual tools are replacing the old

---

30. Hayek, *Constitution of Liberty*, pp. 27–28. (2011 ed.: ch. 2:3)

ones? What if the Marxists are correct, that man is entering a new moral age? As Irving Kristol said in a speech in 1981, one of the important products in all capitalist systems is socialism. Joseph Schumpeter said the same thing in 1942.[31] Why should we resist the obvious and universal transformation of capitalist social orders into socialist orders? We cannot, as methodological individualists, make interpersonal comparisons of subjective utility. People are adopting socialist ideas. Isn't that proof enough of the development of a "new tool," the intellectual tool of socialism? Why fight it?

Darwin argued that species evolved into new species. Marx argued the same thing concerning societies, although he expected a discontinuous leap—revolution—to mark such transitions. Hayek argued that tools are evolved through imitation and competition to deal with environmental changes, or men's new perceptions of environmental possibilities. How could he legitimately argue that socialism is an invalid "tool" in today's Darwinian society, if the planners can predict the future better, arouse moral indignation more efficiently, and erase the flaws of the older, pre-modern capitalist order?

If you cannot legitimately appeal to fixed human nature (evolutionism denies any such thing), and you cannot appeal to fixed moral standards (process philosophy denies any such standards), and you cannot appeal to the greater output of capitalism (no interpersonal comparisons of subjective utility are scientifically valid), then how are you able to defend the free market? Who is going to pay any attention? When mankind faces the possibility of extinction if we fail to compete successfully with other species, isn't it sensible to adopt social, economic, and genetic planning in order to guarantee man's triumph? Aren't we in a war against other species? Can any army be successful that has no chain of command, no centralized leadership? The social impulse of Darwinism is to establish man's position as the new sovereign over nature. *Man as central planner is a powerful image.* How can Hayek's version of evolutionism—analogous to the pre-human, purposeless, undesigned evolutionary process—compete with "the real thing," namely, elitist planning by scientific experts?

Hayek's reasoning has failed to convince men in the marketplace of ideas. What other standard can be used by Hayek or his followers to appeal to beyond the marketplace of ideas? Mises, Hayek's mentor,

---

31. Joseph Schumpeter, *Capitalism, Socialism, and Democracy* (New York: Harper Torchbook, [1942] 1965), especially chapters 12 and 13. See also Benjamin Rogge [ROWEguee], *Can Capitalism Survive?* (Indianapolis, Indiana: Liberty Press, 1979).

knew there was no such appeal for a true Austrian economist, which is why he was incapable of optimism regarding the future of man.

> Whatever is to be said in favor of correct logical thinking does not prove that the coming generations of men will surpass their ancestors in intellectual effort and achievements. History shows that again and again periods of marvelous mental accomplishments were followed by periods of decay and retrogression. We do not know whether the next generation will beget people who are able to continue along the lines of the geniuses who made the last centuries so glorious. We do not know anything about the biological conditions that enable a man to take one step forward in the march of intellectual advancement. We cannot preclude the assumption that there may be limits to man's further intellectual ascent. And certainly we do not know whether in this ascent there is not a point beyond which the intellectual leaders can no longer succeed in convincing the masses and making them follow their lead.[32]

Or, as he wrote in a manuscript as he was about to flee Switzerland in 1940: "Occasionally I entertained the hope that my writings would bear practical fruit and show the way for policy. Constantly I have been looking for evidence of a change in ideology. But I have never allowed myself to be deceived. I have come to realize that my theories explain the degeneration of a great civilization; they do not prevent it. I set out to be a reformer, but only became the historian of decline."[33] The historian of decline: a sad task for an economist. His Darwinian evolutionism was too old-fashioned; it did not honor Man, the central planner, or Man, the new predestinator. Hayek and Mises won few followers among economists.

B. Purposeless Evolutionism

Hayek's most notable contribution to the epistemology of economics is his continuing development of the concept of purposeful action within the legal framework of a free market. It is the *market process* that provides acting men with a maximum of information, especially information necessary to the dovetailing of competing plans by individuals. The focus on purposeful action marks the Austrian School of economists more than any other academic group of economists.

The most influential group of free market economists, generally referred to as the Chicago School (since so many of the members

---

32. Ludwig von Mises, *The Historical Setting of the Austrian School of Economics* (Auburn, Alabama: Mises Institute, [1969] 1984), pp. 17–18.

33. Mises, *Notes and Recollections* (South Holland, Illinois: Libertarian Press, 1978), p. 115.

attended, or have taught at, the University of Chicago), is more forth-rightly empiricist in its epistemology. They want to discuss economic facts. They want economic theory to prove itself by its performance in making verifiable predictions. They regard themselves as defenders of positivist economics: empirical, inductivist economics, as contrasted to logical, deductivist economics (the Austrian School's approach). Because they cling to a scientific idea that is much closer to the logic of the natural sciences, they are less concerned about unmeasurable, unverifiable concepts such as "human purpose." The Kantian dualism between the phenomenal realm of science and the noumenal realm of human personality has led to the formation of rival schools of free market economists. The Chicago School economists are attempting to be "hard" science advocates, so they are less concerned about the "noumenal."

1. Armen Alchian

Chicago School economist Milton Friedman wrote *Free to Choose*, but Armen Alchian was more consistent with the methodology of nat-ural science. He tried to avoid a word like "choice," since it is suppos-edly irrelevant to a discussion based on science.[34] It implies too much independence from the law of cause and effect. Human choice as an independent factor cannot be tested; all we can do is speak about demonstrated preference or actual actions made by men.

Because of his devotion to empirical science, Alchian was com-mitted to a concept of economics that is based on *results* of human actions. He was a committed evolutionist. Nevertheless, Hayek's brand of decentralized but purposeful evolutionism does not appear in Alchian's version of evolutionistic economics. Hayek's system in-volves heavy reliance on the idea of human purposefulness. Alchian's essay relies heavily on the idea that the results of human action are what matter, not purposeful behavior. Alchian returned economics to Stage One of the Darwinian paradigm: *the purposeless competitive process*. This stage, for Darwin and his scientific disciples, was exclusively confined to *pre-human evolution*, meaning a world of cosmic purpose-lessness. Once man appeared on the scene, Darwin and his disciples concluded, the rules of evolution changed. Human purposeful choice

---

34. In a seminar held at Claremont Men's College in June of 1969, sponsored by the Institute for Humane Studies, Alchian lectured graduate students. He explicitly refused to use the word "choice." He said that choice is not economically distinguished from impulsive, instinctively motivated action. There is no choice. I attended the con-ference and kept my notes. That was my choice.

became the new source of evolutionary change. Man the planning being, man the communicator, man the maker of recorded information, became the source of evolutionary directionality. Alchian's approach, therefore, is an anachronism: a throwback to the methodology of pre-human evolution.

The classic statement of this methodology is found in his 1950 article, "Uncertainty, Evolution, and Economic Theory." It should be pointed out from the beginning that few significant new approaches have been achieved through the use of this methodology. One essay by Gary Becker, which I will discuss a bit later, is just about all we have to show for Alchian's pioneering work. But the original article is important, for it points to the all-pervasive nature of the evolutionary paradigm in modern economic thought. No school of economics has escaped from this paradigm. Alchian's article simply presses one phase of the evolutionary model—the pre-human purposeless phase—to a uniquely depersonalized conclusion.[35]

The criterion for success is *survival*, Alchian concluded. This is original Darwinism. *The economic system as a whole determines the survivors.* "It does not matter through what process of reasoning or motivation such success was achieved. The fact of its accomplishment is sufficient. This is the criterion by which the economic system selects survivors: those who realize positive profits are the survivors; those who suffer losses disappear."[36] We are back to right-wing Social Darwinism. Yet Alchian's version is even more radical, for he was not in the least concerned about the motivation of the survivors. "The preceding interpretation suggests two ideas. First, success (survival) accompanies relative superiority; and, second, it does not require proper motivation but may rather be the result of fortuitous circumstances. Among all competitors, those whose peculiar conditions happen to be the most appropriate of those offered to the economic system for testing and adoption will be 'selected' as survivors."[37]

Alchian's language, like Darwin's before him, personalizes an impersonal process. The impersonal economic system, like the equally

---

35. I have read other materials written by Alchian, and they show little or no sign of influence from this pioneer essay. It is possible—I think it is likely—that Alchian wrote the 1950 essay as a kind of intellectual exercise, just to make a scientific and radically theoretical point.

36. Armen Alchian, "Uncertainty, Evolution and Economic Theory" (1950); reprinted in *The Collected Works of Armen A. Alchian*, 2 vols. (Indianapolis, Indiana: Liberty Press, 2006), I, p. 6.

37. *Ibid.*, I, pp. 6–7.

impersonal pre-human process of evolution through natural selection, is described as *adopting* or *selecting* survivors. Yet this process cannot be personal. It surely cannot be purposeful. The cold impersonalism of such a process alienated Darwin, as it alienates his disciples, once man appears on the scene. Alchian was more coldly, rigorously logical in his commitment to cosmic impersonalism. The Kantian ideal of personality must be sacrificed to the Kantian ideal of science. "All individual rationality, motivation, and foresight will be temporarily abandoned in order to concentrate upon the ability of the environment to *adopt* 'appropriate' survivors even in the absence of any adaptive behavior. This is an apparently unrealistic, but never the less very useful, expository approach. . . ."[38]

Survival may very well be chance-based. He spoke about

the richness which is really inherent in chance. First, even if each and every individual acted in a haphazard and nonmotivated manner, it is possible that the variety of actions would be so great that the resulting collective set would contain actions that are best, in the sense of perfect foresight. For example, at a horse race with enough bettors wagering strictly at random, someone will win on all eight races. Thus individual random behavior does not eliminate the likelihood of observing "appropriate" decisions. Second, and conversely, individual behavior according to some foresight and motivation does not necessarily imply a collective pattern of behavior that is different from the collective variety of actions associated with a random selection of actions.[39]

Is the market process really comparable to a large horse race? Is entrepreneurship and the market process that rewards or penalizes various degrees of entrepreneurship really comparable to a game of chance? A zero-sum game has rules: winners win at the expense of losers. It is illogical to assume that a game is the same as the uncertainty-reducing process of the free market. Games of chance are based on probability distributions. They involve *risk*. They rely on the law of large numbers. There is a class probability associated with individual flips of a coin or roll of the dice. But *uncertainty* is different.[40] The class probability aspect of games of chance does not apply to future events that are truly uncertain. They cannot be known in advance through the application of statistics.[41] How could Alchian be sure that the analogy of the horse race applies to the competi-

38. *Ibid.*, I, p. 7.
39. *Ibid.*, I, p. 9.
40. Frank H. Knight, *Risk, Uncertainty, and Profit* (Boston: Houghton Mifflin, 1921).
41. Mises, *Human Action*, ch. 6.

tive struggle of the market—a struggle that is the product of human action? We know that people plan; they also act in terms of plans. They have motivations. Does the logic of impersonal chance apply to the processes of personal decision-making, simply because the market process rewards and punishes? Alchian wrote that "it is possible," but is it probable? Is there any way of testing the probability of his theory? Is there an empirical method that can tell us whether or not the market process is statistically identical to a large game of chance? No empiricist from the economics profession has offered such a test, although Alchian thought that such a test is possible.[42]

The scientism of Alchian's position should be obvious. He was equating men with atoms, biological evolution with market selection. Alchian did not shrink back from his radical methodology.

> It is not even necessary to suppose that each firm acts as if it possessed the conventional diagrams and knew the analytical principles employed by economists in deriving optimum and equilibrium conditions. The atoms and electrons do not know the laws of nature; the physicist does not impart to each atom a willful scheme of actions based on laws of conservation of energy, etc. The fact that an economist deals with human beings who have sense and ambitions does not automatically warrant imparting to these humans the great degree of foresight and motivations which the economist may require for his customary analysis as an outside observer or "oracle." The similarity between this argument and Gibbsian statistical mechanics, as well as biological evolution, is not mere coincidence.[43]

The continuing reliance on the *language of personalism* to describe a *hypothetically impersonal process* is revealing. Alchian dismissed trial and error as a standard of economic success. This is too purposeful a process. It involves "conscious adaptive behavior."[44] This allows far too much importance for the decisions of acting men. Trial and error, he asserted, cannot serve as a success indicator in a changing environment. "As a consequence, the measure of goodness of actions in anything except a tolerable-intolerable sense is lost, and the possibility of an individual's converging to the optimum activity via a trial-and-error process disappears. Trial and error becomes survival or death. It cannot serve as a basis of the individual's method of convergence to a 'maximum' or optimum position. Success is discovered by the economic system through a blanketing shotgun process, not by the indi-

---

42. Alchian, *Collected Works*, I, p. 9.
43. *Ibid.*, I, pp. 10n–11n.
44. *Ibid.*, I, p. 14.

vidual through a converging search."[45] Success is *discovered*—the language of personalism—by the economic system. Survival is the sole criterion. The aggregate process *screens* the survivors. *There is nothing rational or purposeful about this process.* It is altogether impersonal.

What is left as an explanation for economic causation? *Imitation.*[46] Men seek profits. The economic system screens out the successful imitators and innovators from the unsuccessful. "The economic counterparts of genetic heredity, mutations, and natural selection are imitation, innovation, and positive profits."[47] Alchian did not deny purposeful actions on the part of individuals, but he asserted that "the precise role and nature of purposive behavior in the presence of uncertainty and incomplete information have not been clearly understood or analyzed. It is straightforward, if not heuristic, to start with complete uncertainty and nonmotivation and then to add elements of foresight and motivation in the process of building an analytical model."[48]

This sounds scientific, but it is not. To add elements of personalism to an impersonal system undermines the impersonalism of that system. Personalism is like an acid that brings purpose into a purposeless system. This is what Darwinism did to the evolutionary process. Man brings purpose. This completely transformed cosmic impersonalism. It also led to statism: the planning elite.

2. Becker vs. Kirzner

Gary Becker, who later won the Nobel Prize, acknowledged his intellectual debt to Alchian's article. He attempted to do what Alchian had imagined possible: explain economic success apart from human purpose. In a path-breaking essay—although nobody else has followed him down this path—Becker argued that it is not necessary to assume that men act purposefully or rationally in order to conclude that aggregate market demand curves are negatively inclined (that is, that at lower prices, people in the aggregate will purchase more of the scarce resource in question). We do not need to assume that either individuals or households are economically rational—that they, too, have negatively inclined demand curves—in order to demonstrate that market demand curves are negatively sloping. "Hence the mar-

---

45. *Idem.*
46. *Ibid.*, I, p. 13.
47. *Ibid.*, I, p. 15.
48. *Ibid.*, I, pp. 16–17.

ket would act as if 'it' were rational not only when households were rational, but also when they were inert, impulsive, or otherwise irrational."[49] He compared his model to the physicist's model, as Alchian did before him. We can have a rational market even when we have irrational individualistic decisions. "If we may join the trend toward borrowing analogies from the currently glamorous field of physics, the theory of molecular motion does not simply reproduce the motion of large bodies; the smooth, 'rational' motion of a macrobody is assumed to result from the erratic, 'irrational' motions of a very large number of microbodies."[50] The post-Kantian ideal of science is here triumphant. Men are treated as atoms.

Israel Kirzner, the most academically respected member of the Austrian School, subjected Becker's analysis to a withering critique. As an Austrian, Kirzner focused on individuals who must make decisions concerning an uncertain future. The Austrian School begins with *methodological individualism*. When people go to buy a good or service, they make bids. If a man bids too low, he cannot buy all of the scarce resource that he wants. He is outbid by other customers. So, he must revise his plans. "The *essence* of this market process, it will be observed, is *the systematic way in which plan revisions are made as a consequence of the disappointment of earlier plans*."[51] More important for economic theory, "Such a pattern of plan revision can be conceived of only for rational buyers. If buyers were afflicted with chronic inertia, they would presumably come to market each day with the same low bids as yesterday, and return home with the same disappointments. If buyers made bids in a purely random manner, there is again no assurance that 'the' market price would rise at all. Only by assuming that buyers purposefully seek to achieve given goals can we predict that their thwarted plans of yesterday will lead to their systematically offering more attractive choices to sellers today."[52] Acting men are rational. They learn.

Becker relied heavily on the logic of equilibrium. Equilibrium assumes that all men are omniscient about the future, and therefore they are *responders* to the supply and demand conditions of the mar-

---

49. Gary Becker, "Irrational Behavior and Economic Theory," *Journal of Political Economy*, LXX (Feb. 1962), p. 7. This was the lead article for this issue. The *JPE* is published by the University of Chicago.

50. *Ibid.*, p. 8.

51. Israel Kirzner, "Rational Action and Economic Theory," *ibid.*, LXX (Aug. 1962), p. 381.

52. *Ibid.*, p. 382.

ket. They are all price-*takers*. As Kirzner stated, "The essence of the market process is precisely what happens before equilibrium has been reached."[53] Uncertainty prevails in real life. Men are not simply price-takers. They offer new bids, both as buyers and sellers (since every buyer is a seller of something else). "As soon, therefore, as one begins to analyze the consequences of the absence of the conditions for equilibrium, it becomes apparent that plan revisions must be the focus of attention. It is primarily upon the systematic revisions of disappointed plans that the market process depends."[54]

If I understand what Becker was really saying (he never says this explicitly), he was arguing that the market process eliminates those economic decision-makers who waste resources, it rewards those who do not waste resources, and it does not matter why members of each group made their respective decisions. Maybe they were lucky. Maybe they were rational. It makes no difference, so we need not assume rationality. The market will produce the same results. In the *aggregate*, the market will buy more of a good if its price is lower; it makes no difference if individuals act rationally and seek out lower prices. They need not be assumed to be rational seekers of lower prices. The market process is conceivably totally impersonal, even including its randomly acting participants.

Kirzner, as an Austrian, wanted explanations for the rationality of the *market process*. He very carefully avoided speaking, as Becker did, of the rationality of the market itself, as if the market as a whole possessed a supply or demand curve. There were reasons for his unwillingness to speak of "the rationality of the market." He was a methodological individualist. This methodology categorically denies the validity of any aggregate constructs. There are only acting individuals; there are no "acting markets." But individual actions by acting men can be discussed, and Kirzner provides a clear description of the way in which market participants plan ahead, learn from market experiences, and reformulate their plans.

In one sense, the two men were talking at cross purposes. Becker wanted to discuss a hypothetical construct, the market as a whole. Kirzner did not explicitly say so here, but his methodology denies the existence of any such construct, let alone its rationality. Becker did not want to discuss the market process explicitly (how the hypothetically random actions of individuals are merged into an aggregate

---

53. *Ibid.*, p. 384.
54. *Idem.*

which is rational), and Kirzner wanted to discuss nothing else. Becker avoided discussing the market process, and Kirzner avoided discussing market (collective) rationality. Neither man really addressed the central feature of the other's position, namely, the implicit assumptions about the *one* (the aggregate market) and the *many* (acting men). What each scholar refused to come out and say explicitly is the heart of each man's analysis. Such is the fate of scholarly discussions in academic journals.

Why the failure of each man to "go for the throat"? I contend that it stems from a sort of unwritten agreement among humanistic scholars: they will not "expose the nakedness" of their opponents if their opponents politely reciprocate. Humanism cannot solve the problem of the one and the many; so, when discussions involving this fundamental issue arise, neither participant is immune from a devastating attack from the other.

Becker never said in his rebuttal: "Prof. Kirzner, you cannot logically discuss the rationality of the market as an aggregate. There are no aggregates in Austrian School economic theory. All that you can discuss is the individual. All that you can discuss is a market process. You are unable to say anything about whether the market as a whole responds to high or low prices in predictable ways. You have no right even to use a model of 'the market,' since your presuppositions deny the possibility of such a model. In fact, you cannot claim to be an economist at all, since you are far too consistent with your own presupposition about the scientific illegitimacy of making interpersonal comparisons of subjective utility. Any model of the market as a system must abstract from reality, and human action in Austrian School economics is not conceivable in such abstract terms. Without a market model of human action, you ought to get out of the economics profession. Why not sell insurance for a living?"

If Becker had attacked him so forthrightly, Kirzner might have replied: "You cannot explain how a market works. Your system is totally static. You cannot integrate human actions by means of a theory of market process, because acting men are rational, they learn from the past, and they are low price-seekers. You draw a lot of charts that show indifference curves, but no such curves exist in reality; they are all mental constructs. All things never remain equal. Your static system is a sham. You must rely on some version of equilibrium, yet all equilibrium analysis necessarily involves timelessness, not to mention perfect human foresight—the elimination of all unforeseen uncertainty. So, you claim to be building a case for irrational individuals as the foundation for market rationality, but your graphs can only be constructed by means of a presupposition of total, perfect human foresight and rationality. You cannot explain how your inconceivable aggregate market with its hypothetical demand curves ever comes into existence—which it does not do, since it is all a mental construct. So, you ought to get out of the economics profession. But stay out of the insurance business; insurance salesman must deal with acting men, and you refuse to acknowledge that men act rationally anyway. You ought to become a mystic."

In such an exchange, both men would have to deny that the other is a true economist, and in doing so, both men would deny the existence of a science of economics. They would show that neither the a priorists nor the empiricists can deal with the problem of the one and the many. Both sides need to deny the validity of their own presuppositions in order to practice their profession. As Van Til once quipped, each side stays in business by taking in each other's washing. So, to this extent, these men were not talking at cross purposes. They were united in their willingness to let each other stay in the profession; otherwise, both of them would have to get out. And, for that matter, so would the editors of all the scholarly economics journals. There would be no economics profession to write for.

3. Equilibrium

What about equilibrium? Is the concept of equilibrium really crucial to modern free market economics? It has been an implicit aspect of economic reasoning from the beginning, and an explicit aspect since the 1800s. Free market economic models all assume the "tendency toward equilibrium" in the market process. Was Kirzner correct in challenging Becker for having used the concept in an essay that denied the necessity of assuming rational (low price-seeking) individuals? And, if he was correct, does that very equilibrium come back to haunt him?

Equilibrium is an impossibility, since it involves perfect foreknowledge—a world with no surprises, no profits, and no losses.[55] Everyone is a price-taker; everyone responds predictably to market conditions; no one has any independence from all other participants' predictions. In short, *human action is inconceivable in such a universe.* Yet it is this inconceivable standard that undergirds all non-social-

---

55. Mises called this the evenly rotating economy.

ist economic thought, including Kirzner's. He wrote: "It is generally recognized that the market process (whether within a given industry or for an entire economy) is a means of communicating knowledge. The knowledge that a market communicates is made up of precisely those elements of information necessary to bring about the systematic revisions of plans in the direction of equilibrium (whether partial or general). Each market decision is made in the light of market information. Where the decisions of all market participants dovetail completely, all of them can be implemented without disappointments and without subsequent alterations of plans; the market is in equilibrium."[56] So, Kirzner, as with all other market-oriented economists, judged the real world of human action in terms of a hypothetical, intellectually inconsistent world of equilibrium—a world in which forecasting is perfect, everyone's actions are fully known in advance, and men have no freedom of choice. In such a world, humans respond as automatons to stimuli. Cause and effect rule supreme: the triumph of Kant's phenomenal realm of science over Kant's noumenal realm of free human personality. In short, Kirzner had to rely on a limiting concept, equilibrium, in order to judge the success or failure of market institutions in dovetailing the varying plans of acting men. Yet this limiting concept is in total opposition to the methodological individualism (autonomous man) that Kirzner and the Austrian School economists constantly preach. *To explain human action, economists use a model which denies human action.*

Here is one of the important assumptions of Alchian: "Comparability of resulting situations is destroyed by the changing environment."[57] The changing environment in an evolving universe may have changed the rules of survival. This is also true for Hayek's evolving universe. This is the plight of all process philosophy. Hayek relied on the market to guide men in their quest to dovetail their plans, but how can he be sure that the laws of the market process are still supreme? After all, we live in a world of constant change. Where is his measuring rod that tells us whether or not we are progressing according to our individual plans? How could he or Kirzner use equilibrium as the standard, when equilibrium analysis is absolutely contrary to the concept of free, autonomous human action?

Alchian, as a consistent evolutionist, said that survival is the only criterion. This leads us back to the old debate: Who or what is to in-

---

56. Kirzner, "Rational Action and Economic Theory," *op. cit.*, p. 384.
57. Alchian, *Collected Works*, I, p. 14.

sure the survival of mankind? The intellectual appeal of Lester Frank
Ward and all other advocates of central planning is that they argue
that man is different from the animals around him or before him.
Man has a mind. Scientific men, as an elite corps of specialists, can
therefore do what no other animal can: change the environment according to a plan that ensures the survival of their own species. Man
the planner overcomes through central planning the limits that have
constrained all other life forms. Man the planner is a new being, a
being that can adapt evolutionary processes to his own advantage
as a species. No longer is man nothing more than a product of evolutionary, purposeless competition among all the species. Now man
can take control of the processes of evolutionary change. Science has
made this possible. This perspective is widely held. The religion of
humanism teaches it.

Hayek and Kirzner affirmed that man the planning individual can
best achieve control over nature by decentralized planning within the
framework of a market order. But to claim this, they had to rely on
some sort of standard. They asked: How can men, as individuals, be
sure that their plans are working to their advantage? By appealing
to the hypothetical standard of equilibrium? But Hayek's reliance
on the institutions of the free market was founded on his *denial* of
omniscience. Equilibrium analysis affirms universal human omniscience, and it simultaneously denies autonomous human action.[58]
Progress toward equilibrium is the Austrian School's equivalent to
progress toward absolute zero: when we achieve it, we have denied all
progress.[59] It is progress toward man the omniscient being, meaning

58. Mises wrote: "Action is change, and change is in the temporal sequence. But in
the evenly rotating economy change and succession of events are eliminated. Action
is to make choices and to cope with an uncertain future. But in the evenly rotating
economy there is no choosing and the future is not uncertain as it does not differ from
the present known state. Such a rigid system is not peopled with living men making
choices and liable to error; it is a world of soulless unthinking automatons; it is not
a human society, it is an ant hill." *Human Action: A Treatise on Economics* (New Haven,
Connecticut: Yale University Press, 1949), p. 249. In the third edition published by
Regnery in 1966, this appears on page 248.
59. Mises wrote: "The only method of dealing with the problem of action is to conceive that action ultimately aims at bringing about a state of affairs in which there is
no longer any action, whether because all uneasiness had been removed or because
any further removal of felt uneasiness is out of the question. Action thus tends toward
a state of rest, absence of action." *Ibid.*, (1949), p. 245; (1966), p. 244. Mises, however,
insisted that the use of such imaginary and self-contradictory constructs is inescapable
for the science of economics. He did not offer a theoretical defense of static theory; he
used pragmatism. "The method of imaginary constructions is justified by its success,"
(1949), p. 238; (1966), p. 236. Then how can we know whether an imaginary construct

men as totally predictable, cause-and-effect dominated, price-taking non-actors. *The world of equilibrium is a world without autonomous men.* But autonomous man is the universally shared presupposition of all schools of humanistic economics.

Can the decentralized competition of the free market ensure the survival of man? There is no way that Hayek or Kirzner could affirm this scientifically. How can we even speak of species man, when we cannot legitimately make interpersonal comparisons of subjective utility? How can "man, the collective" ever know anything? How can we even speak of such an intellectual abstraction, if we are methodological individualists and subjectivists? Only by denying our premises.

Chicago School rationalists want to avoid such questions, but they are also unable to escape the antinomies of Kantian thought. Their world of economic equilibrium analysis also assumes omniscience. Becker began with equilibrium analysis to prove that in the aggregate, the market is rational, even if individuals are not. Yet, as Kirzner asked, how could he assume the existence of equilibrium conditions? It is men as plan-makers and plan-revisers who create a tendency toward equilibrium. You cannot legitimately argue rationality in an equilibrium market and also deny that men are necessarily rational, since to achieve equilibrium, all men must be perfectly rational and totally omniscient.

Alchian began with the presumption of uncertainty: "The existence of uncertainty and incomplete information is the foundation of the suggested type of analysis; the importance of the concept of a class of 'chance' decisions rests upon it...."[60] Yet Becker began with equilibrium charts to prove his case that a rational market can be the product of irrational decisions. There is something illogical here.

"works"? He had no answer: "The method of imaginary constructions is indispensable for praxeology [the science of human action—G.N.]; it is the only method of praxeological and economic inquiry. It is, to be sure, a method very difficult to handle because it can easily result in fallacious syllogisms. It leads along a sharp edge; on both sides yawns the chasm of absurdity and nonsense. Only merciless self-criticism can prevent a man from falling headlong into these abysmal depths," (1949), p. 238; (1966), p. 237. But, we must ask, self-criticism according to what standards? How do we link our hypothetical and self-contradictory constructs (human action without human action) to the external realm of events? Mises does not say. No economist can say. The only way we can do this is through intuition, as Mises and Milton Friedman agree: North, "Economics: From Reason to Intuition," *Foundations of Christian Scholarship, op. cit.,* reprinted as Appendix A, North, *Christian Economics: Scholar's Edition* (Dallas, GA: Point Five Press, 2020).

60. Alchian, *Collected Works,* I, p. 17.

Conclusion

The dualisms of Kantian thought are inescapable. To evaluate change, you need a fixed standard. To evaluate the success of human action, you need a model that denies human action, whether you call it equilibrium or "the evenly rotating economy," as Mises did. To measure the progress of mankind, you need a changeless standard which thwarts the progress of mankind. (How can we have progress in a static order?) To assert that personal irrationality is compatible with market rationality, you need an equilibrium model that rests on personal infallibility. By arguing that we need a decentralized market order to preserve and expand human knowledge, the evolutionist winds up affirming that no one can understand the market order. The laws of the market order are said to be the result of eons of development—the product of human action but not of human design—yet we are asked to believe that this order is as useful to mankind as a whole (when we can legitimately say nothing as methodological individualists about mankind as a whole) as if it had been designed specifically for mankind as a whole. We are asked to affirm cause and effect in a world that is the product of chance. We are asked to affirm that man the planning individual cannot effectively make decisions for other men, because no man has sufficient knowledge to integrate the knowledge of other acting men, yet we are also supposed to affirm that the market is a reliable institution for the progress of the species, when we do not know how the market ever developed, and we cannot speak of an aggregate like "man, the species." We want the one (the market order) to conform to the needs of the many (acting individuals), yet we cannot, as methodological individualists, make any scientifically legitimate statements about the needs of the many. (One man "needs" to stick pins in others, while others insist that they "need" to avoid being stuck.) We make our case for the market in terms of imperfect knowledge (Alchian and Hayek), yet we are then forced to make judgments about evolution as a process, the best interests of mankind as a species, the reliability of the market in a world of evolutionary change, and so forth. From ignorance (we need the market to integrate and expand knowledge) to near-omniscience (we know that the market will provide us with this needed knowledge). From irrationality (Becker's irrationality thesis) to rationality (Becker's equilibrium analysis). The logic of humanistic economics is hopelessly self-contradictory.

Christian economics is the only answer. We have a source of rationality. We have a guarantee of economic laws. We have confidence that the market order is fully conformable to the needs of individuals, and also to the needs of mankind as a whole. We know that we do not need perfect knowledge (omniscience) in order to have reliable knowledge. We know that the logic of our minds, despite its limitations when pushed, is a reliable device for interpreting and moulding external reality. We know that the market is historically the product of human action, precisely because it is transcendentally the product of God's design.

The dominion covenant offers us all these needed intellectual requirements. It makes economic thought possible. Without the presupposition of the dominion covenant, and the revelation of God's design for economic institutions and relationships, there can be no logical, consistent, reliable, self-attesting science of economics, whether deductivist (logical) or inductivist (empirical). Any economic theory based on evolutionism must fail; its own internal contradictions cannot support it. *Evolution is process philosophy, and process philosophy is relativism, lawlessness—the kingdom of whirl.* All humanistic systems of economics are evolutionistic: Marxism, Austrianism, Chicagoism, and Keynesianism. If we are to have a reliable concept of economics, we need reliable concepts of God, man, law, causation, and progress. Humanism provides us with unreliable concepts of God, man, law, causation, and progress. It is time to abandon humanism as the foundation of economic analysis.

I have argued that the humanists must borrow heavily from Christianity in order to build their economic systems. They deny omniscience, yet they must affirm it as an ideal in order to create an equilibrium model which serves as a standard toward which human action moves. They affirm structure in the midst of change. They affirm progress for the species as a whole, despite the fact that they cannot speak of progress for the species as a whole if they are faithful to the principle of methodological individualism.

The free market's advocates are united in their belief that there is an inherent rationality in the market order, yet neither Hayek nor Alchian could explain why such rationality can exist in a world of flux and irrationality. They denied the epistemological necessity of the doctrine of providence, yet they spoke of market processes as if these processes were providential in nature: *selecting* survivors, *adopting* species, *integrating* conflicting plans of individuals, and so forth. The very features of their individualistic systems that demand aggregate coherence cannot be affirmed without abandoning the logical requirements of methodological individualism. They did not wish to speak of methodological covenantalism, yet they were forced to adopt the conclusions of covenantalism in order to escape the clutches of methodological collectivism. They wrote as though they were living in a world of cosmic personalism, yet they explicitly denied the existence of any such universe. They wanted the fruits of a Christian world-and-life view, but not the roots.

We cannot enjoy forever the fruits of Christian civilization, including the free market social order, without the roots: the biblical doctrines of God, creation, law, sanctions, and inheritance. We must affirm the doctrine of man as the image of God. We must affirm the dominion covenant. We must abandon the evolutionists' various defenses of the free market if we are successfully to defend the market from the evolutionistic opponents of the free market.

APPENDIX C

COSMOLOGIES IN CONFLICT:
CREATION VS. EVOLUTION

Gertrude Himmelfarb, in her superb study, *Darwin and the Darwinian Revolution* (1959), quoted an amusing and highly revealing section from Benjamin Disraeli's 1847 novel, *Tancred*. Disraeli, who later became England's Prime Minister, caught the new evolutionistic spirit of some of Britain's upper classes—pre-Darwinian evolution, and a perspective universally condemned by scientists everywhere prior to Darwin's *On the Origin of Species* (1859). A fashionable lady urges Tancred, the hero, to read a new book, *Revelations of Chaos* (actually, Robert Chambers' anonymously printed and enormously popular *Vestiges of Creation*): "You know, all is development. The principle is perpetually going on. First, there was nothing, then there was something; then—I forget the next—I think there were shells, then fishes; then we came—let me see—did we come next? Never mind that; we came at last. And at the next change there will be something very superior to us—something with wings. Ah! that's it: we were fishes, and I believe we shall be crows. But you must read it. [Tancred protests, mentioning that he had never been a fish. She goes on:] Oh! but it is all proved.... You understand, it is all science.... Everything is proved—by geology, you know."

It was people like this lady who bought 24,000 copies of *Vestiges of Creation* from its publication in 1844 until 1860—not the scientists, but good, upstanding Anglican Church members. When Darwin's *Origin* was published, the entire edition of 1,250 copies was sold out to booksellers in one day. The doctrine of evolution, rejected by scientists in 1850, was the universal orthodoxy in 1875. The idea of natural selection over millions of years had become the catch-all of the sciences. The entire universe is a chance operation in this perspective.

437

Chance brought all things into existence (if in fact all things were not always in existence), and chance presently sustains the system. The utterly improbable laws of probability provide creation with whatever piecemeal direction it possesses. This cosmology was a return to the cosmologies of ancient paganism, though of course it is all dressed up in its scientific white smock and footnotes.

The reigning cosmologies of the non-Christian world have always had one feature in common: they do not distinguish between the being of God and the being of the universe. In all these cosmogonies—stories of the original creation—a finite god created the world out of a pre-existing "stuff," either spiritual or material. This god, only comparatively powerful, faced the contingent (chance) elements of the ultimately mysterious "stuff" in a way analogous to the way we now face a basically mysterious creation. *Chance is therefore ultimate in most non-biblical systems.* Some "primitive" cosmogonies affirm creation from an original cosmic egg (Polynesian, eighth-century Japan).[1] A large number of the creation stories were creation out of water (Maori, certain California Indian tribes, the Central Bantu Tribe of the Lunda Cluster, Mayan Indians in Central America, Babylon).[2] The Egyptian text, "The Book of Overthrowing Apophis," provides an excellent example of a water cosmogony: "The Lord of All, after having come into being, says: I am he who came into being as Khepri (i.e., the Becoming One). When I came into being, the beings came into being, all the beings came into being after I became. Numerous are those who became, who came out of my mouth, before heaven ever existed, nor earth came into being, nor the worms, nor snakes, were created in this place. I being in weariness, was bound to them in the Watery Abyss. I found no place to stand."[3] After planning in his heart the various beings, he spat them out of his mouth. "It was my father the Watery Abyss who brought them up and my eye followed them (?) while they became far from me." This god is not the sovereign God of the biblical creation story. The Bible's God did not spring from a watery abyss, nor did He create the world from His own substance. He created it out of nothing.

---

1. Mircea Eliade (ed.), *From Primitives to Zen* (New York: Harper & Row, 1967), pp. 88, 94.

2. *Ibid.*, pp. 86, 88, 90, 91, 93, 98.

3. *Ibid.*, p. 98.

A. Greek Speculation

Hesiod, who probably wrote his classic poems in the eighth century B.C., sketched a cosmogony that sought the source of creation in the infinite void (chaos), in much the same way as modern science searches for the origin of the universe. Chaos is the source of all that is.[4] As was the case and is the case in most non-Christian cosmologies, he held to a theory of eternal cycles: the original Age of Gold is inevitably followed by a process of deterioration into new ages: Silver, Bronze, and finally Iron.[5] (A similar outline is given by Daniel to King Nebuchadnezzar in Daniel 2; Daniel's exposition to the king's vision is not cyclical, however, for a fifth kingdom—God's eternal kingdom—finally replaces the fourth and final earthly kingdom.) Pagan cyclical theories held to a faith that the grim age of iron could be regenerated back into a new age of gold through the application of ritual acts of chaos. Our present age is characterized by law and order—the opposite of life—so that by violating established social and political laws, societies can be regenerated from below. Thus, the ancient pagan cultures had annual or seasonal chaos festivals. Metaphysical regeneration rather than ethical regeneration was basic to their cosmologies. Not a return to covenantal law, as in the Hebrew-Christian perspective, but an escape from law: here was the alternative to the biblical perspective.[6] This dialectic between order and chaos was universal in the Near Eastern and classical civilizations. Ethics was therefore primarily political, for it was the state, as the supposed link between heaven and earth, that was the agency of social and personal salvation.[7]

In examining the history of the universe, Greek scientists were not noticeably superior to their predecessors, the poets, or the cosmologists of other ancient cultures. In an extremely important study, *The Discovery of Time* (1965), the authors concluded: "For all the rationality of their concepts, they never put down firm intellectual roots into the temporal development of Nature, nor could they grasp the timescale of Creation with any more certainty than men had done before.

---

4. Hesiod, "Theogony," *ibid.*, p. 115.

5. Hesiod, *Works and Days*, lines 109-201.

6. Eliade, *Cosmos and History* (1958); *The Sacred and the Profane* (1957). See also Roger Caillois, *Man and the Sacred* (Glencoe, Illinois: Free Press, 1959).

7. R. J. Rushdoony, *The One and the Many* (Vallecito, California: Ross House, [1971] 2007), chaps. 3, 4. Cf. Charles N. Cochrane, *Christianity and Classical Culture* (New York: Oxford University Press, [1944] 1957), p. 323. This has been reprinted by Liberty Press, Indianapolis.

In the *History of Nature*, therefore, the continuity between the ideas of the Greek philosophers and those of the preceding era is particularly striking: here, even more than elsewhere, one may justly speak of their theories as 'radical myths.'"[8]

Hecateus of Miletos, an historian of the mid-sixth century, B.C., attempted to link human history with natural history. His conclusions were still being quoted by Diodorus of Sicily five centuries later, in the latter's *Historical Library*. "When in the beginning, as their account runs, the universe was being formed, both heaven and earth were indistinguishable in appearance, since their elements were intermingled: then, when their bodies separated from one another, the universe took on in all its parts the ordered form in which it is now seen...."[9] Life sprang from "the wet" by reason of the warmth from the sun; all the various forms were created at once. The creation of the elements was therefore impersonal. The creation of life was spontaneous, instantaneous, and fixed for all time. It was a purely autonomous development.

Plato was caught in the tension between order and chaos. Two of the pre-Socratic philosophers, Heraclitus and Parmenides, had set forth the case for each. Heraclitus had argued that all is flux, change, and process; Parmenides had argued that all is rational, static, and universal. This so-called dialectic between structure and change, order and chaos, was expressed in terms of the Form (Idea)-Matter dualism.[10] Plato, in the *Timaeus* dialogue, began with a contrast between exact, eternal mathematical concepts and the temporal flux of history. As Toulmin and Goodfield commented: "The Creation of the cosmos was the process by which the eternal mathematical principles were given material embodiment, imposing an order on the formless raw materials of the world, and setting them working according to ideal specifications."[11] It is the vision of a Divine Craftsman. Plato was non-committal about the timing of this creation or the order of the creation; it was, at the minimum, 9,000 years earlier. In response to Aristotle's attack on this theory, Plato's pupils argued that it was

---

8. Stephen Toulmin and Jane Goodfield, *The Discovery of Time* (New York: Harper Torchbook, 1965), p. 33; cf. p. 37.

9. *Ibid.*, p. 35.

10. Rushdoony, *One and the Many*, ch. 4; Herman Dooyeweerd, *In the Twilight of Western Thought* (Philadelphia: Presbyterian and Reformed, 1960), pp. 39–42; Cornelius Van Til, *A Survey of Christian Epistemology*, Volume II of *In Defense of the Faith* (Den Dulk Foundation, 1969), ch. 3.

11. Toulmin and Goodfield, *Discovery of Time*, p. 42.

only an intellectual construct, not something to be taken literally.[12] They were correct. Plato's god, as his other dialogues indicate, was an impersonal Idea of the Good, itself a fragmented universal.[13]

Aristotle's cosmology was different. His god was a totally impersonal, totally aloof being—thought contemplating itself—and therefore indifferent to the world. The affairs of the world are determined by autonomous processes. Both god and the world are eternal (*Physics*, VIII). His god was therefore "Unmoved Perfection," totally independent. The creation was equally independent.[14] God's existence does not explain why other beings exist, or why they exist in a particular way.[15] There had never been a temporal beginning; time is unbounded. History operates in terms of cycles.[16] Aristotle was intensely skeptical concerning questions about some hypothetical and unknowable original creation.

The later Greek philosophical schools known as the Stoics (deterministic) and Epicureans (skeptical, atheistic) also held to a cyclical view of history. Their curiosity about the universe's origins went unsatisfied. When Paul confronted members of both schools of thought on Mars' Hill in Athens, he was unable to convince them to believe in the Bible's Creator God—the God in whom we live and have our being (Acts 17:24–28, 32). Paul's concept of God was utterly foreign to their belief in an independent, autonomous universe. They preferred to believe that an impersonal world of pure chance (luck) battles eternally for supremacy over pure determinism (fate), equally impersonal.[17]

Christianity offered a solution to this eternal tension. The Creator of heaven and earth is a God of three Persons: eternal, omnipotent, exhaustive in self-revelation. The revelation of the Bible, not the logic of the self-proclaimed autonomous human mind, serves as the foundation of this belief.[18] This belief overcame the dualism of classical

---

12. *Ibid.*, p. 43.

13. Arthur O. Lovejoy, *The Great Chain of Being* (New York: Harper Torchbook, [1936] 1965), pp. 38, 48–53; Van Til, *Survey*, pp. 37–38.

14. Toulmin and Goodfield, *Discovery of Time*, pp. 44–45. For Aristotle's arguments against the Greek "creationists," see *Meteorologica*, Bk. II, ch. I, par. 1.

15. Lovejoy, *Great Chain of Being*, p. 55.

16. Aristotle, *Meteorologica*, II: XIV: 352a, 353a. Haber has concluded that Aristotle was essentially a uniformitarian: Francis C. Haber, "Fossils and Early Cosmology," in Bentley Glass, et al. (eds.), *Forerunners of Darwin: 1745–1859* (Baltimore: Johns Hopkins Press, 1959), pp. 9–10. Cf. Toulmin and Goodfield, *Discovery of Time*, pp. 45–46.

17. Cochrane, *Christianity and Classical Culture*, p. 159.

18. *Ibid.*, p. 237.

thought by denying the impersonalism of the cosmos. It provided an alternative to the collapsing classical civilization, for it offered a wholly new cosmology. As Cochrane says, "The fall of Rome was the fall of an idea, or rather of a system of life based upon a complex of ideas which may be described broadly as those of Classicism; and the deficiencies of Classicism, already exposed in the third century, were destined sooner or later to involve the system in ruin."[19]

B. Eastern Monism

The major philosophical religions of China and India are Buddhism and Hinduism. Both are ultimately monistic faiths. They hypothesize an ultimate oneness of being underlying all reality. This total oneness became plural at some point in the past, thus producing the creation out of itself; at some later point in history, it will overcome this dualism to become unified again. The change and multiplicity of life are therefore maya—illusions. Only unity can be said truly to exist. Somehow, the ultimate reality of one has included in itself the illusion of plurality. Swami Nikhilananda, a respected Hindu scholar whose article appears in a symposium of Darwinian evolutionists, tried to explain his system's cosmology.

> According to the Upanishads, which form the conclusion and the essence of the Vedas and are also the basis of the Vedanta philosophy, Atman, or the unchanging spirit in the individual, and Brahman, or the unchanging spirit in the universe, are identical. This spirit of consciousness—eternal, homogeneous, attributeless, and self-existent is the ultimate cause of all things.... Vedanta Philosophy speaks of attributeless reality as beyond time, space, and causality. It is not said to be the cause of the Saguna Brahman [first individual] in the same way as the potter is the cause of the pot (dualism), or milk of curds (pantheism). The creation of Saguna Brahman is explained as an illusory superimposition such as one notices when the desert appears as a mirage, or a rope in semi-darkness as a snake. This superimposition does not change the nature of reality, as the apparent water of the mirage does not soak a single grain of sand in the desert. A name and a form are thus superimposed upon Brahman by maya, a power inherent in Brahman and inseparable from it, as the power to burn is inseparable from fire.... According to Vedanta, maya is the material basis of creation; it is something positive. It is called positive because it is capable of evolving the tangible material universe.[20]

---

19. *Ibid.*, p. 355.

20. Swami Nikhilananda, "Hinduism and the Idea of Evolution," in *A Book that Shook the World* (University of Pittsburgh, 1958), pp. 48–49. The position of philosophical

The one of Atman-Brahman produces something different, maya, which really is not different in reality from the one, and maya in turn evolves the material universe, although it is not itself material. It is an illusion. The universe is therefore an illusion. The process is cyclical:

> Evolution or manifestation is periodical or cyclic; manifestation and non-manifestation alternate; there is not continuous progress in one direction only. The universe oscillates in both directions like a pendulum of a clock. The evolution of the universe is called the beginning of a cycle, and the involution, the termination of the cycle. The whole process is spontaneous, like a person's breathing out and breathing in. At the end of a cycle all the physical bodies resolve into maya, which is the undifferentiated substratum of matter, and all individualized energy into prana, which is the cosmic energy; and both energy and matter remain in an indistinguishable form. At the beginning of the new cycle, the physical bodies separate out again, and the prana animates them. Evolution and involution are postulated on the basis of the indestructibility of matter and the conservation of energy. [The swami seems to be throwing a sop to the evolutionists here, since matter really cannot exist, for all is one—spirit.—G.N.] From the relative standpoint, the creation is without beginning or end. A cycle is initiated by the power or intelligence of God. According to Hindu thinkers, the present cycle commenced about three billion years ago. It appears from some of the Upanishads that all beings—superhuman, human, and subhuman—appear simultaneously at the beginning of a cycle.[21]

There can be no true separation or distinction between the Creator and the creation. All is ultimately one substance: spirit. If matter is eternal, this means that illusion is eternal. Yet the attainment of Nirvana implies an escape from the process of time and change, so it would appear that not everything is matter eternally, i.e., illusion. Something—one's soul—escapes from this eternal illusion to return to the oneness. Thus, both Hindus and Buddhists developed systems of ascetic practices by which the souls of men, or at least the surviving deeds of men (Buddhism), could escape from creation. In this sense, the asceticism of the East was similar to the monistic (not necessarily monastic) asceticism of the West's gnostic sects, desert mystics, or other neoplatonic groups.[22]

Buddhism is similar: D. T. Suzuki, *Outlines of Mahayana Buddhism* (New York: Schocken Books, [1907] 1963), pp. 46–47.

21. *Ibid.*, p. 51.

22. R. J. Rushdoony, "Asceticism," in *The Encyclopedia of Christianity* (Wilmington, Delaware: National Foundation for Christian Education, 1964), I, pp. 432–36; Rushdoony, *One and the Many*, pp. 164–70; Rushdoony, *The Flight from Humanity: A Study of the Effect of Neoplatonism on Christianity*, 2nd ed. (Vallecito, California: Chalcedon, [1973]

During the first half of the twentieth century, English language readers had to rely almost exclusively on the voluminous researches of Daisetz Teitaro Suzuki for their knowledge of Zen Buddhism. His studies of the more orthodox and scholarly Mahayana Buddhism were also influential. Both systems are ultimately monistic, as is Hinduism, from which Buddhism developed. Paralleling the almost scholastic Mahayana form of Buddhism is Hinayana, or ascetic-magical Buddhism, but Western readers are far less concerned with this less speculative offshoot, however important it may have been in practice. As might be expected, Suzuki tried to come to grips with the ultimate oneness—Absolute Suchness—but his explanation was by definition hopeless. "Absolute Suchness from its very nature thus defies all definitions."[23] The ground of all existence is therefore nonrational, incommunicative, mysterious. As with Hinduism, diversity is viewed as a result of finite consciousness.[24] There can be no answer of the eternal one-many distinction; we can never know how the one became many.[25]

Certain conclusions utterly foreign to Western, Christian thought result from this monism. For example, *there can be no personal responsibility in such a system.* Suzuki explained that "Buddhism does not condemn this life and universe for their wickedness as was done by some religious teachers and philosophers. The so-called wickedness is not radical in nature and life. It is merely superficial."[26] All things are at bottom one; thus, there can be no murder. "It is true that Mahayanism perfectly agrees with Vedantism when the latter declares: 'If the killer thinks that he kills, if the killed thinks that he is killed, they do not understand; for this one does not kill, nor is that one killed.' (*The Katopanishad*, II, 19.)"[27] Furthermore, according to Suzuki, there is no personal immortal soul in Mahayana Buddhism.[28] There is no personal God.[29] There is no grace; all merit is earned.[30] One's deeds—not the person—are carried into eternity through karma, or reincar-

2008), chaps. 1–5. An example of heretical Christian monistic asceticism almost Eastern in its perspective was the medieval mystic, Meister Eckhart. See Raymond Bernard Blakney, *Meister Eckhart: A Modern Translation* (New York: Harper Torchbook, [1941]).

23. D. T. Suzuki, *Outlines of Mahayana Buddhism*, pp. 101–2.
24. *Ibid.*, p. 112.
25. *Ibid.*, p. 114.
26. *Ibid.*, p. 128.
27. *Ibid.*, p. 135n.
28. *Ibid.*, p. 164.
29. *Ibid.*, p. 219.
30. *Ibid.*, pp. 184–85.

nation, ascending or descending along the scale of being.[31] The deeds survive, not an individual soul.[32] Yet somehow it is possible to distinguish good deeds from bad deeds, in spite of the fact that at bottom all things are one, and all distinctions are illusions.[33] There is no Creator, no Fall, and no hell.[34] In the final analysis, there is no knowledge:

> Human consciousness is so made that at the beginning there was utter not knowing. Then there was the eating of the fruit of the tree of knowledge— the knowledge that consists in making the knower different from what he knows. That is the origin of this world. The fruit separated us from not-knowing in the sense of not knowing subject and object. This awakening of knowledge resulted in our ejection from the Garden of Eden. But we have a persistent desire to return to the state of innocence prior, epistemologically speaking, to creation, to the state where there is no division, no knowledge—prior to the subject-object division, to the time when there was only God as He was before He created the world. The separation of God from the world is the source of all our troubles. We have an innate desire to be united with God.[35]

He deliberately used Western and Christian terms to describe a completely non-Western concept of God—impersonal, without attributes. But the thrust of Buddhist monism should be clear: *the goal is universal, eternal unity.* The Creator must be unified with the creature. We are to unite with God metaphysically, as equals, not ethically, as subordinates. We are to share God's attribute of divinity and oneness, rather than be united ethically to Christ in His perfect humanity.

The idea of creation out of nothing, and hence the Creator-creature distinction, is repugnant to Eastern thought. While the following quotation from Suzuki is chaotic, it is no worse than an extract from Hegel, Tillich, or Bonhoeffer, whose book, *Creation and Fall*, must rank as one of the truly perverse, contorted efforts in modernist biblical exegesis.

> When God created the world outside Himself, He made a great mistake. He could not solve the problem of the world as long as He kept it outside of Himself. In Christian theological terminology, God, to say "I am," has to negate Himself. For God to know Himself He must negate Himself, and His negation comes in the form of the creation of the world of particulars.

---

31. *Ibid.*, pp. 187, 192.
32. *Ibid.*, p. 193.
33. *Ibid.*, p. 200. Capitalism, for example is evil: pp. 188–89.
34. *Ibid.*, p. 253.
35. Suzuki, "The Buddha and Zen" (1953), in *The Field of Zen* (New York: Harper and Row Perennial Library, 1970), pp. 15–16.

To be God is not to be God. We must negate ourselves to affirm ourselves. Our affirmation is negation, but as long as we remain in negation we shall have no rest; we must return to affirmation. We must go out into negation of ourselves and come back. We go out but that negation must come back into affirmation. Going out is coming back. But to realize that going out is coming back we have to go through all kinds of suffering and hardship, of trials and disciplines.[36]

The use of intense mystical contemplation of total absurdities, sometimes followed by acts of asceticism, or physical beatings, is the Zen Buddhist means of achieving satori, the heart of Zen.[37] Nothing has meaning or purpose: this is the gateway to satori, or pure religious freedom. Total chaos rules supreme, and in chaos there is perfect peace.[38] All aspects of life must be accepted.[39] True existence is timeless.[40] By abandoning one's own individuality, man links himself to the infinite—infinite possibilities, infinite responsibilities, unlimited freedom.[41] Total annihilation means total perfection.

Given such a philosophy, it is not surprising that the East should have produced a stagnant culture in which men seek escape in earthly routine and the timelessness of satori: "The only thing that makes Buddhists look rather idle or backward in so-called 'social service' work is the fact that Eastern people, among whom Buddhism flourished, are not very good at organization; they are just as charitably disposed as any religious people and ready to put their teachings into practice. But they are not accustomed to carry on their philanthropic undertakings in a systematic way...."[42] This stands in contrast to Puritans of the sixteenth and seventeenth centuries, who built charitable institutions that still exist today, and which transformed the character of English life.[43] Eastern people can organize successfully, as the Communists have shown, but only under the influence of a Western philosophy of progress and triumph. Monism is a religion of stagnation and retreat.

---

36. *Ibid.*, p. 15.
37. *Zen Buddhism: Selected Writings of D. T. Suzuki* (Garden City, New York: Doubleday Anchor, 1956), chaps. 3, 4.
38. *Ibid.*, ch. 1.
39. *Ibid.*, pp. 105, 256.
40. *Ibid.*, pp. 250, 264.
41. *Ibid.*, pp. 265–66.
42. *Ibid.*, p. 274. For a critique of Zen, see Lit-sen Chang, *Zen-Existentialism* (Nutley, New Jersey: Craig Press, 1967).
43. W. K. Jordan, *Philanthropy in England, 1480–1660* (London: George Allen & Unwin, 1959; New York: Russell Sage Foundation).

C. Cosmological Evolution

God is not part of the creation, according to Christianity. He is the Creator. He existed before time began. The Bible offers a unique concept of time. There was a beginning; there is linear development; there will be a final judgment. The first philosopher to develop this concept of linear history was Augustine.

1. Augustine's Cosmology

The concluding chapter of Charles Norris Cochrane's superb study, *Christianity and Classical Culture* (1944), deals with the philosophy of St. Augustine and his concept of history.[44] Augustine marks the transition between the shattered world of classical civilization and the new Christian society. Augustine reshaped the historical vision of Western Civilization, a monumental intellectual feat. Augustine's twin vision of predestination and linear line—both explicitly Pauline concepts—gave Western culture the idea of history. All human history is directional. It began with the creation, and it shall end with the final judgment. Earthly kingdoms rise and fall, but God's kingdom (which Augustine saw, unfortunately, as exclusively spiritual and ecclesiastical in impact) is permanent. The doctrine of historical cycles is therefore false.[45] Furthermore, creation was not a process extending back into the mists of time; it was a fiat creation within the time span of human records:

> In vain, then do some babble with most empty presumption, saying that Egypt has understood the reckoning of the stars for more than a hundred thousand years. For in what books have they collected that number who learned letters from Isis their mistress, not much more than two thousand years ago?... For as it is not yet six thousand years since the first man, who is called Adam, are not those to be ridiculed rather than refuted who try to persuade us of anything regarding a space of time so different from, and contrary to, the ascertained truth?[46]

Sadly for the condition of the besieged Church in the early decades of the twenty-first century, Christian scholars must spend whole

---

44. On the importance of his philosophy of history, see Lynn White, Jr., "Christian Myth and Christian History," *Journal of the History of Ideas*, III (1942), p. 147; Theodore Mommsen, "St. Augustine and the Christian Idea of Progress," *ibid.*, XII (1951), pp. 346–74; Robert A. Nisbet, *Social Change and History* (New York: Oxford University Press, 1969), ch. 2; Herbert A. Deane, *The Political and Social Ideas of St. Augustine* (New York: Columbia University Press, 1963), pp. 71–73.

45. Augustine, *City of God*, Bk. XII, chaps. 14–16.

46. *Ibid.*, XVIII: 40.

lifetimes in refuting that which is, in Augustine's term, ridiculous—worthy of ridicule rather than refutation.

Augustine's world was a universe of cosmic personalism. God's providence brings all things to pass. This was his answer to the cosmic impersonalism of the classical world. "By thus discarding characteristic prejudices of classical mentality, Augustine opens the way for a philosophy of history in terms of the logos of Christ; i.e. in terms of the Trinity, recognized as the creative and moving principle."[47] In short, wrote Cochrane, "For Augustine, therefore, the order of human life is not the order of 'matter,' blindly and aimlessly working out the 'logic' of its own process, nor yet is it any mere reproduction of a pattern or idea which may be apprehended *a priori* by the human mind."[48] Process is not the source of structure or meaning. "The *logos* of Christ thus serves to introduce a new principle of unity and division into human life and human history."[49]

The world has a fixed order. The Greeks believed this with respect to the creation of the various species, as do the Hindus. They were not so rigorous in applying a theology of process to the world. They hesitated to follow the implications of their view of cycles. They refused to question fully the firmness of a fixed order of creation that is not the product of a sovereign Creator. But Christians do have a foundation for their trust in natural laws. From the time of Augustine in the early fifth century through the sixteenth and seventeenth centuries, the Christian West stood in confidence before a nature which is under the control of God.[50]

2. Medieval Cosmology

The medieval view of the earth was still basic to Western men's understanding of the universe as late as 1600. Because of the centrality of the earth in the order of God's creation, and because of the drama of the Fall of man and the Incarnation of the Son of God in Jesus Christ, their view of the universe was understandably geocentric. But they took the Ptolomaic construction of the universe as physically geocentric as a valid representation of the *covenantal* geocentricity of earth in the creation. The earth was understood as round. (The incredible portolano maps of the Middle Ages rival the accuracy of modern maps;

---

47. Cochrane, *Christianity and Classical Culture*, p. 480; cf. p. 474.
48. *Ibid.*, p. 484.
49. *Ibid.*, p. 487.
50. Toulmin and Goodfield, *Discovery of Time*, p. 68. Cf. the works of the French historian, Pierre Duhem.

they were probably pre-Phoenician in origin.)[51] But it was supposedly placed at the center of a huge system of translucent spheres, to which the sun, planets, and stars were attached, all rotating in perfect spherical harmony around the earth. While the existence of comets should have warned them against the translucent spheres, it did not. Galileo's telescopes, not comets, smashed these spheres.

Some commentators, such as J. B. Bury, have argued that this geocentricity gave men a sense of importance and power in the universe. This was supposedly destroyed by the advent of modern astronomical theories.[52] Others, such as Arthur O. Lovejoy, have argued just the opposite: the earth, was seen as the garbage dump of the universe, with hell at its center. "It is sufficiently evident from such passages that the geocentric cosmography served rather for man's humiliation than for his exaltation, and that Copernicanism was opposed partly on the ground that it assigned too dignified and lofty a position to his dwelling-place."[53] The fact seems to be that man's escape from the geocentric universe could be viewed either as a contraction of man's physical (and therefore historical) place in creation, or as an elevation, ethically, because of one's escape from the wrath of the God of the formerly confined creation. On the other hand, men might view the universe as majestically huge, and therefore the God who created it must be infinite. This is metaphysically humbling, but for the regenerate it can be the promise of triumph. The key is not the size or shape of the universe, but the reliability of the revelation of the God of creation. The problem is not size, but ethics, not geographical position, but ethical position. The great danger, soon witnessed, of the expanded size of God's universe was the next step, wholly illegitimate: *infinite time*.[54]

---

51. Charles H. Hapgood, *Maps of the Ancient Sea Kings* (Philadelphia: Chilton, 1966). This is one of the most startling books ever published. Ignored by professional historians and geographers, it produces evidence that accurate maps of the world, including Antarctica, were available to explorers in the sixteenth century, probably in the twelfth century, and very likely long before the Phoenicians. Antarctica was not rediscovered—discovered, given the standard textbook account—until the eighteenth century. The book is an eloquent rebuttal of cultural and historical evolutionists: if anything, it indicates cultural devolution. No wonder it is ignored by modern scholars!

52. J. B. Bury, *The Idea of Progress* (New York: Dover, [1932] 1955), p. 115. The book first appeared in 1920.

53. Lovejoy, *Great Chain*, p. 102; cf. Alexander Koyré, *From the Closed World to the Infinite Universe* (Baltimore: Johns Hopkins Press, [1957] 1970), pp. 19, 43. This garbage-dump cosmology was an Aristotelian conception of the world: *Great Chain*, p. 104.

54. The crucial aspect of time in cosmological speculation will be discussed more fully in the section dealing with geological evolution.

3. Renaissance Cosmology

Modern historians have often been remiss, lazy, or deliberately misleading in their unwillingness to comment on another aspect of the conflict between medieval Roman Catholic orthodox science and the Renaissance discoveries. Renaissance speculation was not the product of a group of armchair college professors. It was deeply involved in magic, demonism, and the occult arts. C. S. Lewis was correct when he observed that it was not the Middle Ages that encouraged grotesque superstitions; it was the "rational" Renaissance. These men were searching for *power*, like Faustus, not truth for its own sake.[55] For example, it is generally today accepted that the first late-medieval or early modern figure to advance the old Greek concept of an infinite universe was Giordano Bruno.[56] Yet it was Bruno's reputation, well-deserved, as a magician, a Kabbalist, and an astrologer that brought him to his disastrous end.[57] It was not simply that Copernicus, in the name of mathematical precision, placed the sun at the center of the universe. Ptolemy's system was as accurate in its predictions as Copernicus' system (for Copernicus erroneously favored circular planet orbits instead of ellipses).[58] Copernicus was involved in a neoplatonic, Pythagorean revival against the Aristotelian universe of the late-medieval period. Mathematics governs everything, this tradition teaches, contrary to Aristotle's teachings.[59] It was also a deeply mystical and magical tradition. Kepler, the mathematical genius who discovered that planetoid motion is elliptical, was a sun-worshipper and an astrologer.[60] The leaders of the institutional church understandably were disturbed by these theologically and cosmologically heretical individuals.

The debate over whether or not the universe is infinite is still with us today. Einstein's curved (in relation to what?) and finite universe is obviously not in harmony with the absolute space of Newton's cosmol-

---

55. C. S. Lewis, *The Abolition of Man* (New York: Macmillan, [1947] 1965), pp. 87–89. The attempt of modern science to fuse rational scientific technique and magical power is the theme of Lewis' magnificent novel, *That Hideous Strength* (1945).

56. Lovejoy, *Great Chain*, pp. 116–17; Koyré, *Closed World*, p. 39.

57. Frances Yates, *Giordano Bruno and the Hermetic Tradition* (New York: Vintage, [1964] 1969). This is required reading for anyone who still believes the myth of the "rational" Renaissance.

58. E. A. Burtt, *The Metaphysical Foundations of Modern Physical Science* (Garden City, New York: Doubleday Anchor [1925] 1954), p. 36. This is a very fine study of the mind-matter dualism of modern scientific and philosophical thought.

59. *Ibid.*, p. 52–56.

60. *Ibid.*, pp. 56–58, 69. Kepler's Platonism was tempered by his Christian faith.

ogy. Prior to the sixteenth century, however, European scholars had not raised the question. Aristotle's rejection of the idea was considered final. The problem is exceedingly intricate, as anyone understands who has attempted to struggle through Alexander Koyré's book, *From the Closed World to the Infinite Universe* (1957). Copernicus and Kepler rejected the idea, although their speculations vastly expanded men's vision of the creation. Galileo, whose telescopes shattered the transluscent spheres as comets never had, was content to affirm an indeterminate universe. Descartes, who above all other men of his era believed in a totally mathematical universe, and whose vision in this regard was crucial for the development of modern science, said that space is indefinite. He was always cautious on theological or semi-theological topics. The limit, he thought, may well be in our minds; we should therefore avoid such disputes. In fact, Descartes' refusal to postulate limits (due to men's inability to conceive such limits) really served as an assertion of an infinite space.[61] Descartes' god was simply pure mind, having nothing in common with the material world.[62]

Henry More (not Sir Thomas More), in the latter part of the seventeenth century, was converted to a belief in an infinite void space, identifying this with God's omnipresence. The limited material universe is therefore contained in this infinite void. Space is eternal, uncreated, and the necessary presupposition of our thinking. He identified the spatiality of God and the divinity of space.[63] Space is an attribute of God in this perspective—a dangerous linking of Creator and creature. (This position, by the way, was also held by Jonathan Edwards in his youth.[64]) More is not that crucial a figure in the history of Europe, but his opinion on the infinity of space was shared by Isaac Newton.[65] Newton's affirmation of Absolute Space and Absolute Time as postulates of all physics was to open the door to a conclusion which he personally opposed: an autonomous universe.

Leibniz identified Newton's Absolute Space with the material universe, a step Newton did not take, but one which few others seemed able to resist after 1700. It was the crucial step in severing God from His universe. Thus, concluded Koyré,

---

61. *Ibid.*, p. 124.

62. Koyré, *Closed World*, p. 124.

63. *Ibid.*, pp. 150–53.

64. R. J. Rushdoony, *This Independent Republic* (Vallecito, California: Ross House, [1964] 2001), p. 6. Rushdoony cited Edwards' youthful notebooks: "Notes on Natural Science, Of Being."

65. Koyré, p. 159; Burtt, pp. 260–61.

At the end of the [seventeenth] century Newton's victory was complete. The Newtonian God reigned supreme in the infinite void of absolute space in which the force of universal attraction linked together the atomically structured bodies of the immense universe and made them move around in accordance with strict mathematical laws. Yet it can be argued that this victory was a Pyrrhic one, and that the price paid for it was disastrously high. . . . Moreover, an infinite universe existing only for a limited duration seems illogical. Thus the created world became infinite both in Space and in Time. But an infinite and eternal world, as [Dr. Samuel] Clarke had so strongly objected to in Leibniz, can hardly admit creation. It does not need it; it exists by virtue of this very infinity.[66]

From a closed world to an infinite universe means, therefore, *a universe closed to God.* There is nothing to which men can appeal beyond the creation itself. But without God there can be no meaning. Max Weber was correct: modern science removes meaning from the world.[67] Koyré ended his book with this statement: "The infinite Universe of the New Cosmology, infinite in Duration as well as Extension, in which eternal matter in accordance with eternal and necessary laws moves endlessly and aimlessly in eternal space, inherited all the ontological [being] attributes of Divinity. Yet only those—all the others the departed God took away with Him."[68] This is cosmic impersonalism. We are back to the ancient pagan cosmology, only now there is no doubt about the randomness of the universe; it is aimless.

This did not mean that those holding the new cosmology abandoned the idea of linear time. Now that God was officially removed, the linearity of time was secularized and thereby ostensibly humanized. The universe would now be cosmically personal in terms of man. The secular idea of progress was born in the seventeenth century, paralleling the advent of a resurgence of orthodox Protestant (especially Calvinistic and Puritan) optimism. Nothing has characterized this secularization of Christian providence any better than Nisbet's comment: "By the late 17th century, Western philosophers, noting that the earth's frame had still not been consumed by Augustinian holocaust, took a kind of politician's courage in the fact, and declared bravely that the world was never going to end (Descartes, it seems, had proved this) and that mankind was going to become ever more knowledge-

66. Koyré, pp. 274–75.
67. Max Weber, "Science as a Vocation," (1919), in H. H. Gerth and C. Wright Mills (eds.), *From Max Weber: Essays in Sociology* (New York: Oxford University Press, 1946), pp. 139–42.
68. Koyré, p. 276.

able and, who knows, progressively happy. Now, of a sudden, the year 2000 became the object of philosophical speculation."[69] They had not yet become fully consistent with their own philosophy of randomness.

Bernard de Fontenelle's *Conversations on the Plurality of Worlds* (1686) became the great popular work announcing the new infinity of creation, as well as its new-found autonomy. In 1755, Immanuel Kant took these speculations and became the first systematic evolutionist. Process theology came into its own. Wrote Toulmin and Goodfield: "The fame of Immanuel Kant's three Critiques has obscured his striking contributions to cosmology. In fact, his earlier work on the *General History of Nature and Theory of the Heavens* (1755) was the first systematic attempt to give an evolutionary account of cosmic history. In it, he spoke of the whole Order of Nature, not as something completed at the time of the original Creation, but as something still coming into existence. The transition from Chaos to Order had not taken place all at once."[70] Creation, argued Kant, had taken millions of centuries. Time may somehow be linear and infinite, but the process of creation is cyclical. The world will run down, only to be reformed once again out of the climactic conflagration at the end. As he put it, "Worlds and systems perish and are swallowed up in the abyss of Eternity; but at the same time Creation is always busy constructing new formations in the Heavens, and advantageously making up for the loss." So, what we have here, in his words, is a "Phoenix of Nature, which burns itself only in order to revive again in restored youth from its ashes, through all infinity of times and spaces...."[71] Kant, on whose speculations modern philosophy is built, also set forth the presuppositions in terms of which supposedly neutral "eternal oscillation" astronomers have constructed their footnoted cosmologies. Religious presuppositions govern modern astronomical science and modern geological science.

Men have abandoned the revelation of God. In the name of science, they inform us that the belief in a creation by God a few thousand years ago is preposterous—reversing St. Augustine's dictum. In place of this creation account, physicist George Gamow asked us to believe that the universe began its existence as a condensed droplet of matter at an extremely high density and temperature. This primordial egg—the "ylem"—generated fantastic internal pressures and

---

69. Robert A. Nisbet, "The Year 2000 and All That," *Commentary* (June 1968), p. 61.
70. Toulmin and Goodfield, *Discovery of Time*, p. 130.
71. Quoted in *ibid.*, p. 134.

exploded. As it expanded its temperature dropped. As Robert Jastrow summarized Gamow's theory: "In the first few minutes of its existence the temperature was many millions of degrees, and all the matter within the droplet consisted of the basic particles—electrons, neutrons and protons.... According to the big-bang theory, all 92 elements were formed in this way in the first half-hour of the existence of the universe."[72] Jastrow offered this as a serious possibility. He was the Director of the Goddard Institute for Space Studies, and the lectures were originally viewed over CBS television in 1964 as a *Summer Semester*. The public is expected to believe this, but not expected to take seriously the biblical account of creation.

We are told that the laws of probability probably govern the universe. The universe evolved in terms of these laws. Prof. Charles-Eugene Guye once estimated the probability of evolving an imaginary (but given) random assortment of atoms into an equally imaginary protein molecule containing a minimum of four atoms: carbon, hydrogen, nitrogen, and oxygen. He did not assume the coming of all 92 elements or even life itself—just the components of a single protein molecule. The volume of original random atomic substance necessary to produce—randomly—the single protein molecule would be a sphere with a radius so large that light, traveling at 186,000 miles per second, would take 10^{82} years to cover the distance (10, followed by 81 zeros). The outermost limits of the known universe today, however, is about ten billion light-years, or 109 light-years. The probability that this imaginary molecule might be formed on a globe the size of the earth, assuming vibrations of the random electrons and protons on the magnitude of light frequencies, is next to nil. It would take—get this!—10^{243} years. The universe is supposedly a minimum of 10 billion years old, or 109 years.[73] Obviously, modern scientists dismiss Guye's estimates as impossible, but if he is even remotely correct (within 50 or 60 zeroes), the laws of probability simply do not account for the existence of the universe. Yet scientists regard the creation story of

---

72. Robert Jastrow, *Red Giants and White Dwarfs* (New York: New American Library, 1969), p. 69. This happened 10 billion years ago, wrote Jastrow. This figure has been revised to 13.7 billion. This remains the commonly accepted date, give or take a few hundred million years.

73. Guye's figure of probability is 2.02×10^{321}; cited in Lecomte du Nouy, *Human Destiny* (New York: Longmans, Green, 1947), p. 34. A "far less" impossible figure has been computed by Prof. Edward Blick: 10^{67} to one. Henry M. Morris, et al. (eds.), *Creation: Acts, Facts, Impacts* (San Diego: Creation Life Publishers, 1974), p. 175. For a lighthearted discussion of the mathematics of the evolution of life, see Fred Reed, "Fredwin on Evolution" (March 7, 2005).

the Bible as utterly fantastic, the cultic tale of a primitive Semitic tribe. Of course, what they fail to point out is that the theory that the universe sprang from the random impact of atoms in motion was first developed by Epicurus and Democritus; the theoretical presuppositions of the "new cosmology" are very ancient indeed. In the area of speculation concerning ultimate origins, the scientists of today have contributed very little improvement over Greek speculation twenty-three centuries ago. The fact that Kant propounded it in 1755 does not make it automatically modern.[74]

D. Geological Evolution

Renaissance science broadened the conception of the universe that had been inherited from Aristotelian science. The physical boundaries of the universe seemed immeasurably gigantic, inconceivably large, and finally infinite. Enlightenment thinkers, most notably Kant, then hypothesized the infinity of time to match the hypothetical infinity of the spatial universe. From the Christian point of view, this constituted the "evolutionary wedge" by which the creation account of the Bible was steadily shoved into the realm of myth and fable. Mechanical laws replaced personal providence, thus seemingly negating the necessity of believing in "creation as sustaining." Next, the expansion of men's temporal horizon seemingly negated the necessity of believing in "creation as origin." *Cosmological* evolution provided the hypothetical framework for *geological* evolution; geological evolution was to make possible the hypothesis of *biological* evolution. But all three required *vast quantities of time* to make them plausible. Loren Eiseley, perhaps the most successful popularizer of biological evolutionary concepts within America's intellectual circles in the mid-twentieth century, made this point repeatedly: "No theory of evolution can exist without an allotment of time in generous quantities. Yet it is just this factor which was denied to the questioning scientist by the then current Christian cosmology. A change as vast as that existing between the Ptolemaic and Copernican systems of the heavens had to be effected in Western thinking upon the subject of time before one could even contemplate the possibility of extensive organic change; the one idea is an absolute prerequisite to the other."[75]

---

74. John C. Greene, *The Death of Adam: Evolution and Its Impact on Western Thought* (Ames: Iowa State University Press, 1959), pp. 8, 28–30.

75. Loren Eiseley, *Darwin's Century: Evolution and the Men Who Discovered It* (Garden City, New York: Doubleday Anchor, [1958] 1961), p. 58.

In the year 1750, there were still very few scientists, let alone average citizens, who believed that the earth was much older than 6,000 years. By 1850, a majority of scientists were convinced that the earth was far older. *The Origin of Species*, which sold out in one day (1,250 copies) in 1859, would probably not have been published, and certainly would not have been popular, apart from a revolution in men's conception of the earth's chronology. How had this revolution come about?

1. Buffon's System

If any man deserves the distinction of having set forth the outlines of geological evolution in a scientific framework, it is probably the French scholar and literary figure, the Comte de Buffon. Named as a member of the Royal Academy at age 26 (1733), appointed keeper of the Royal Cabinet of Natural History in 1739, Buffon published the first volume of his *Natural History* in 1749. He published 35 more volumes before his death in 1788, one year before the outbreak of the French Revolution. His cosmological presupposition was straight-forward: "Time is the great workman of Nature."[76] In the next sentences, he outlined the doctrine of uniformitarianism: "He [time] moves with regular and uniform steps. He performs no operation suddenly; but, by degrees, or successive impressions, nothing can resist his power. . . ." Buffon personalized the impersonal. His universe was the same as an American popular song's: "We run our race in an hourglass of space; but we're only the toys in time's great game: time gives and time takes away."[77] Only his fear of the French censors kept his language even remotely orthodox.

Buffon also abandoned one of the fundamental beliefs of orthodox Christianity and non-Christian Aristotelian speculation (fused temporarily in one of Thomas Aquinas' proofs of God): the doctrine of final causes. The universe, Buffon believed, is not headed anywhere in particular. This is one of the crucial tenets of all modern science: teleology cannot be assumed by or proved by modern science. In fact, it was only by Charles Darwin's rejection of teleology—final cause, ultimate direction, etc.—that modern biological evolutionism became possible. As we shall see, the earlier systems of biological evolutionism assumed to some degree a teleological framework. Buffon set the standard over a century before the publication of Darwin's *Origin*.[78]

---

76. Buffon, cited by Greene, *Death of Adam*, p. 148.
77. "Toys in Time," by Bob Kimmel and Ken Edwards, BMI.
78. Buffon was not a biological evolutionist, however: Lovejoy, "Buffon and the

Furthermore, Buffon rejected the idea that the present order of existence was set immutably by God in the original creation. As John C. Greene summarized Buffon's position, "it tried to conceive organic phenomena as the outcome of temporal process rather than a static expression of a pattern of creation."[79] *Providence disappears*, and with it, the idea that each kind reproduces after its own kind indefinitely (Gen. 1:24). He did not take this next step, Greene said, but he could not dismiss the idea of the mutability of species from his mind.

Thus, by removing God from the realm of science, Buffon thought he had transferred sovereignty to man. "There is no boundary to the human intellect. It extends in proportion as the universe is displayed. Hence man can and ought to attempt everything: He wants nothing but time to enable him to obtain universal knowledge."[80] Greene's comments are significant: "Buffon had come a long way from the Christian concept of the earth as a stage for the drama of man's redemption by divine grace. Burning with the thirst for knowledge and intoxicated with the sense of man's potential control over nature, he proclaimed man's power to be master of his own fate. Hitherto, he declared, man had pursued evil more energetically than good, amusement more diligently than knowledge, but there was reason to hope that he would at last discover peace to be his true happiness and science his true glory."[81]

Buffon offered a "scientific" conclusion that it had taken about 72,000 years for the globe to cool enough to allow the appearance of life.[82] We have about 70,000 years ahead of us before the planet chills to lifelessness. This is neither far enough back in time to please mod-

---

Problem of Species," in Glass, (ed.), *Forerunners of Darwin*, ch. 4. He did not believe in the mutability of the species. Writing as he did before the development of stratigraphy—an early nineteenth century science—he did not feel compelled to deal with the problem of fossils in some temporal succession. The question had not yet arisen. He could have both time and stable species.

79. Greene, *Death of Adam*, p. 145.

80. Quoted in *ibid.*, p. 154.

81. *Ibid.*, p. 155.

82. Eiseley, *Darwin's Century*, p. 42. Haber pointed out that in the unpublished manuscript copy of Buffon's *Epoques de la Nature*, he admitted that his estimate of 72,000 years to cool the molten earth was conservative; it may have taken as much as a million years, possibly more: Francis C. Haber, "Fossils and the Idea of a Process of Time in Natural History," in Glass (ed.), *Forerunners of Darwin*, p. 256. Buffon saw that the Newtonian view of infinite space could serve as an intellectual wedge for his concept of extended time: "And why does the mind seem to get lost in the space of duration rather than in that of extension, or in the consideration of measures, weights and numbers? Why are 100,000 years more difficult to conceive and to count than 100,000 pounds of money?" *Ibid.*, p. 235. The obvious answer—obvious in the mid-eighteenth century—

ern geologists nor far enough ahead to please evolutionary humanists, but the break between 6,000 years and 72,000 was all that was
necessary; 13 billion more years was easy enough, once the 6,000-year
barrier was breached.

He did not believe in organic evolution; instead, he offered a theory of repeated spontaneous, though naturalistic, appearances of new
life-forms. He allowed God to be present only at the very beginning,
far back in the mists of time, and far ahead in the final, unspecified,
end.[83] By his prestige, Buffon offered man the apostate gift of Godless
time. Time was the needed dwelling place of uniformitarian change,
and the zone of safety from a personal God. Providence was removed
from space by autonomous laws of nature and pushed back into an-
tiquity by the newly discovered time machine.

2. Hutton's Uniformitarianism

Geology, as a specialized profession, came into being with mining
and metallurgy. As men burrowed into the earth, a few of them began
to notice the fact that the earth's crust often appears to be layered, like
a multi-tiered cake without frosting. Prior to the uniformitarian geology, the two generally accepted explanations were: (1) Neptunism,
that is, deposition by water (either at the flood of Noah or in some
great sea of creation); (2) Vulcanism, that is, the deposits of volcanic action. An influential pioneering work was Johann G. Lehmann's
Investigation into the History of Stratified Mountains (1756). The author
believed that Noah's Deluge was the crucial event in the past that reshaped the earth's crust. Another German, Abraham Werner, was an
influential teacher of stratigraphy. He was a Neptunist, but his focus
was a great primeval sea, and he did not explicitly profess faith in a
six-day creation. It was against Werner's theories that James Hutton
reacted.[84]

In all of these theories—Neptunism, Vulcanism, and even Buffon's—
there were elements of catastrophism. James Hutton set out to refute
this presupposition. He accepted the earth at face value; all changes
on earth have always occurred at the leisurely pace observable today.
He first offered the results of his investigations in 1785; his two-vol-
ume *Theory of the Earth* appeared in 1795. He held defiantly to a to-

---

was that by no stretch of the language of Genesis 1 could a period of 100,000 years be
obtained. In 1750, that was important. A century later it was not.

83. Greene, *Death of Adam*, p. 138.
84. On Werner and Lehmann, see *ibid.*, pp. 59–62, 70–72.

tally mechanistic view of geological processes; all forces and changes produce counter-forces and compensating changes. In his famous sentence, Hutton announced to the world: "The result, therefore, of this physical inquiry is, that we find no vestige of a beginning,—no prospect of an end."[85]

Eiseley stated categorically: "He discovered, in other words, time—time boundless and without end, the time of the ancient Easterners...."[86] Indeed he did; as Eiseley also had to admit, Hutton's time bears traces of cyclicalism. There is no linear development in Hutton's self-compensating world machine. "Hutton was thus a total uniformitarian."[87] There have never been any catastrophic changes, Hutton believed, because there have never been any significant change at all. But there has been time—countless eons of time; the checkbook might even be large enough for biological evolutionists to draw the needed time reserves for their cosmologies. The cosmic judgment of God was pushed forward into the endless recesses of time's comforting womb.

Toulmin and Goodfield, in an otherwise excellent study, could not seem to grasp the threat to Christianity which Hutton's system represented. They said that "his fundamental aims were conservative and devout." He was just an honest observer of facts, letting them carry him to some cosmically neutral conclusion. They asked: Why did his contemporaries attack him? For one thing, it was not simply theology that motivated his opponents; his position was undermining Vulcanism's catastrophism, while simultaneously undermining Neptunism, since Hutton laid great emphasis on the power of slowly acting subterranean heat.[88] He was stepping on everyone's methodological toes. But some of the opposition was theological. Naively, Toulmin and Goodfield remarked: "Yet there was, in fact, nothing in Hutton's system—apart from the unbounded chronology—that could legitimately give offense."[89] That, however, was precisely the point, as Eiseley understood so well:

> The uniformitarians were, on the whole, disinclined to countenance the intrusion of strange or unknown forces into the universe. They eschewed final causes and all aspects of world creation, feeling like their master Hutton that such problems were confusing and beyond human reach. The uni-

85. *Ibid.*, p. 78.
86. Eiseley, *Darwin's Century*, p. 65.
87. *Ibid.*, p. 74.
88. Greene, *Death of Adam*, p. 84.
89. Toulin and Goodfield, *Discovery of Time*, p. 156.

formitarian school, in other words, is essentially a revolt against the Christian conception of time as limited and containing historic direction, with supernatural intervention constantly immanent [immanent—"inherent, operating within"—not imminent—"about to happen"—G.N.]. Rather, this philosophy involves the idea of the Newtonian machine, self-sustaining and forever operating on the same principles.[90]

There should be no confusion on this point: the great theological debate centered around the question of time. All good men—Frenchmen excepted, naturally—believed in a personal God in the period 1750–1850. This God was allowed to be a creator in some sense or other. But, by pushing the time or order of God's creative acts back into a misty past, men were relegating this God into a mere intellectual construction—a kind of useful myth, rather like Plato's creator god. *One's concept of time is fundamental in defining one's concept of God.*

Prior to Lyell's hesitating conversion to Darwinism, his view of time was almost static. Some geological forces tend to raise portions of the earth's crust; there are forces elsewhere which tend to allow land to sink. If elevation is happening in one region, leveling or erosion is taking place somewhere else. It has been this way indefinitely. The forces are evenly balanced. "If we ask what of significance has happened in this expanse of time, the answer is, 'Nothing.' There have been no unique events. There have been no stages of growth. We have a system of indifference, of more or less meaningless fluctuations around an eternal mean."[91] As Walter Cannon pointed out, this is not developing time—the time of the modern historian. It is simply unlimited, meaningless time. We might say that his impersonal time is like an infinitely long geometrical line, composed of an indefinite number of identical points. Uniformitarian time does not, in or of itself, give us a theory of evolution, for evolution implies growth, and the eighteenth-century world machine could not grow. It was a gyroscope, not a seed. But it was an exceedingly old gyroscope, and that was to prove crucial.

There is a distinctly religious impulse undergirding uniformitarianism. Eiseley was correct when he said that Hutton was proposing an anti-Christian concept of time. Charles C. Gillispie concluded that "The essence of Huttonianism lay not in specific details of weathering, denudation, or uplift, but in its attitude towards natural his-

---

90. Eiseley, *Darwin's Century*, p. 114. Cf. Nisbet, *Social Change and History*, p. 184.

91. Walter F. Cannon, "The Basis of Darwin's Achievement: A Revaluation," *Victorian Studies*, V (1961); reprinted in Philip Appleman (ed.), *Darwin: A Norton Critical Edition* (New York: Norton, 1970), p. 42.

tory."[92] Consider what Hutton was saying. On the basis of his own limited wanderings and observations around Edinburgh, Hutton announced a new theory of change to the world. In doing so, modern commentators have concluded, he created the first truly historical natural science, geology. Hutton challenged the biblical account of Noah's flood, the researches and conclusions of the Neptunists and the more cataclysmic Vulcanists, and concluded that what he had seen—slow, even imperceptible geological change—is all men now know. Furthermore, we can assume that such imperceptible change is all any man can know—past, present, and future. Because he had never seen the universal flood, obviously no one has ever seen one. His operational presupposition was about as sophisticated as the opinion of the Soviet Union's cosmonaut who announced, after returning from a few revolutions above the earth's atmosphere, that he had not seen God up there! What Hutton imposed, all in the name of rational historical insight, was the most arrogant and blatant form of what historians call "the tyranny of the present." What was true in Edinburgh in 1780 was true for the whole world throughout endless eons of time. If any other historical data refute such a claim—the Bible, the almost universal pagan myths concerning a universal flood, the astoundingly precise calendars of the Babylonians and other ancient cultures, the equally astounding Babylonian astronomical records— then they must be disregarded as insufficiently historical. History is what we can observe here and now, not what primitive people used to think they were observing. Or, as Van Til summarized it, "what my net won't catch aren't fish." Yet what Hutton and his endless troops of defenders have claimed is that he alone was truly empirical, truly concerned with the "facts." But no fact is allowed which seems to come into direct conflict with Hutton's deeply religious presupposition that rates of change today have always existed, or at the very least, that we have no evidence that indicates that the rates of change have ever been different.

The prolix, unreadable writing of James Hutton did not convince men to believe in the uniformitarian religion. It was not the testimony of the rocks near Edinburgh that converted the world to a theory of an ancient earth. It was rather the built-in desire of men to escape the revelation of a God who judges men and societies, in time and on earth, as well as on the final day of judgment. They prefer to believe

---

92. Charles Coulston Gillispie, *Genesis and Geology* (New York: Harper Torchbook, [1951] 1959), p. 83.

in the tyranny of the present because the past indicates the existence of a God who brings immense, unstoppable judgments upon sinners. *Men prefer the tyranny of the present to the sovereignty of God.* Nothing less than a deeply religious impulse could lead men to accept a presupposition as narrow, parochial, and preposterous as the theory of uniformitarian change. Hutton announced, "today Edinburgh; tomorrow the world—past, present, and future," and men rushed to join the new anti-millennial religion. Like the Soviet cosmonaut, Hutton just could not see any sign of God in the Edinburgh rocks, and those were the rocks men soon wanted.

3. Lyell's Uniformitarianism

James Hutton is long forgotten, except by specialists in the history of geology. But his most famous follower, Sir Charles Lyell, cannot be ignored, for it is Lyell's book, *Principles of Geology* (1830–33), which gave Charles Darwin his operating presuppositions. The son of a botanist, Lyell was by profession a lawyer. He studied geology on the weekends. He was in his early thirties when his multi-volume work was published, and it became an instant classic—indeed, the definitive book. He had been a catastrophist until 1827; three years later, he was the premier uniformitarian in the English-speaking world.

It is not easy to summarize Lyell's work. He opposed the theory of biological evolution until the late 1860s, yet it was sometime around 1860 that the evangelical Christianity of his youth returned to him.[93] His commitment to uniformitarian principles of interpretation led him to view geological processes as if they were part of a huge mechanism. He was familiar with the young science of paleontology; he was aware of the fact that lower strata ("older") often contained species that did not appear in the higher ("younger") strata. This seemed to point to both extinct species and completely new ("recent") species, indicating biological development, given the "fact" of eons of time in between the geological strata. Yet Lyell resisted this conclusion until 1867—nine years after Darwin and Wallace had published their first essays on natural selection and biological evolution. Lyell's opposition to evolution had long vexed Darwin; he could not understand why Lyell resisted the obvious conclusion of the uniformitarian position. As recently as 1958, scholars were still as confused over this as Darwin had been. Lyell's correspondence indicates that he was com-

---

93. William Irvine, *Apes, Angels, and Victorians: The Story of Darwin, Huxley, and Evolution* (New York: McGraw-Hill, 1955), p. 139.

mitted to the idea of final causation—teleology—like most other scientists of his day. He spoke of a *"Presiding Mind"* in an 1836 letter to
Sir John Herschel.[94] This divine intelligence directed any extinctions
or new appearances of species that might have taken place in the past.
He called these "intermediate causes," and let it go at that. But such
interventions by God, direct or indirect, violated the principle of uniformitarian change, since no such intervention is visible today. Thus,
concludes the meticulous scholar, A. O. Lovejoy, "once uniformitarianism was accepted, evolutionism became the most natural and most
probable hypothesis concerning the origin of the species."[95] But Lyell
insisted (in the 1830s through 1863) on the recent origin of man and
the validity, respecting mankind, of the Mosaic record. "He simply
did not see," wrote Lovejoy, "that a uniformitarian could not con-
sistently accept special-creationism, and must therefore accept some
form of evolutionism."[96] In the tenth edition of *Principles* (1867), Lyell
finally capitulated, becoming a full Darwinian.

Lyell's ultimate faith was in uniformitarianism: unlimited geological time and slow, continuous geological change. This was to override
his commitment to special creation (or some unnamed nonevolution-
ary natural process of species transformation). It was an inescapable
either/or situation. Nineteenth-century geological and biological scientists could not forever cling to a God who intervened to rewrite the
book on living species, eon after eon, letting the "geological clock"
tick for ages in between interventions. *If creationism was not a one-time
fiat act of God, it was ludicrous.* The ridiculousness of such a God could
not forever be avoided. Here was a God who created creatures, then
let them perish; intervening, He created new creatures, and some
of them perished. In order to keep the balance of nature going, He
intervened over and over through countless ages, adding ever more
complex creatures to the earth. Some of these became extinct, but
cockroaches and ants survived. He behaved, in Lovejoy's words, like
a very lazy and befuddled architect, intervening with endless *ad hoc*
plans to reconstruct the jerry-built structure. As Lovejoy wryly com-

---

94. Quoted by Greene, *Death of Adam*, p. 373, note #6.

95. Lovejoy, "The Argument for Organic Evolution Before the Origin of the Species,
1830–1858," in Glass (ed.), *Forerunners of Darwin*, p. 367.

96. *Ibid.*, p. 373. Gertrude Himmelfarb believed that Lyell was an evolutionist in
private. But his private letters also indicate his belief in a "Presiding Mind." He was
certainly ambivalent—or epistemologically schizophrenic—but I do not think he was
dishonest. See Himmelfarb, *Darwin and the Darwinian Revolution* (Gloucester, Massachusetts: Peter Smith [1959] 1967), pp. 189–93.

mented, "no man outside of a madhouse ever behaved in such a manner as that in which, by this hypothesis, the Creator of the universe was supposed to have behaved."[97] Yet such a view was orthodox, both theologically and geologically, from 1820–30. Enlightenment rationalism had eroded the Christian foundation of knowledge; Christians had built on a foundation of sand. Darwinism destroyed the structure, but only because the "creationists" had long before gone bankrupt, leasing the grounds temporarily to Lyell until Darwin foreclosed, bringing in the demolition equipment.

What is both baffling and appalling is that so many Christians still cling to Lyell's temporary and hopeless compromise—a compromise he had to abandon in 1867. Geologists who profess orthodoxy still argue that we must accept the results of uniformitarian geology, yet assure us that we do not have to accept organic evolution. In a scholarly journal of a modern Calvinistic seminary we read:

> We believe that Scripture does not permit the interpretation of the theistic evolutionist. We do believe that the data of Scripture permit, although they do not require, the view that the days of Genesis one were periods of time of indefinite length. Hence we believe that the products of creation of the various days one through six were not necessarily instantaneously produced in a mature state but were formed over a long period of time. This view does have the advantage of permitting the Christian geologist to interpret intelligibly the actual data of geology.[98]

This has the advantage of allowing a geologist who is a Christian to interpret the Bible in terms of the geology and theology of 1840, when some men could still believe in numerous special creations. The geology of 1859 or later, devoid of final causes, purpose, interventions by God, or the need of reconciliation with the Bible, has no space for God's activity in between the autonomous strata of the earth.

Galileo had begun the steady removal by autonomous men of God from His universe. By the 1840s, God's last place of refuge among scientists was in the realm of biology. Uniformitarianism after 1830

---

97. *Ibid.*, p. 413.

98. Davis A. Young, "Some Practical Geological Problems in the Application of the Mature Creation Doctrine," *Westminster Theological Journal*, XXXV (Spring 1973), p. 269. He was the son of Edward J. Young, author of *Studies in Genesis One*. A reply to Young's article appeared in the subsequent issue: John C. Whitcomb, Jr., "The Science of Historical Geology in the Light of the Biblical Doctrine of a Mature Creation," *ibid.*, XXXVI (Fall 1973). Young's doctorate was in geology; Whitcomb's was in theology. Whitcomb was co-author of *The Genesis Flood* (1961), the most important book in the revival of the six-day creation view of Genesis, for it helped to develop the market for numerous additional studies along these lines in the 1960s.

had finally removed Him from the rocks. He was allowed His various "special creations" from time to time among living beings. Lovejoy commented: "And while all these miraculous interpositions were taking place in order to keep the organic kingdom in a going condition, the Creator was not for a moment allowed, by most of these geologists (including, as we shall see, Lyell and his followers) to interfere in a similar manner in their own particular province of the inorganic processes. . . . So, in the opinion of most naturalists the only officially licensed area in which miracles might be performed by the Creator was the domain of organic phenomena."[99] Charles Darwin's *On the Origin of Species* repealed the license even here. Thus, it is a sign of the demoralization and naivete of modern uniformitarian geologists who claim to be Christian in their scholarship, that they expect the methodology of uniformitarianism to be easily restrained. It is supposedly fine for geologists to assume as valid this uniformitarian methodology (as it was in 1840), but biologists nevertheless have to be anti-evolutionists, denying therefore Darwin's overwhelmingly successful—pragmatically speaking—fusion of uniformitarianism and biology. But Darwinianism is not to be denied by compromising Christian biologists today, any more than he could be denied by uniformitarian scholarship in the 1870s. Uniformitarian concepts of time are far too potent for half-measures.

The important humanist study, *Forerunners of Darwin* (1959), published on the centenary of the publication of *Origin of Species*, opens with a crucial quotation from the uniformitarian geologist, George Scrope, who in 1858 wrote these memorable words: "The leading idea which is present in all our researches, and which accompanies every fresh observation, the sound which to the ear of the student of Nature seems continually echoed from every part of her works, is—Time! Time! Time!"[100]

E. Biological Evolution: Pre-Darwin

The seventeenth century had seen the reappearance of postmillennial eschatology—out of favor ever since the fifth century—which offered Christians new hope. The preaching of the gospel and the establishment of Christian institutions would eventually transform the world ethically, and this ethical transformation would eventually be accompanied by external personal and cultural blessings. This had been the

---

99. Lovejoy, in *Forerunners of Darwin*, p. 365.
100. Cited by Francis C. Haber, "Fossils and Early Cosmology," *ibid.*, p. 3.

vision of many English Puritans and most of the American colonial Puritans until the pessimism of the 1660s, symbolized by the poetry of Michael Wigglesworth, set in. This vision was to have a revival, unfortunately in more antinomian, "spiritual" forms, through the influence of Jonathan Edwards in the eighteenth century.[101]

1. The Idea of Progress

Paralleling this biblical optimism was the secular idea of progress of Enlightenment thinkers, especially Frenchmen. By the 1750s, this perspective was becoming a part of the European climate of opinion.[102] The idea of stages of historical development fascinated the writers of the day. The cosmological evolutionary schemes of Kant and Laplace were discussed as serious contributions, and Maupertuis and Diderot, the French secularists, offered theories of biological development—"transformism."[103] Three important features were present in these new theories; without these theoretical axioms, there would have been no reason to assume the evolutionary perspective. First, *change* (not stability) is "natural"—one of the key words of the Enlightenment.[104] Second, the natural order is regular; nature makes no leaps. This is the doctrine of *continuity* (uniformitarianism). Finally, in the late eighteenth and early nineteenth centuries, the method of investigation selected by the progressivists was the *comparative method*. Classification preceded the demonstration of evolutionary change.[105]

---

101. On the Puritans' postmillennial impulse, see the articles by James Payton, Aletha Gilsdorf, and Gary North in *The Journal of Christian Reconstruction*, VI (Summer 1979); Iain Murray, *The Puritan Hope* (London: Banner of Truth, 1971); Ernest Lee Tuveson, *Redeemer Nation: The Idea of America's Millennial Role* (Chicago: University of Chicago Press, 1967); Alan Heimert, *Religion and the American Mind* (Cambridge, Massachusetts: Harvard University Press, 1966). One of the representative documents of the colonial American period is Edward Johnson's *Wonder-Working Providence*, ed. J. Franklin Jameson (New York: Barnes & Noble, 1952). Until quite recently, postmillennial thought was a neglected—indeed, completely misunderstood—factor in American history.

102. J. B. Bury, *The Idea of Progress* (1920), is a standard account of secular optimism.

103. Bentley Glass, "Maupertuis, Pioneer of Genetics and Evolution," and Lester G. Crocker, "Diderot and Eighteenth Century Transformism," in Glass (ed.), *Forerunners of Darwin*.

104. On the importance of the word "nature" to the eighteenth century, see Carl Becker, *The Heavenly City of the Eighteenth-Century Philosophers* (Ithaca: Cornell University Press, 1932). On the way in which "natural history" was used, see Nisbet, *Social Change and History*, ch. 4. It meant, essentially, *conjectural history*, that is, how events would automatically develop "naturally" if there were no "artificial" restraints on them. Developmentalism became biological evolutionism in the nineteenth century.

105. Frederick J. Teggart, *Theory of History* (New Haven, Connecticut: Yale University Press, 1925), pp. 129–32.

Classification: this was all-important. Because of the influence of the Greek concept of the *chain of being*, men had long regarded all life as a harmonious interdependence of every species, from God at the top of the chain (or ladder) to the lowest creature. (This presented problems in theory: Are Satan and his angels therefore metaphysically necessary for the operation of the cosmos? Is Satan at the bottom of the scale because of his ethical depravity, or just under God Himself because of his metaphysical power? In fact, if he is totally evil, can he be said to have true existence at all? Questions like these destroyed the jerry-built "medieval synthesis" of Greek philosophy—itself self-contradictory—and biblical revelation. Even in the eighteenth century, much of the original potency of the concept of the "great chain of being" remained.) But this chain of being was made up of fixed species. There was progress possible *within* one's species, but *not between* the fixed categories. Part of the magical impulse of alchemy was the desire to change lead into gold, not primarily for the sake of wealth, but for the power involved. The magical "philosopher's stone" would enable the magician-scientist to transcend the limits of creation. Thus, the search for the magical talisman; thus, the quest for magical salvation: *metaphysical manipulation* rather than ethical repentance and regeneration was the magician's means of grace.[106] To break the limits of creaturehood!

Enlightenment progressivists now offered a new theory: there had been progress of species through time. There had been development, and to Enlightenment thinkers, it was easy to assume that biological modification implied ethical improvement. There had been progress! And there would continue to be progress, not just politically and economically, but in the very nature of mankind. The religious impulse was clear enough: *there are no longer any fixed barriers in the creation, given sufficient time to transcend them.* The great chain of being could now be temporalized. Heaven was no longer above men; it was in front of mankind chronologically. Genetics would serve as a substitute for the alchemical talisman.

Not many thinkers were convinced by the biological evidence in 1750, or even in 1850. But the *comparative method* which had always been implied in the concept of the great chain of being was now emphasized by a newly developed discipline, *natural history*. The crucial figure in this field in the eighteenth century was the Swedish naturalist, Linnaeus. He possessed an unparalleled reputation in 1750; in-

---

106. Yates, *Giordano Bruno and the Hermetic Tradition*, chaps. 2, 3.

deed, after the publication of the first edition of his *Systema Naturae* in 1735, he became world-famous, "a phenomenon rather than a man," as Eiseley put it.[107] He had a mania for naming things, and he created the system of dual names which still exists today, generic and species (which H. L. Mencken used in classifying the *boobus Americanus*). He was not an evolutionist in any sense, but by popularizing comparative anatomy as the means of classification—a method to be applied to every living organism—he added the crucial third axiom of the developmental hypothesis.[108]

Buffon's researches also added prestige to the taxonomic research of the mid-eighteenth-century naturalists. But the next major step was half a century away. An obscure mining engineer, William Smith, had created a system of classifying strata in terms of the placement of organic fossils in each layer. "Strata" Smith's system would be popularized by Rev. William Townsend after 1800. (Ministers would have an important role in natural science for well over a century. Rev. John Ray was the first popular classifier, four decades before Linneaus published. Rev. John Playfair would be the popularizer of James Hutton's uniformitarianism after 1800. Even Charles Darwin himself had once studied to be a minister.) Smith avoided any theoretical explanation of his system. He hated both speculating and publication. He was a convinced catastrophist. Nevertheless, he had provided the uniformitarians with their necessary yardstick. By fusing Hutton's time scale and Smith's progressive fossil beds ("older" fossils in the lower layers), uniformitarians could now argue that they could measure the slow, steady history of the earth.

By 1820, there was hardly a single reputable scientist in the British Isles who was committed to a six-day creation. Both the Neptunists (flooders) and Vulcanists (heaters) believed in long ages preceding man's appearance on the earth. The Hutton time scale was common property among all the groups. All geologists therefore faced a disturbing problem: the fossil record demonstrated clearly that animals and plants appearing in one layer of the earth often did not appear in lower or higher layers—dinosaurs, for example. This implied extinction. It also implied a series of special creations over eons of time. The "creationism" of the 1820s, by clinging to Hutton's time scale,

---

107. Eiseley, *Darwin's Century*, p. 16.

108. Linnaeus did admit, in later years, that nature had a "sportiveness" about her, that is, surprising variations within species. But not even Eiseley or Greene concluded that he ever leaned toward biological developmentalism.

was involved in a whole series of difficult, self-imposed dilemmas. We have already discussed them in the previous section: God the lazy architect; uniformitarianism with too many supernatural interventions; catastrophism with too much time to explain and too little emphasis on the great Noahic flood. (Not that it was ignored, but it was regarded as only one of many important crises; after 1830, the Flood had become a local disaster in Palestine, or the Near East, at most.)

2. Organic Evolution

The doctrine of organic evolution was advocated by two thinkers at the turn of the century, Jean Baptiste Lamarck and Erasmus Darwin. Their speculations never proved popular among scientists or laymen. Each came to the conclusion that members of the various species adapted themselves to changes in their environments. This process of adaptation was supposedly hereditary; thus, *the doctrine of acquired characteristics* was born. It was never to be taken seriously officially; unofficially, it became an escape hatch in the later editions of Charles Darwin's *On the Origin of Species*. But their major premise, namely, the *unlimited possibility of species variation*, did become the touchstone of Darwinian evolution. It was this premise that broke the spell of the great fixed chain of being.

One of the most important books of the early nineteenth century was Rev. William Paley's *Natural Theology* (1802). Paley's work synthesized many of the then-prominent arguments for God's providence on earth. He argued that Newton's clock-like universe offers us testimony to God's sustaining providence. We can see it if only we look at nature's intricate design; the harmonious interdependence of the infinite number of parts assures us that only an omnipotent Creator could have designed, created, and sustained it for all these years. The language of design had become universal by Paley's day, and his book only reinforced an established dogma. Darwin himself had been greatly influenced by Paley's providentialism in his college days, as he admitted much later: "I do not think I hardly ever admired a book more than Paley's 'Natural Theology.' I could almost formerly have said it by heart."[109] At the heart of all these schemes of God's mechanistic providence was the doctrine of final causation: the whole universe was designed to serve the needs of man. All things were planned

---

109. Darwin to John Lubbock (Nov. 15, 1859); in Francis Darwin (ed.), *The Life and Letters of Charles Darwin*, 2 vols. (New York: Appleton, 1887), II, p. 15.

in advance to further man's affairs; in every being created in the mists of time there were the materials available to deal with the survival of the species. (This posed a serious theoretical problem: how to explain extinct fossils.) The evolutionary form of this doctrine is obviously Lamarckianism: species have the power of adaptation, individual by individual, organ by organ. *Unconscious adaptation* is the mechanism of organic evolution. When Darwin finally broke with Rev. Paley, he therefore also had to break with Lamarckianism, a position which he had never held anyway. Only later, under criticism, did he return to partial Lamarckianism.

3. The Concept of Purpose

Providence implies control by God; control implies purpose. The doctrine of final causation had provided Western man with philosophical purpose since the days of Aristotle.[110] For as long as scientists were able to cling to the concept of purpose, science would never become fully autonomous. It is safe to say that *the struggle over Darwinian evolution was, above all, a struggle over the concept of purpose.*

Darwin is regarded as the Newton of biological science. Why? Most of his arguments and data had been offered by others much earlier; the crucial arguments had been provided in the much maligned *Vestiges of Creation* (1844).[111] The answer would appear to be in the purposeless quality of the doctrine of natural selection; it is based on the philosophy of random variations. Biological processes, in theory, can now be subjected to the rigors of mathematical logic, just as Newton subjected all astronomical changes to mathematical law—or thought he had. It was no longer necessary, Darwin and his followers believed, to hypothesize the existence of creation, providence, or final causes. *Therefore, God was seen as no longer a part of the operating hypothesis of biological science.* From the observation that final causes are not necessary for the operations of modern science, it was easy—almost automatic—to conclude that there can be no final causes. "Whatever my net doesn't catch aren't fish," and the net of modern science excludes final causes, both impersonal and personal, but especially personal.

---

110. F. S. C. Northrop, "Evolution and Its Relation to the Philosophy of Nature," in Stow Persons (ed.), *Evolutionary Thought in America* (New York: George Braziller, 1956), pp. 48–54. This was first published in 1950 by Yale University Press. It is a compilation of lectures delivered to the American Civilization Program at Princeton University, 1945–46.

111. Lovejoy, "The Argument for Organic Evolution Before the Origin of Species, 1830–1858," in Glass (ed.), *Forerunners of Darwin*, pp. 381–410.

Final causation points to God; so does design; hence, let us abolish final causation from the domain of logic and science. If God is to confront us, He must do so only through the non-logical communication of mysticism, ecstasy, encounter, the tongues movement, or some other way which does not confront us in our external, intellectual apostasy. God, being unnecessary to science, was shaved away by the logic of Occam's razor: needless propositions in any logical statement may be safely ignored.

Lamarck was a representative of the French Enlightenment. In England, after 1789 had brought the French Revolution, it was not popular to be identified with French revolutionaries. After the advent of Napoleon in 1799, it was not popular to be identified with the French, unless it was the "orthodox" comparative anatomist, Cuvier. Lamarck's arguments were not compelling to conservative Christians or even vague Anglican scholars. He had broken with theological and biological orthodoxy by offering the theory of organic evolution (as had Erasmus Darwin), thus alienating conservatives. Yet he held to the idea of purpose, however remote, in arguing for the unconscious adaptation of species to the environment. He had not gone far enough to propose a true "scientific revolution." Too heretical for the conservatives, too providential for any potential atheists and "total autonomy" investigators, the doctrine of the inheritance of acquired characteristics died for want of takers. It survived after 1859 only because Charles Darwin's mechanism of natural selection had washed all traces of purpose from its exterior, and after 1900, the rediscovery of Mendelian genetics finally buried it.

There were other possibilities for an earlier conversion to biological evolution, but none took hold. Hegel's thought was one of these, but the discontinuous "leaps" of nature that he proposed alienated uniformitarians.[112] In Germany, the close association of romanticism and evolutionary thought alienated the professional biologists, most of whom were increasingly mechanistic in outlook.[113] Darwin's theory was truly a scientific revolution.

4. A "Higher" View of God

The defeat of orthodox creationism was not an overnight event. One of the most interesting features of this steady retreat between

---

112. Northrop, *Evolutionary Thought*, pp. 61–68.

113. Owsei Temkin, "The Idea of Descent in Post-Romantic German Biology: 1848–1858," *Forerunners of Darwin*, ch. 12.

1750 and 1859 was the rallying cry of each successive capitulation: the "higher" view of God involved, or the "deeper" understanding of His providence. Six days just did not do justice to God; He must have showered His providence on His creation for millions of extra years. If only we accept the action of God's primeval sea, the Neptunists said, plus a less comprehensive impact of the flood. If only we accept God's activity in unleashing volcanoes and internal heat, said the Vulcanists. If only we will admit the effects of the flood and earthquakes, said the catastrophists of the 1820s. If only we allow God the right to create new species from eon to eon, the uniformitarians said. If only we do these things, then the introduction of vast geologic time will not harm us. *At each step, the name of God was invoked.* Men were not to be limited by the confines of God's six-day creation; God is unlimited.

The "unlimited" God of geologic time steadily retreated from the scene. The "unlimited" God was steadily replaced by unlimited time. Time was not seen as personal; time was not seen as calling men to repentance. Time seemed holy and magnifying, but most of all, it seemed *safe.* This centrality of time is understood by today's evolutionists; "respectable" Christian geologists—geologists who may be regenerate—have never grasped the fact. Wrote Gillispie:

> From both the empirical and the interpretative points of view, the progress of geological science in the first half of the nineteenth century was an essential prelude to the formulation of a successful theory of biological evolution. There had, of course, been a number of more or less fanciful evolutionary schemes suggested ever since the middle of the eighteenth century. In [Thomas H.] Huxley's opinion, however, these speculative proposals had little influence on scientific thinking, and it was rather Lyell's work which was primarily responsible for smoothing the road for Darwin, so that from this standpoint it is James Hutton and not Lamarck who ought to be considered Darwin's intellectual ancestor.... But uniformitarianism as an attitude toward the course of nature could not be carried to its logical conclusion in a theory of organic evolution until a formulation sufficiently scientific to be compelling could attack the idea of a governing Providence in its last refuge, the creation of new species, and drive it right out of the whole field of natural history.[114]

Men abandoned creationism step by step, not overnight.

Gillispie went on to argue that it was the commitment to providentialism that kept the idea of immutable species in the canons of biological orthodoxy: design implied fixed species. *Step by step,*

---

114. Gillispie, *Genesis and Geology*, pp. 217–18. See also Francis C. Haber, *The Age of the World: Moses to Darwin* (Baltimore, Maryland: Johns Hopkins Press, 1959).

uniformitarianism removed God from the earth's history. "And after each successive retreat, providential empiricists took up positions on new ground, which their own researches were simultaneously cutting out from under them."[115] Not starting with God as the presupposition of their empirical researches, not starting with God's self-justifying revelation in the Bible, the supposedly neutral scientists—operating as they were in terms of non-Christian methodologies—found that their own logic drove them into the waiting arms of infinite time and random change. Not starting with God, they could not logically wind up with God—not the God of the Bible, at least.

No document can be found that better demonstrates this "higher view of God" than Robert Chambers' *Vestiges of Creation*. More than any other scientific work, though produced by an amateur scientist, this one prepared the public's mind for Darwin. Not even Herbert Spencer's evolutionism was more important. How did Chambers defend his researches? First, he defended the Mosaic record as being most in conformity with his views. Then he said that it was God's expressions of will, not His direct activities, that brought forth the creation. (He ignored, of course, the orthodox doctrine of the verbal creation, that is, the response out of nothing to the command of God.) God created all life; Chambers stated that he took this for granted. "In what way was the creation of animated beings effected? The ordinary notion [that is, the debased doctrine of successive creations over endless ages—G.N.] may, I think, be described as this,—that the Almighty Author produced the progenitors of all existing species by some sort of personal or immediate exertion." So, he allowed God to create life. But he then proceeded to ridicule the "orthodox" creationism of his day, that disastrous fusion of geologic time, uniformitarian change with successive creations:

> How can we suppose an immediate exertion of this creative power at one time to produce zoophytes, another time to add a few marine mollusks, another to bring in one or two crustacea, again to produce crustaceous fishes, again perfect fishes, and so on to the end? This would surely be to take a very mean view of the Creative Power.... And yet this would be unavoidable; for that the organic creation was thus progressive through a long space of time, rests on evidence which nothing can overturn or gainsay. Some other idea must then be come to with regard to *the mode* in which the Divine Author proceeded in the organic creation.[116]

---

115. *Ibid.*, p. 221.

116. [Robert Chambers], *Vestiges of the Natural History of Creation*, 4th ed. (Soho, London: John Churchill, 1845), pp. 157–58. It sold 24,000 copies, 1844–60: Eiseley, *Dar-*

It should be obvious that the progression described by Chambers is correct: given the idea of vast geological time, fossils distributed in layers, and uniformitarian change—and it was, by 1840, a single idea—God's creative interventions do look foolish. So, he offered new mode of creation: *organic evolution.* In two sentences, Chambers took his readers from Newton's cosmic impersonalism for the heavens (not that Newton intended such a conclusion) into a hypothetically impersonal world of biological law: "We have seen powerful evidence, that the construction of this globe and its associates, and inferentially that of all the other globes of space, was the result, not of any immediate or personal exertion on the part of the Deity, but of natural laws which are expressions of his will. What is to hinder our supposing that the organic creation is also a result of natural laws, which are in like manner an expression of his will?[117] Only one thing was to inhibit such a supposition: *there was too much of God's will in the picture.* When Darwin substituted natural selection through random variation, there would no longer be any hindrance to the supposition in the minds of "liberated" scientists—liberated from the doctrine of final causation or design. Chambers prepared the way for Darwin among the public even as John the Baptist prepared the way for Jesus. And, like John the Baptist, he did it in the name of God, he thought.

> To a reasonable mind the Divine attributes must appear, not diminished or reduced in any way, by supposing a creation by law, but infinitely exalted. It is the narrowest of all views of the Deity, and characteristic of a humble class of intellects, to suppose him constantly acting in particular ways for particular occasions. It, for one thing, greatly detracts from his foresight, the most undeniable of all the attributes of Omnipotence. It lowers him towards the level of our own humble intellects.... Those who would object to the hypothesis of a creation by the intervention of law, do not perhaps consider how powerful an argument in favour of the existence of God is lost by rejecting this doctrine.[118]

Men adopted heresy in the name of a "higher orthodoxy."

Odd, is it not? With every so-called strengthening of the idea of God, He became less and less important to the affairs of men. With each "elevated concept" of God's sovereign power, He became less and less relevant for the activities of empirical scientists. This "exalted" conception of God was to collapse into oblivion a decade and a half later, when Charles Darwin finally made biology autonomous.

F. Biological Evolution: Darwinism

Early in the year 1858, Alfred Russel Wallace lay on his bed on the island of Ternate in the Dutch East Indies, suffering from what he later described as "a sharp attack of intermittent fever." Because of hot and cold fits, he had to lie down, "during which time I had nothing to do but think over any subjects then particularly interesting to me." So, in the midst of some tropical fever, with nothing else to while away his time, Wallace discovered the principle of organic development through natural selection, the theory which shook the world. Somewhere in between 98.7 degrees Fahrenheit and delirium, modern secularism's most important theory of human autonomy was born. It was an auspicious beginning.[119]

Wallace had been thinking about the problem for almost a decade. He had wondered why some men live and some men die. "And the answer was clearly, that on the whole the best fitted live." He might have said simply, those who survive do, in fact, survive. But that would never have satisfied a scientist like Wallace. "From the effects of disease the most healthy escaped"—you can't fault his logic here, certainly—"from enemies, the strongest, the swiftest, or the most cunning; from famine, the best hunters or those with the best digestion; and so on." A skeptic might not be very impressed so far, but you have to remember that the man was suffering from a fever. "Then it suddenly flashed upon me that this self-acting process would necessarily *improve the race*, because in every generation the inferior would inevitably be killed and the superior would remain-that is, *the fittest would survive*."[120] This is the Darwinian theory of evolution, without its footnotes, intricate arguments, flank-covering, and graphs.

There are two answers to this perspective. *First*, the absolute sovereignty of God: "So then it is not of him that willeth nor of him that runneth, but of God that sheweth mercy" (Rom. 9:16). The other is that of the *philosophy of pure contingency*, described so wonderfully in Ecclesiastes: "I returned, and saw under the sun, that the race is not to the swift, nor the battle to the strong, neither yet bread to the wise, nor yet riches to men of understanding, nor yet favour to men of skill; but time and chance happeneth to them all. For man also knoweth

---

119. Alfred Russel Wallace, *My Life* (New York: Dodd, Mead, 1905), I, p. 361.
120. *Ibid.*, I, p. 362.

not his time: as the fishes that are taken in an evil net, and as the birds that are caught in the snare; so are the sons of men snared in an evil time, when it falleth suddenly upon them" (Eccl. 9:11–12).[121]

Pure contingency or God's sovereignty: neither satisfied Alfred Russel Wallace, Charles Darwin, and the myriad of their monograph-writing followers. Somewhere in the randomness that overtakes the individual, the evolutionists believe, there has to be some stability: impersonal, laws-of-probability-obeying stability. Thomas Huxley, Darwin's unofficial hatchet-man and progenitor of that remarkable family of professional skeptics—skeptics except where evolution was concerned—stated his faith quite eloquently: chance is really quite orderly, all things considered, and totally sovereign in any case. Here is the testament of modern evolutionary thought.

> It is said that he [Darwin] supposes variation to come about "by chance," and that the fittest survive the "chances" of the struggle for existence, and thus "chance" is substituted for providential design.
>
> It is not a little wonderful that such an accusation as this should be brought against a writer who has, over and over again, warned his readers that when he uses the word "spontaneous," he merely means that he is ignorant of the cause of that which is so termed; and whose whole theory crumbles to pieces if the uniformity and regularity of natural causation of illimitable past ages is denied. But probably the best answer to those who talk of Darwinism meaning the reign of "chance" is to ask them what they themselves understand by "chance"? Do they believe that anything in this universe happens without reason or without a cause? Do they really conceive that any event has no cause, and could not have been predicted by anyone who had a sufficient insight into the order of Nature? If they do, it is they who are the inheritors of antique superstition and ignorance, and whose minds have never been illuminated by a ray of scientific thought. The one act of faith in the convert to science, is the confession of the universality of order and of the absolute validity in all times and under all circumstances, of the law of causation. This confession is an act of faith, because, by the nature of the case, the truth of such propositions is not susceptible of proof. But such faith is not blind, but reasonable; because it is invariably confirmed by experience, and constitutes the sole trustworthy foundation for all action.[122]

At least he called this view what it was: *faith.*

---

121. Gary North, *Autonomy and Stagnation: An Economic Commentary on Ecclesiastes* (Dallas, Georgia: Point Five Press, 2012), ch. 35.

122. T. H. Huxley, "On the Reception of 'Origin of Species'" (1887), in Francis D. Darwin (ed.), *Life & Letters of Charles Darwin*, 2 vols. (New York: Appleton, 1887), I, p. 553.

This is one of the endearing qualities about science, especially nineteenth-century, pre-Heisenberg science: its candid lack of modesty.[123] We know where Huxley stood—at the vanguard of irrefutable truth—because he told us so.

Wallace was so confident in the truth of what he had discovered that he could hardly contain himself. "I waited anxiously for the termination of my fit so that I might at once make notes for a paper on the subject." His fit-induced paper was completed post-haste and sent to his acquaintance, Charles Darwin, who was working on the same problem that had occupied Wallace's mind for so long.

1. Darwin's Response: Despair

When Darwin read the paper, he was crestfallen. He wrote despondently to Charles Lyell:

> Your words have come true with a vengeance—that I should be forestalled. You said this, when I explained to you here very briefly my views of "Natural Selection" depending on the struggle for existence. I never saw a more striking coincidence; if Wallace had my MS. [manuscript] sketch written out in 1842, he could not have made a better short abstract! Even his terms now stand as heads of my chapters.... So all my originality, whatever it may amount to, will be smashed....[124]

Actually, Darwin should not have worried about Wallace's paper and its possible effects on Darwin's claim of originality. The theory had already been offered back in 1813 by William Wells, in a paper delivered before the Royal Society of London, and it immediately sank into oblivion. Furthermore, another obscure writer, Patrick Matthew, had outlined a very similar theory in an appendix to an 1831 book on timber.[125] But in 1858, few scientists remembered these papers.

---

123. Werner Heisenberg, an influential physicist of the early twentieth century, destroyed the Newtonian view of the universe. Instead of a mathematically regular, precise world, the modern conception is that of a world governed by the highly improbable laws of probability. Radical contingency was substituted for Newtonian order. Individual events are random; only aggregates can be dealt with statistically—order in the aggregate out of chaos in the individual. Huxley's faith is, by twentieth-century standards, hopelessly naive. For a superb study of modern physics, see the article by the Nobel prize winner, Eugene Wigner, "The Unreasonable Effectiveness of Mathematics in the Natural Sciences," *Communications on Pure and Applied Mathematics*, XIII (1960), pp. 1–14. Basically, the pessimism of Ecclesiastes 9:11–12 comes closer to modern temper than Huxley's optimism.

124. Darwin to Lyell (June 18, 1858), *Life & Letters*, I, p. 473.

125. Darwin gave belated recognition to Wells and Matthew (among a long list of others, thereby downplaying their importance) in his "Historical Sketch," added to the third (1861) edition of the *Origin*.

He offered to have Wallace's paper added to a summary of his own—carefully selected from a pre-1858 pile of notes, just to make certain that nobody would forget who had the idea first—and they were published in the *Journal of the Linnean Society*, Zoology, Vol. III (1858).[126] The fate of these path-breaking, revolutionary papers was identical to those published by Wells and Matthew: they sank beneath the surface without a trace. No angry rebuttals, no outraged theologians, nothing. So much for the impact of scholarly journals on nineteenth-century society (and perhaps today).

The matter might have ended there, an obscure footnote in some obscure Ph.D. dissertation (which is the fate of most scholarly articles published in obscure academic journals), had it not been for Darwin's willingness to bring his *Origin of Species* to a conclusion. It was published on November 24, 1859, and it sold out the entire edition of 1,250 copies in one day.[127] This must have surprised the publisher, John Murray, who had begged Darwin to write a book on pigeons instead.[128] The reading public, which had purchased 24,000 copies of *Vestiges of Creation*, in marked contrast to the subscribers to the *Journal of the Linnean Society*, obviously was in tune to the times. (Or, in Darwinian terminology, was better adapted to the intellectual environment.)

2. Why Such Success?

There can be no question about the book's impact. It launched an intellectual revolution. Many historians and scientists have tried to grasp this instant success, and few can. It was an unpredictable fluke, by human standards. Thomas Huxley remarked years later that the principle of natural selection was so clear, so obvious, that he could not understand why he had not thought of it before. This was the reaction of most of the academic community. For about a year, the reviews in professional magazines were hostile. One exception—"by chance"—was the review in the *Times*, which had been assigned to a staff reviewer, and had in turn been referred to Huxley when he had

---

126. Reprinted in Appleman (ed.), *Darwin*, pp. 81–97. Arnold Brackman argued persuasively that Charles Lyell and Joseph Dalton Hooker, Darwin's friends, set up the "delicate arrangement" whereby Darwin got the credit for discovering the principle of evolution through natural selection. They had the extracts from Darwin's notes read at the Linnean Society meeting, along with Wallace's paper. Brackman, *A Delicate Arrangement: The Strange Case of Charles Darwin and Alfred Russel Wallace* (New York: Times Books, 1980).
127. *Life & Letters*, II, p. 1.
128. Himmelfarb, *Darwin*, p. 252.

decided that it was too technical for him to review. Thus, the December 26, 1859 review was very favorable.[129] Yet at first it had not appeared that Darwin's victory would prove so easy. Huxley wrote much later: "On the whole, then, the supporters of Mr. Darwin's views in 1860 were numerically extremely insignificant. There is not the slightest doubt that, if a general council of the Church scientific had been held at that time, we should have been condemned by an overwhelming majority."[130] By 1869, the Church scientific (except in France) was in Darwin's camp.[131]

Darwin knew in 1859 just what is needed to pull off an academic revolution: younger scientists and the support of laymen. He went after both, and he won. As he wrote to one correspondent within two weeks of the publication of the *Origin*, "we are now a good and compact body of really good men, and mostly not old men. In the long run we shall conquer."[132] He was like a troop commander, sending copies with accompanying personal letters to most of the eminent scientific figures in Europe and America.[133] Laymen may not have converted the scientists, as Himmelfarb noted, but they helped to create the climate of opinion in which both laymen and professionals worked.[134]

Good tactics will seldom win a world war. Why did Darwin and his book succeed so completely? *Because the various geological theories had already undermined the traditional faith of Christians in the historical accuracy of the Bible.* Huxley may have been correct in his complaint that nine-tenths of the civilized world was Christian in 1860; he was not correct when he also complained that the Bible was accepted "as the authoritative standard of fact and the criterion of the justice of scientific conclusions, in all that relates to the origin of things, and, among them, of species."[135] If it had been true, then Huxley's 1871 pronouncement would not have been very likely: "...this much is certain, that, in a dozen years, the 'Origin of Species' has worked as complete a revolution in biological science as the 'Principia' [of Isaac Newton] did in astronomy...."[136] Himmelfarb's assessment is closer to the mark: "Thus the 1850s, which have been apotheosized as

129. *Ibid.*, p. 264.
130. *Life & Letters*, I, p. 540.
131. Himmelfarb, *Darwin*, pp. 304–9.
132. Darwin to Carpenter (Dec. 3, 1859), *Life & Letters*, II, p. 34.
133. Irvine, *Apes, Angels & Victorians*, p. 114.
134. Himmelfarb, *Darwin*, p. 296.
135. Huxley, *Westminster Review* (1860); in Appleman (ed.), *Darwin*, p. 435.
136. Huxley, *Quarterly Review* (1871); *ibid.*, p. 438.

the most tranquil, prosperous, and assured of all decades in English history, were, in fact, a period of intense spiritual anxiety and intellectual restlessness."[137] The geology question had disturbed many thinking Christians. As a specialist in the history of Victorian England, her words have to be taken seriously: "What the Origin did was to focus and stimulate the religious and nihilist passions of men. Dramatically and urgently, it confronted them with a situation that could no longer be evaded, a situation brought about not by any one scientific discovery, nor even by science as a whole, but by an antecedent condition of religious and philosophical turmoil. The Origin was not so much the cause as the occasion of the upsurge of these passions."[138] With this kind of religious and spiritual assessment of Darwin's impact, it is not surprising to find, as late as 1969, a deservedly obscure evolutionary scientist warning his readers to "beware" of books like Himmelfarb's.[139] She points to the religious roots of Darwin's success.

3. A Slow Starter

Charles Darwin had not been a bright child; he had not been ambitious, either. His father had despaired of him for years. He had studied to be a physician, like his father, but had given it up. He had studied to be a minister, but had given that up, too. At the end of his university career, he had developed a fondness for natural science under the direction of Prof. J. S. Henslow, the Cambridge botanist. Henslow secured for Darwin a position as naturalist for the voyage of the H. M. S. *Beagle*, a five-year cruise which changed Darwin's life, as he freely admitted. Henslow also recommended that Darwin read Lyell's newly published first volume of *Principles of Geology*, although Henslow warned against its uniformitarian thesis. The warning went unheeded. At the first port of call for the ship, in early 1832, Darwin's observation of the St. Jago volcanic mountains and boulders, coupled with the uniformitarian vision of Lyell, converted him.

The voyage lasted from late 1831 through the fall of 1836. During that time Darwin collected, classified, made many notes, read books, speculated endlessly, and vomited (he was seasick throughout the trip). He sent reports back to England about his findings, and the ready market made by the geologizing mania saw to it that these es-

---

137. Himmelfarb, *Darwin*, p. 239.
138. *Ibid.*, p. 400.
139. Michael T. Ghiselin, *The Triumph of the Darwinian Method* (Berkeley & Los Angeles: University of California Press, 1969), p. 8, and footnote #19, p. 251.

says were published and read. He returned to England a mildly prominent fellow. And, like other slow-starting sons, he undoubtedly could face his father—who had opposed the trip in the first place—with a good deal more confidence.

Darwin always regarded himself as a truly empirical investigator, a man in the tradition of Francis Bacon, the philosopher of scientific empiricism. He wanted to be known as a "fact man." He freely admitted in his autobiography that he had difficulty in following long, abstract arguments.[140] Commenting many years later on his early researches, he proclaimed: "My first note-book was opened in July 1837. I worked on true Baconian principles, and without any theory collected facts on a wholesale scale. . . ."[141] Nevertheless, he wrote to Wallace in 1857 that "I am a firm believer that without speculation there is no good and original observation."[142] In 1860, he wrote to Lyell that "without the making of theories I am convinced there would be no observation."[143] Thus, we can side safely with Himmelfarb's judgment: "As the notebooks amply demonstrate, he was speculating boldly from the very beginning of this period [1837], and his speculations were all directed to a particular theory—that of mutability. What is impressive about these early notebooks is not the patient marshaling of the evidence, which in fact was conspicuously absent, but rather the bold and spirited character of his thought. What clearly urged him on was theory capable of the widest extension and a mind willing to entertain any idea, however extravagant."[144]

In the fall of 1838, Darwin read Rev. Thomas Malthus' classic study in political economy, *An Essay on the Principles of Population* (1798). This, he later said, transformed him. Malthus' hypothesis of a geometrically expanding population pressing against an arithmetically expanding food supply convinced him that the key to the species question is the struggle for existence. It is doubly interesting that Wallace admitted that it was his recollection of Malthus' theory, during his fever, that triggered his formulation of the theory of natural selection. Once again, a minister had been crucial—indirectly, this time—in the steady progress of the theory of evolution. Darwin's theory was basically complete as early as 1838. Lest we forget the circumstances of this intellectual breakthrough:

---

140. *Life & Letters*, I, p. 82.
141. *Ibid.*, I, p. 68.
142. *Ibid.*, I, p. 465.
143. *Ibid.*, I, p. 108.
144. Himmelfarb, *Darwin*, p. 156.

Darwin was only twenty-nine and barely out of his apprenticeship, so to speak, when, by this second leap of imagination, his theory took full shape. If this chance reading—or misreading—of Malthus, like his first general speculations about evolution, seems too fortuitous a mode of inspiration, the fault may lie not with Darwin but with the conventional notion of scientific discovery. The image of the passionless, painstaking scientist following his data blindly, and provoked to a new theory only when the facts can no longer accommodate the old, turns out to be, in the case of Darwin as of others, largely mythical.[145]

There was another relevant coincidence during this period. Between 1836 and 1839, Darwin simultaneously lost his early faith in the accuracy of the Bible,[146] and he became afflicted with an unnamed physical sickness that remained with him for the remainder of his life, some 45 years. The sickness weakened him, so that he seldom left his home, could see few visitors, and could work only a few hours each day.[147] Thomas Huxley was also afflicted with a lifelong "internal pain" and "hypochondriacal dyspepsia," and, like Darwin's burden, it had come upon him within a year or two after he had abandoned his faith (a loss which occurred when he was eleven or twelve years old).[148] Most of Darwin's children suffered from this same affliction (one son, his namesake, was feeble-minded, and died very young—not a surprising event in the family life of a man who had married his first cousin). William, his eldest son, like his father, was never one to take needless chances with the weather. At his father's funeral in Westminster Abbey, which was unfortunately conducted under cloudy skies, William sat with his gloves on top of his bald head, keeping out unnecessary drafts.[149]

It took Darwin 20 years to piece together the evidence for the theory he had decided was true at age 29, including eight years in classifying barnacles. (Non-evolutionists may fault his biological theory, but

---

145. *Ibid.*, p. 66. See also Thomas Kuhn, *The Structure of Scientific Revolutions*, 2nd ed. (Chicago: University of Chicago Press, [1962] 1970) and James D. Watson, *The Double Helix* (New York: New American Library, 1969). This last book is an autobiographical account of one of the co-discoverers of the DNA molecule, the second major breakthrough of modern genetics (Mendel's was the first). Watson shows how many unscientific factors, including (humanly speaking) pure luck, go into a major intellectual discovery.

146. *Life & Letters*, I, p. 227.

147. Irvine, *Apes*, pp. 53, 124, 162, 200, 229.

148. *Ibid.*, pp. 11–12. Irvine thought that it was Huxley's witnessing of an autopsy at age 14 that triggered his life-long physical disturbances, an odd feature in the life of a self-proclaimed expert in biology. I think Irvine was incorrect.

149. *Ibid.*, p. 229; Himmelfarb, *Darwin*, p. 441.

one thing is certain: that man knew his barnacles!) He had published an account of his voyage, plus numerous articles and monographs, but he told only close friends of his doubts concerning the fixity of the species. In the early stages of his labors, all he claimed to be asking was fair hearing for his theory as one among many.[150] He admitted the "many huge difficulties on this view" to Asa Grey, the noted American scientist.[151] Cautious, patient, modest to a fault: this is the legend of Charles Darwin. And modesty was a wise tactic, given the paucity of his position. In 1863, four years after the publication of the *Origin*, he wrote to one correspondent: "When we descend to details, we can prove that no one species has changed [i.e. we cannot prove that a single species has changed]—[*note*: apparently added by Francis Darwin, the editor]; nor can we prove that the supposed changes are beneficial, which is the groundwork of the theory. Nor can we explain why some species have changed and others have not."[152] Therefore, he warned, we must "always remember our ignorance." But in 1871, his *Descent of Man* carefully defined the "neutral" ground on which the discussion of species would henceforth be conducted: "But it is a hopeless endeavor to decide this point, until some definition of the term 'species' is generally accepted; and the definition must not include an indeterminate element such as an act of creation."[153] His modesty had earlier overcome him in the *Origin*: "Thus, on the theory of descent with modification, the main facts with respect to the mutual affinities of the extinct forms of life to each other and to living forms, are explained in a satisfactory manner. And they are wholly inexplicable on any other view."[154] However, he was quite willing to debate the details with all comers, so long as they were willing to be truly scientific. Therefore, let all good men join hands and march under the banner unfurled in 1969 by Michael Ghiselin, when he reminded us all that "Darwin was a master of scientific method."[155] Let us all "beware" of Miss Himmelfarb's book, taking care to read the one book Dr. Ghiselin thinks is an adequate biography of Darwin, in which we learn of the "extremes of hypocrisy and self-contradiction" of Darwin's nineteenth-century critics, as well as the "venomous and

---

150. Darwin to Jenyns (1845?), *Life & Letters*, I, p. 394.
151. Darwin to Gray (July 20, 1856), *ibid.*, I, p. 437.
152. Darwin to G. Bentham (May 22, 1863), *ibid.*, II p. 210.
153. Darwin, *The Origin of Species and the Descent of Man* (Modern Library, 2 vols. in one): Descent, ch. 11, p. 268.
154. Darwin, *Origin*, ch. 11, p. 268.
155. Ghiselin, *Triumph*, p. 4.

confused counterattacks" these men used.[156] If we do all these things, we shall become truly adapted to our intellectual environment, and we shall prosper—for as long as that climate of opinion survives.

4. Indeterminacy

The technical details of Darwin's thought are best left to professional biologists. But we can consider the operating presuppositions and practical conclusions that Darwin set forth. Three of these are *indeterminacy*, *continuity*, and *cosmic impersonalism*.

The heart of the Darwinian system is *indeterminacy*. The universe is a chance event. Darwin was self-conscious in his commitment to randomness. Take, for example, his definition of species, the origin of which his book was intended to demonstrate. *There is no definition of species*.[157] This is Darwin's chief contribution to biological science. He denied that there are any limits on genetic variation within the arbitrarily defined group called species. "Slow though the process of selection may be, if feeble man can do much by artificial selection, I can see no limit to the amount of change...."[158] The great chain of being, with its separate and permanent links, has become a multi-tiered escalator. The second chapter of the *Origin* reiterates this theme over and over: there are no reliable definitions (although, as we have already seen, there are unreliable definitions: creationists' definitions). "Nor shall I here discuss the various definitions which have been given of the term species. No one definition has satisfied all naturalists; yet every naturalist knows vaguely what he means when he speaks of a species." (This is vaguely reminiscent of the old line, "I can't define art, but I know what I like." Unfortunately, Darwin is regarded as the Newton of biology.)

We are no better off when we seek his definition of that other crucial term, "variety": "The term 'variety' is almost equally difficult to define...."[159] In short, to clear things up once and for all: "From these remarks it will be seen that I look at the term species as one arbitrarily given, for the sake of convenience, to a set of individuals closely resembling each other, and that it does not essentially differ from the term variety, which is given to less distinct and more fluctuating forms. The term variety, again, in comparison with mere individual

---

156. Irvine, *Apes*, p. 88; Ghiselin's recommendation: p. 8.
157. This is comparable to Karl Marx's refusal ever to define "class."
158. Darwin, *Origin*, ch. 4, p. 82.
159. *Ibid.*, ch. 2, p. 38.

differences, is also applied arbitrarily, for convenience' sake."[160] Got
that? Excellent!

The biblical account of Genesis 1:24–25 indicates one very good
definition: reproduction. Buffon's definition corresponded with this
one fairly closely: no infertile progeny. A perfect definition may no
longer be possible in a post-Fall age; the ground has been cursed, and
"nature" is no longer normative, even as a fool-proof pointer to the
truth. But Buffon's position is so vastly superior for operational purposes in day-to-day experiments that one can only conclude that the
professional preference for Darwin's indeterminate definition rests on
a deeply religious commitment: *evolutionary change in an indeterminate
universe*. When a variety is simply an "incipient species,"[161] and species
is undefined, it is no feat of genius to conclude that it is possible for
varieties to vary and species to change. Everything is in flux.

5. Continuity

Darwin was a theologian of the continuity of life. While he never
faced the issue squarely, later evolutionists have concluded that organic life stemmed from inorganic matter. Thus, *Darwinism is the theology of the continuity of everything*. All "being" is basically one. Huxley
was quite correct when he called Darwinian evolution "the revivified
thought of ancient Greece."[162] This is the old Greek denial of a fundamental difference between God and the creation. *This doctrine of continuity destroyed the semi-creationism of the early nineteenth century*. There
could be no special creations in the world's history. To argue that
such events could have occurred was to argue against the logic of uniformitarian science. Modern "Theistic evolutionists" and "successive
creationists" may not grasp this fact, but Darwin and his followers
did. God's activities could no longer have any measurable effect in
time. Eiseley made his point forcefully:

> As one studies these remarks, and many like them, one can observe that
> the continuity in nature which had been maintained by Sir Charles Lyell
> against the catastrophists in geology has now been extended to the living
> world. The stability of natural law, first glimpsed in the heavens, had been
> by slow degrees extended to the work of waves and winds that shape the
> continents. Finally, through the long cycles of erosion and the uneasy stir-
> ring of the ocean beds, it was beginning dimly to be seen that life itself had

160. *Ibid.*, ch. 2, p. 46.
161. *Ibid.*, ch. 2, p. 51.
162. Huxley, "On the Reception of the 'Origin of Species,'" *Life & Letters of Darwin*
(ed.), I, p. 534.

passed like a shifting and ephemeral apparition across the face of nature. Nor could that elusive phantom be divorced from man himself, the great subject, as even Darwin once remarked. If fin and wing and hoof led backward toward some ancient union in the vertebrate line, then the hand of man and ape could be scanned in the same light. Even had they wished, the scientists could not stop short at the human boundary. A world, a dream world which had sustained human hearts for many centuries, was about to pass away. It was a world of design.[163]

The continuity of change was as dear to Darwin as the continuity of being. Uniformitarianism pervaded all of his writings. Nature, he asserted, "can never take a great and sudden leap, but must advance by short and sure, though slow steps."[164] Admittedly, "The mind cannot possibly grasp the full meaning of the term of even a million years; it cannot add up and perceive the full effects of many slight variations, accumulated during an almost infinite number of generations." But even though the mind cannot grasp this, we are expected to drop our unwarranted prejudices against what we cannot grasp, and accept it. "Whoever is led to believe that species are mutable will do good service by conscientiously expressing his conviction; for thus only can the load of prejudice by which this subject is overwhelmed be removed."[165] We should not "hide our ignorance" by using terms like "plan of creation" or "unity of design." Instead, we should stand firm alongside those "few naturalists, endowed with flexibility of mind, and who have already begun to doubt the immutability of species," and wrap our newly flexible minds around a concept of uniformitarian change which no mind can grasp.[166] This, you understand, is the scientific method.

6. Cosmic Impersonalism

The third feature of Darwin's thought is cosmic impersonalism. Obviously, this is the product of both his philosophy of indeterminacy and uniformitarianism. They are intertwined. There is no personal God in Darwin's system who can in any way affect the operations of random variation and statistical natural law. In general, this is regarded as the heart of the system. Biology, the last refuge of a personal God, was finally cleared of this embarrassing influence.

While he regarded nature as wholly impersonal, Darwin was never

---

163. Eiseley, *Darwin's Century*, p. 194.
164. Darwin, *Origin*, ch. 6, p. 144.
165. *Ibid.*, ch. 15, p. 368.
166. *Idem.*

able to escape the language of personification in describing natural processes. The very phrase "natural selection" implied an active power, as he admitted, but he reminded his readers that this was simply a metaphor. But metaphors are powerful devices, however candid Darwin's admission may have been. It made the transition from cosmic personalism to cosmic impersonalism that much easier. "So again it is difficult to avoid personifying the word Nature; but I mean by Nature, only the aggregate action and project of many natural laws, and by laws the sequence of events as ascertained by US."[167] The obvious conclusion is that his doctrine of natural law is completely nominalistic: we humans make the laws, since we observe and interpret the data of observation. We hope that the regularities "out there" conform to our vision of them, but how do we know? As he had written to his old teacher, Henslow, after five months at sea on the *Beagle*: "One great source of perplexity to me is an utter ignorance whether I note the right facts, and whether they are of sufficient importance to interest others."[168] And how do we know our theories are correct, once we have selected the facts? Furthermore, "it is lamentable," as he wrote to Wallace, "how each man draws his own different conclusions from the very same facts."[169] Charles Darwin had a naive view of law, or else a grimly skeptical estimation of the public's ability to bother about its intellectual nakedness, one way or the other.

To erase God from the universe of phenomena, he had to erase teleology, the doctrine of final causation. He went as far as the following admission to sweep away any trace of final cause: "There is no evidence, as was remarked in the last chapter, of the existence of any law of necessary development."[170] No necessary law of development; no necessary anything: the whole universe is random. How long should a species survive? "No fixed law seems to determine the length of time during which any single species or any single genus endures."[171] We are quite ignorant concerning the laws of variation within species.[172] (He need not have been so ignorant; Mendel's famous paper on genetics was available in 1865, prior to the sixth edition of the *Origin*, but none of Darwin's contemporaries ever saw the significance of it, although reprints were sent to many scientific men. This truly great

---

167. *Ibid.*, ch. 4, p. 64.
168. Darwin to Henslow (May 18, 1832), *Life & Letters*, I, p. 208.
169. Darwin to Wallace (May 1, 1857), *ibid.*, I, p. 453.
170. Darwin, *Origin*, ch. 12, p. 281.
171. *Ibid.*, ch. 11, p. 259.
172. *Ibid.*, ch. 6, p. 147.

advance in biological science was not spectacular enough to be visible amidst the evolution controversy.) Darwin's view of nature's laws was indeterminate, however much he disliked the implications. *He suffered with indeterminacy in order to maintain his cosmic impersonalism.*

He was convinced that chance governs the variability of any genetic (he did not use the term, of course) inheritance.[173] Time, he said, is important only to give scope to selection.[174] And, wonder of wonders, "We have almost unlimited time...."[175] (He was forced to give up his open checkbook of time when Lord Kelvin, the physicist, offered his theory of heat loss for the earth, which Darwin thought he had to accept: 300,000,000 years of organic life in the first edition of the *Origin* disappeared in later editions. Instead, we read: "Unfortunately we have no means of determining, according to the standards of years, how long a period it takes to modify a species...."[176]) Yet it appalled him to argue for an indeterminate universe, with or without unlimited quantities of time in which chance could operate. To Asa Gray, who never abandoned his faith in God's design in nature, he confessed: "I am conscious that I am in an utterly hopeless muddle. I cannot think that the world, as we see it, is the result of chance; and yet I cannot look at each separate thing as the result of Design.... Again, I say I am, and ever shall remain, in a hopeless muddle."[177] And so he remained. *To abandon a non-teleological universe would have meant abandoning his life's work.*

How did he view his labors? What did he think was the significance of those years in the laboratory and the study? In his autobiography, written in 1876, he was forced to reflect upon the meaning of his life. What impressed him was his victory over Rev. William Paley, whose *Natural Theology* had influenced him so greatly before his voyage on the *Beagle*. First, he took Paley's argument from the regularity of the universe and reversed it; for once, he returned to a vision of impersonal, totally sovereign natural law—in contrast to his former doubts, which favored the randomness of nature. He had long ago abandoned faith in the miracles of Christianity, for "the more we know of the fixed laws of nature the more incredible do miracles become." Nevertheless, he admits, "I was very unwilling to give up my

173. Darwin to Hooker (Nov. 23, 1856), *Life & Letters*, I, p. 445.
174. *Idem.*
175. Darwin to Gray (Sept. 5, 1857), *ibid.*, I, p. 479.
176. Darwin, *Origin*, ch. 11, p. 239. On Lord Kelvin's criticism, see Eiseley, *Darwin's Century*, ch. 9.
177. Darwin to Gray (Nov. 26, 1860), *Life & Letters*, II, p. 146.

belief.... Thus disbelief crept over me at a very slow rate, but was at last complete. The rate was so slow that I felt no distress." (Even his loss of faith was uniformitarian, in his recollections!) This was sent just one year after the publication of the *Origin*. At last he was free from Paley: "The old argument from design in Nature, as given by Paley, which formerly seemed to be so conclusive, fails, now that the law of natural selection has been discovered."[178] What little cosmic personalism that still remained in Paley's rationalistic universe was now officially rejected.

When challenged by Asa Gray to defend his anti-teleological attitude, Darwin did not call forth his notes on barnacles or some new theory of coral reef formation. He replied from his heart, and his heart was exceedingly religious. *What he really hated was the Christian doctrine of a totally sovereign God.* He hated this God more than he feared a random universe.

> With respect to the theological view of the question. This is always painful to me. I am bewildered. I had no intention to write atheistically. But I own that I cannot see as plainly as others do, and as I should wish to do, evidence of design and beneficence on all sides of us. There seems to me too much misery in the world. I cannot persuade myself that a beneficent and omnipotent God would have designedly created the Ichneumonidae with the express intention of their feeding within the living bodies of Caterpillars, or that a cat should play with mice. Not believing this, I see no necessity in the belief that the eye was expressly designed. On the other hand, I cannot anyhow be contented to view this wonderful universe, and especially the nature of man, and to conclude that everything is the result of brute force. I am inclined to look at everything as resulting from designed laws, with the details, whether good or bad, left to the working out of what we may call chance. Not that this notion at all satisfies me. I feel most deeply that the whole subject is too profound for the human intellect. A dog might as well speculate on the mind of Newton.[179]

He could not believe that the eye was designed, despite the inescapable difficulty that it is a totally complex element of the body that needs to be complete before it can function at all. How could this organ have evolved? What good was it during the countless millennia before it was an eye? Darwin was familiar with this objection, but he could not believe in specific design. However, in order to save his hypothetical universe from the burden of total randomness—from "brute force"—he was willing to admit that natural laws had been

---

178. *Ibid.*, I, p. 278.
179. Darwin to Gray (May 22, 1860), *ibid.*, II, p. 105.

designed, a conclusion wholly at odds with his own theoretical methodology. But he was not satisfied with this conclusion, either.

So, he feigned modesty. These questions are beyond human intellect. Questions of biology, factual and theoretical, are answerable,
but not questions that are raised as a direct product of the biological answers. This has been a tactic of "neutral" scientists for years:
challenge the conclusions of a culture's presuppositions by referring
to neutral science, but claim honest ignorance when discussing the
presuppositions of the methodology of neutral science. As he wrote
to W. Graham, two decades later, contradicting his earlier defense of
designed natural laws: "You would not probably expect anyone fully
to agree with you on so many abstruse subjects; and there are some
points in your book which I cannot digest. The chief one is that the
existence of so-called natural laws implies purpose. I cannot see this."
Here is the dilemma of modern, Kantian philosophy: Law or no law?
When defending the *total reliability and stability of "autonomous" natural science* against the claims of Christians in favor of God's miraculous interventions, natural law is absolute. But when faced with *the
totalitarian implications of absolute natural law*—a law so complete and
systematic that it indicates design rather than randomness as its foundation—the "neutral" scientist throws out "so-called natural laws."
God may neither thwart absolute natural law, nor claim credit for the
existence of such law, because it really is not absolute after all. Absolute randomness is therefore a philosophical corollary of absolute,
impersonal law, and Darwin was uncomfortable with both horns of
his dilemma. So, he appealed once again to ignorance, since he had
to agree that chance is not sovereign:

> But I have had no practice in abstract reasoning, and I may be all astray.
> Nevertheless you have expressed my inward conviction, though far more
> vividly and clearly than I could have done, that the Universe is not the
> result of chance. But then with me the horrid doubt always arises whether
> the convictions of man's mind, which has been developed from the mind
> of the lower animals, are of any value or at all trustworthy. Would anyone
> trust the convictions of a monkey's mind, if there are any convictions in
> such a mind?[180]

Notice Darwin's implicit faith. He has absolute confidence in his
"monkey-descended" (or, for the purists, "ancestor-of-monkey-de-
scended") mind when it concluded that his mind had, in fact, descended from some lower animal. But when the implications of this

---

180. Darwin to W. Graham (July 3, 1881), *ibid.*, I, p. 285.

religiously held belief came into direct conflict with a belief that man's mind can be relied upon precisely because man is made in the image of God, then he doubted the capacity of his monkey-descended mind to grapple with such abstract questions. We are intelligent enough to know that we are not intelligent enough to know; we can have sufficient confidence in our minds to rest assured that we can have no confidence in our minds. God is locked out of His universe by man's simultaneous confidence and lack of confidence in his own logic. Neither doubt nor confidence is allowed to point to God. Cosmic impersonalism is thereby assured; autonomous man is defended by his supposedly autonomous science. Like the universe around man, his own thought processes are simultaneously absolute (man is descended from lower animals; no other theory is valid[181]) and contingent (man cannot trust his own speculations when they concern absolutes).

Anyone who imagines that the implications for philosophy of Darwinism are not both widespread and important in modern life is embarrassingly naive. It was not the details of the Darwinian system that captivated European thought—Darwin had to repudiate much of his system anyway. He once admitted to his earliest supporter, J. D. Hooker, that he was proficient "in the master art of wriggling."[182] Few biologists could follow all of his arguments; if they had done so, they would have grasped the fact that his retreat into the categories of "use and disuse" represented a revival of Lamarckianism. But they did not read his works that closely. Liberated men scarcely question the logic or fine points of their liberator's scriptural canon. *What did capture the minds of intellectuals, and continues to captivate them, is Darwin's rejection of meaning or purpose; the Darwinian universe has no traces of final or ultimate causation.*

A marvelous statement of the Darwinian faith was presented in the *Britannica Roundtable* (Vol. I, #3, 1972), a slick magazine which was on the intellectual level of the Sunday newspaper's magazine insert, but which paraded under the banner of high culture. C. P. Snow, widely ballyhooed in the early 1960s because of his propaganda favoring the fusion of the "two cultures"—autonomous rational science and the equally autonomous humanities—offered us his personal credo in "What I Believe."

> I believe life, human life, all life, is a singular chance. A fluke, which depended on all manner of improbable conditionings happening at the same time, or in the same sequence of time. Between ten and twenty billion years

---

181. Darwin, *Origin*, ch. 11, p. 268; quoted earlier.
182. Darwin to Hooker (Dec. to, 1866), *Life & Letters*, II, p. 239.

ago there was a big bang, and the universe started. Before that, time did not exist: this is something our minds are not able to comprehend. . . . It has all been a very unlikely process, with many kinds of improbability along the way. . . . If any asked me on what basis I make these assumptions, I have no answer. Except to affirm that I do. Some will say I am making them because, under all the intellectual qualification, I am a residual legatee of the Judeo-Christian tradition. I doubt that. I have a nostalgic affection for the Anglican Church in which I was brought up, but for me its theological formulations have no meaning. Nor have any theological formulations of any kind.

"Nobody in here but us non-theologians," Snow affirmed. His little credo went out to those who purchased their *Encyclopedia Britannicas* in the hope of upgrading their minds and their children's social position. In fact, I would guess that it is likely that they read through this slick magazine more often than they looked up references in their dust-covered set of encyclopedias. Sooner or later, ideas have consequences.

Most modern commentators, both philosophers and professional scientists (Himmelfarb excepted), see Darwin's denial of teleology as his most important intellectual contribution. It is not simply that science can *see* no traces of purpose or design in the universe; science now affirms that it has *shown* that there is no design or purpose in the universe. If there is, it is wholly internal to the non-rational recesses of the human personality, and the behaviorist psychologist B. F. Skinner did his best to reduce *that* noumenal realm of mystery. George Gaylord Simpson, the world-famous Darwinian paleontologist, stated quite forthrightly that "Man is the result of a purposeless and natural process that did not have him in mind. He was not planned."[183] You just cannot make it any plainer than that.

Darwin's work, wrote Loren Eiseley, "had, in fact, left man only one of innumerable creatures evolving through the play of secondary forces and it had divested him of his mythological and supernatural trappings. The whole tradition of the parson-naturalists had been overthrown. Mechanical cause had replaced Paley's watch and watch maker."[184] Man has to view this mechanical cause as essentially random, however, since man's mind is finite. Nevertheless, in spite of this lack of omniscience, *man can see the random universe as sufficiently orderly and absolute to remove God from the premises.* So we are now at last set free from God: "The evolutionists discovered that nature 'makes things

---

183. George Gaylord Simpson, *The Meaning of Evolution* (New Haven: Yale University Press, [1949] 1967), p. 345.
184. Eiseley, *Darwin's Century*, pp. 195–96.

make themselves' and thus succeeded in apparently removing the need of a Master Craftsman."[185] Impersonal, random biological variation within the framework of an impersonal, random, passively pruning environment is the key to all purposeful, orderly life. But man now makes his own purpose; or, as C. S. Lewis warned, some elite men now seek to define and impose purpose and meaning for all the others.[186]

7. Darwinian Man

The cosmic impersonalism, the indeterminacy, and the continuity of natural processes have all combined to produce a remarkably discontinuous leap: *Man.* Man now is to take over the direction of the processes of evolution. Man is now to make the cosmos personal; he shall determine it. As Simpson said, "Plan, purpose, goal, all absent in evolution to this point, enter with the coming of man and are inherent in the new evolution, which is confined to him."[187] Julian Huxley said the same thing.[188] Cosmic impersonalism is now transcended. Man, the product of nature (immanence), now takes control of nature (transcendence). Freed from God's sovereignty by nature's random, impersonal sovereignty, man now affirms his own sovereignty, to impart meaning and purpose to the formerly random forces of evolutionary process. Our first true god has come at last!

Darwinian man is simultaneously transcendent and immanent with respect to nature, just as orthodox Christian man has been. But there is this fundamental difference: Christian man gained his claim of transcendence over some of nature's physical processes only by maintaining his meekness under God and His laws. *He achieved limited sovereignty over nature by means of his complete dependence on God's total sovereignty.* But Darwinian man has dispensed with God's sovereignty in order to grant such sovereignty (temporarily and as a theoretical limiting concept) to random, impersonal nature. Once this transfer of sovereignty has taken place, Darwinian man reclaims his sovereignty as the legitimate heir of nature. Man then becomes the official king of nature, and like Napoleon Bonaparte, he has been careful to place the crown on his own head (not relying on the Pope or any other theological agent).

Eiseley was quite correct when he said that Darwin's work destroyed

---

185. *Ibid.*, p. 198.
186. C. S. Lewis, *Abolition of Man*, ch. 3.
187. Simpson, *Meaning of Evolution*, pp. 345–46.
188. J. Huxley, "Evolutionary Ethics," (1943): in Appleman (ed.), *Darwin*, pp. 406–7.

the labors of the parson-naturalists. This did not keep the parsons from flocking to him in droves, bearing symbolic frankincense and myrrh, in his later years. This typical yet pathetic development only served to intensify his hostility to religion. His cousin remarked that he was far more sympathetic to religious critics than the fawning ecclesiastics who lauded his work.[189] Preposterously,

> The religious managed to find in Darwinism a variety of consolations and virtues not dreamed of even in natural theology. One distinguished botanist bewildered Darwin by declaring himself a convert on the grounds that the theory finally made intelligible the birth of Christ and redemption by grace. A clergyman was converted on the grounds that it opened up new and more glorious prospects for immortality. And theologians declared themselves ready to give up the old doctrine of "the fall" in favor of the happier idea of a gradual and unceasing progress to a higher physical and spiritual state.[190]

Himmelfarb hit the nail on the head when she wrote that *the Darwinian controversy was not between theists and evolutionists, but between the reconcilers and irreconcilables on both sides of the controversy.*[191] In the West, the irreconcilable Christians (and, I gather, Orthodox Jews) have diminished in number. The new evolutionists do not care enough one way or the other whether Christians do or do not rewrite their religion to conform to the Darwinian universe. The historian John C. Greene bent over backward to say nice things about the various theological compromises of men like Russell Mixter and James O. Buswell III, but he was only stating an inescapable fact (from the consistent Darwinian point of view) when he concluded:

> These theories may help to conserve belief in the inspiration of the Bible, but it is difficult to see how they can be of much scientific value.... [When Greene referred to the inspiration of the Bible, he had in mind the heretical Barthian variety, as he said two pages later.] As science advances, moreover, the maintenance of what these writers call "verbal inspiration" is likely to prove possible only by continual reinterpretation of the Bible. In the long run, perpetual reinterpretation may prove more subversive of the authority of Scripture than would a frank recognition of the limitations of traditional doctrines.[192]

The compromisers are trapped.

---

189. Himmelfarb, *Darwin*, p. 386.
190. *Ibid.*, p. 394.
191. *Ibid.*, p. 397.
192. John C. Greene, *Darwin and the Modern World View* (New York: Mentor, 1963), p. 34.

The best summary was made by Richard Holt Hutton back in 1879, and the fact that hardly a pastor in the conservative churches today sees the truth of this statement constitutes one of the most chilling facts of contemporary religious life. "The people who believe today that God has made so fast the laws of His physical universe, that it is in many directions utterly impenetrable to moral and spiritual influences, will believe tomorrow that the physical universe subsists by its own inherent laws, and that God, even if He dwells within it, cannot do with it what He would, and will find out the next day, that God does not even dwell within it, but must, as Renan says, be 'organized' by man, if we are to have a God at all."[193] From the natural law of the parson-naturalists, to Robert Chambers' "Christian" evolution, to Charles Darwin's autonomous law, to Julian Huxley's evolving human master of the evolutionary process: the development has seemed almost irreversible. It has led us into three cultural quagmires: the modern chaotic world of impotent existentialism, the modern bureaucratic world of the planners, and the modern retreatist world of visionless, compromised religion.

G. Christianity and Evolutionism

There is only one accurate doctrine of creation: *creation out of nothing.* All other systems partake either of pantheism or deism, both implying a finite creator. The Bible's account avoids both pitfalls. A totally sovereign God created the universe out of nothing in six days, according to His own trinitarian counsel. He then placed man, His subordinate representative, in authority over the creation. Man rebelled against the Creator, thereby bringing the wrath of God upon himself and, to some extent, on the creation itself. But, in His grace, God revealed Himself to men, both in the creation (the testimony of which is always rejected by rebellious men) and in His verbal, written word, the Bible. He has informed men of His creative acts in bringing all things into existence in six days—a period of time identical to the six days in which men are to labor at their vocations. Men arc to subdue the earth to the glory of God and in terms of His natural laws, as interpreted by His written word. Man is subordinate to God, operating entirely in terms of His ethical laws, and he is both under and over laws of nature. Nature responds to mankind's authority in terms of mankind's ethical relationship to God, especially with respect to

---

193. Cited in Himmelfarb, *Darwin*, pp. 398–99.

man's obedience to the external laws of God. God's law, both natural and revealed through the Bible, is man's tool of godly subduing.

All other systems place man in a position either of total impersonal autonomy (transcendence), or total impersonal passivity (immanence), or—as in the case of Darwinian thought—both simultaneously. The deist's god is on vacation, leaving man in full control of the semi-autonomous world machine. The pantheist's god is indistinguishable from the organic, living creation. *In either case, God is silent concerning ethics.* The deist's god ignores the world; the pantheist's god is impotent to speak in a voice separate from the world. Thus, man is seen as rationally autonomous from God (eighteenth-century Continental deism) or irrationally immersed in and part of God. In neither case is there a final ethical judgment by a self-contained, sovereign, personal God in whose image man is created. Man either rules over nature as a totalitarian despot, or else he is completely subservient to nature, like some oriental slave. The universe is closed to any judgment outside itself in both pantheism and deism; man has no higher court of appeal than nature itself. In both cases, *nature ignores ethics.* As Simpson put it: "Discovery that the universe apart from man or before his coming lacks and lacked any purpose or plan has the inevitable corollary that the workings of the universe cannot provide any automatic, universal, eternal, or absolute ethical criteria of right or wrong."[194]

H. Rival Methodologies

What should be inescapably clear by now is this: *there is no doctrine of ultimate origins that is not intensely religious.* Similarly, there is no philosophical system that does not possess a doctrine of creation—the origin of all things and the constitution which presently sustains all things. For Christians to tamper with the plain meaning of the Bible in order to make it conform to the latest findings of this or that school of evolutionary thought is nothing short of disastrous. It means an amalgamation of rival and irreconcilable religious presuppositions. Neither Darwin nor the orthodox Christian can escape the philosophical and theological implications of methodology. Both Darwin and the compromising Christians tried to push questions of philosophy and epistemology (knowledge) into the background, as if there could be some universally shared scientific methodology that is inde-

---

194. Simpson, *Meaning of Evolution*, p. 346.

pendent of philosophical presuppositions. But when the chips were down, Darwin always sided with atheism; he refused to acknowledge that the God of the Bible could have created or influenced the world in the ways explicitly affirmed by the Bible. *Evolutionism is methodological atheism,* whether Hindu, or Buddhist, or Lamarckian, or Darwinian. It always was; it always will be.

Darwinian thought is fundamentally Greek paganism. This was recognized very early by Darwin's hatchet-man, Thomas Huxley. In Huxley's assessment of the impact of Darwin's thought, which Huxley wrote for the *Life and Letters of Charles Darwin* in 1887, he expressed his opinion:

> The oldest of all philosophies, that of Evolution, was bound hand and foot and cast into utter darkness during the millennium of theological scholasticism. [Actually, scholastic philosophy lasted only from the twelfth century through the fifteenth as a cultural force in Europe, but Huxley means simply medieval Christian thought in general–G.N.] But Darwin poured new lifeblood into the ancient frame; the bonds burst, and the revivified thought of ancient Greece has proved itself to be a more adequate expression of the universal order of things than any of the schemes which have been accepted by the credulity and welcomed by the superstition of seventy later generations of men.

Indeed; all three of the accepted "scientific" evolutionary cosmologies today are simply footnoted revivals of Greek cosmological thought.

First, consider George Gamow's "primeval atom" or "big bang" theory—the exploding "ylem" of matter-energy that created all the elements of the universe in the first half-hour of its existence. Plato's theory of creation outlined in the *Timaeus* dialogue was its analogue in Greek thought. *Second,* there is the so-called steady-state theory (Fred Hoyle, the famous British astronomer, used to believe in this one). Matter and energy are continuously being created out of nothing. Everything continues today as it always has. This is the Aristotelian outlook, and it undergirded the geology of Hutton and Lyell. It is the uniformitarian theory. *Finally,* there is the theory of the oscillating universe: big bang, explosion outward, slowing, imploding inward, crash, and new big bang. Marx's partner, Engels, held this faith. It is quite similar to the Stoic theory of a cyclical cosmos. As Toulmin and Goodfield noted: "The disagreement between supporters of these views today is just about complete. Nor does there seem to be any real hope of reaching an accommodation without abandoning elements which are regarded as indispensable to the theories."[195] In short, rival pagan faiths are no less in opposition to each other, despite their unity against cosmic personalism. It was true in the days of Greece; it is equally true today.

"Details apart," wrote Toulmin and Goodfield, "the *general* resemblances between twentieth-century cosmology and its ancestors are no mere coincidence. Rather, they prompt one to look for an equally general motive." There is not sufficient evidence today to prove any theory of the earth's history, so the same old a priori refrains are repeated, generation after generation. As the authors concluded, "cosmological theory is still basically philosophical," and certain "obstinate and insoluble" problems and objections "still face us which cannot be evaded by dressing them up in twentieth-century terminology."[196] Either time had an origin, thereby making discussion of what happened "before" impossible; or else time is infinite in both directions, thus forcing us to ask forever, "Before then, what?"

Secularists, who too often spend little or no time thinking about the internal contradictions of their own presuppositions, like to ridicule Christians with stupid questions like "Who created God?" or "Where did God get the 'stuff' to build the universe?" as if they had some non-theistic answer to these questions. They do not. They have a tendency to ignore their own rootless systems of philosophy, however, which gives them great confidence in challenging the revelation of the Scripture. They prefer to have faith in the impersonal "ylem" or impersonal, infinite, steady-state time or impersonal cosmic cycles; a personal Creator God is too preposterous for their sophisticated tastes.

Yet if we are compelled to regard secular opponents of the biblical doctrine of the six-day creation as naive, then those Christians who try to amalgamate Genesis 1 and one (or all) of the secular cosmologies are doubly naive. Philosophically, the concept of process undergirds the secular positions. Toulmin and Goodfield recognized this. R. J. Rushdoony, in his study, *The Mythology of Science*, recognized this. Instead of the fiat word of God—a discontinuous event which created time and the universe—we are expected to believe in the creativity of impersonal process. As Rushdoony argued, "the moment creativity is transferred or to any degree ascribed to the process of being, to the inner powers of nature, to that extent sovereignty and power are

---

195. Toulmin and Goodfield, *Discovery of Time*, p. 255.
196. *Ibid.*, p. 258.

transferred from God to nature. Nature having developed as a result of its creative process has within itself inherently the laws of its being. God is an outsider to Nature, able to give inspiration to men within Nature but unable to govern them because He is not their Creator and hence not their source of law."[197] Is it any wonder, then, that the first modern cosmological evolutionist, Immanuel Kant, was also the premier philosopher of the modern world? Is it any wonder that his theory of the two realms—autonomous external and random "noumena" vs. scientific, mathematically law-governed "phenomena"—is the foundation of modern neo-orthodox theology, which has eroded both Protestantism and Catholicism? Is it any wonder that Kant's "god" is the lord of the noumenal realm, without power to influence the external realm of science, without even the power to speak to men directly, in terms of a verbal, cognitive, creedal revelation? This is the god of process theology, of evolution, of the modern world. It is the only god that humanists allow to exist. The God of Deuteronomy 8 and 28, who controls famines, plagues, and pestilences in terms of the ethical response of men to His law-word, is not the God of modern, apostate evolutionary science. He is not the god of process theology. The Christian with the Ph.D. in geology who says that he just cannot see what process has to do with the sovereignty of God is telling the truth: he cannot see. Had he been able to see, no "respectable" university would ever have granted him a Ph.D. in geology, at least not in historical geology.[198]

The Bible does not teach the theology of process. It does not tell us that an original chaos evolved into today's order, and will become even more orderly later. That is the theology of the Greeks, of the East, and the modern evolutionist. It is not a part of the biblical heritage. Even the so-called "chaos" of Genesis 1:2—"And the earth was without form and void"—does not teach a "chaos into order" scheme. Prof. Edward J. Young offered considerable proof of the fact that the Hebrew phrase translated "without form and void" should be rendered, "desolation and waste." It signifies that "God did not create the earth for desolation, but rather to be inhabited... Such an earth has not fulfilled the purpose for which it was created; it is an earth created in vain, a desolate earth."[199] Young cited Isaiah 45:18, which con-

---

197. Rushdoony, *The Mythology of Science* (Vallecito, California: Ross House, [1967] 1995), p. 53.

198. Davis Young, *Westminster Theological Journal* (Spring 1973), p. 272.

199. Edward J. Young, *Studies in Genesis One* (Philadelphia: Presbyterian & Reformed, 1964), p. 33. See also pp. 13, 16, 34.

tains the same Hebrew words: "For thus saith the LORD that created the heavens; God himself that formed the earth and made it; he hath established, he created it not in vain, he formed it to be inhabited: I am the LORD; and there is none else." What is described in Gen. 1:2 is a great primeval sea, which was uninhabitable and therefore desolate. (See verse 9: "let the dry land appear.") The "chaos" factor, so heavily relied upon by compromising biblical expositors, not only does not conform to Greek speculation, but is intensely anti-modern: the desolation implies purpose, that great bugaboo of modern science. Any attempt to view Genesis 1:2 in terms of some original chaos plays into the hands of the Darwinians, for it compromises the element of purpose in the creation.

One popular variation on this theme is the so-called "gap hypothesis," which argues that in Genesis 1:1 God created the earth, only to shake up the elements in Genesis 1:2 as a result of Satan's fall. He then created the new, six-day earth in Genesis 1:3–27. There are three things wrong with this view, at the very least. *First,* the Bible does not teach anything like this; it is obviously a jerry-built interpretation that has become popular in order to give an explanation for the apparent age of the uniformitarians' earth. *Second,* the uniformitarians are entitled to dismiss it, since a true "chaos" would have been a complete erasure of the previously existing earth, thus removing the "precious" traces of age that the "gapologists" so desperately desire. *Third,* as already mentioned, it compromises the explicit traces of purpose in the creation's original desolation. A *fourth* reason is at least possible: Satan fell on the seventh day, after God had pronounced the whole creation "good."

The step-by-step retreat of Christian thinkers from the six-day creation—universally acknowledged in 1725, and generally believed until 1800—has been a disastrous, though temporary, setback for Christian orthodoxy. Sadly, Christians were not usually dragged, kicking and screaming, into Lyell's uniformitarian and Darwin's purposeless evolution. They accepted each new scientific "breakthrough" with glee. At best, each resistance attempt was a three-stepped process: (1) it is not true; (2) it is not relevant, anyway; (3) we always knew it was true, and Christianity teaches it, and teaches it better than any other system. No wonder Darwin was irritated; a good, purposeless universe could not be left in peace by these silly people!

The battle lines should be clear: Christianity or error, the six-day creation or chaos, purpose and meaning or cosmic impersonalism and randomness. It is not hard to understand why the religion of modernism clings to Darwinian thought. It is also not surprising why occultist Max Heindel could write *The Rosicrucian Cosmo-Conception or Mystic Christianity: An Elementary Treatise upon Man's Past Evolution, Present Constitution and Future Development* (1909). But why Christians should give one second's consideration of the possibility of evolution—ancient or modern, occultist or scientific—is a mystery.

The compromise with uniformitarian principles has been a steady, almost uniformitarian process within Christian circles. Gillispie, describing the steady capitulation of early nineteenth-century Christian naturalists, shows how disastrous the retreat was for orthodoxy. At each stage, the Christians, copying the mythical act of King Canute, shouted "thus far and no farther" to uniformitarianism. "And at every stage except the last, progressives admitted that a further step, the possibility of which they disavowed while they unwittingly prepared it, would indeed have had serious implications for orthodox religious fidelity."[200] But each new uniformitarian "discovery" was assimilated into the supposedly orthodox framework nonetheless, despite the fact that at every preceding capitulation, the proponents of that compromise admitted that the next step (now greeted passively or even enthusiastically) would be unnecessary, impossible, and utterly wrong. (Any similarity between nineteenth-century Christian progressives and today's Christian progressives is hardly coincidental.) The progressivists of the 1840s, like the compromisers of today, would not face up to reality. They could not admit to themselves or their few orthodox opponents the fact that Robert Nisbet has called to our attention: "It is hard today to realize the degree to which the attack on Christianity obsessed intellectuals of rationalist and utilitarian will. Christianity had much the same position that capitalism was to hold in the first half of the twentieth century. It was the enemy in the minds of most intellectuals. Uniformitarianism, above any other single element of the theory of evolution, was the perfect point of attack on a theory that made external manipulation its essence and a succession of 'catastrophes' its plot."[201]

Conclusion

Thomas H. Huxley, the scientist who helped spread the gospel of Darwinism more than any other man in the second half of the nine-

---

200. Gillispie, *Genesis and Geology*, p. 221.
201. Nisbet, *Social Change and History*, p. 184.

teenth century, was vitriolic in his hostility to orthodox Christianity, with its insistence on the doctrine of creation. He knew there could never be any compromise between Darwinism and creationism. He announced in his important defense of Darwin in 1859:

> In this nineteenth century, as at the dawn of modern physical science, the cosmogony of the semi-barbarous Hebrew is the incubus of the philosopher and the opprobrium of the orthodox. Who shall number the patient and earnest seekers after truth, from the days of Galileo until now, whose lives have been embittered and their good name blasted by the mistaken zeal of Bibliolators? Who shall count the host of weaker men whose sense of truth has been destroyed in the effort to harmonise impossibilities— whose life has been wasted in the attempt to force the generous new wine of Science into the old bottles of Judaism, compelled by the outcry of the same strong party?[202]

Huxley was totally confident in the long-term success of Darwinism. In fact, he believed that this victory of science (which he dutifully capitalized, as one should do when spelling out the name of any divinity one worships) had already been secured. He viewed this triumph as the result of an intellectual war.

> It is true that if philosophers have suffered, their cause has been amply avenged. Extinguished theologians lie about the cradle of every science as the strangled snakes beside that of Hercules; and history records that whenever science and orthodoxy have been fairly opposed, the latter has been forced to retire from the lists, bleeding and crushed if not annihilated; scotched, if not slain. But orthodoxy is the Bourbon [referring to the French monarchy, the House of Bourbon—G.N.] of the world of thought. It learns not, neither can it forget; and though, at present, bewildered and afraid to move, it is as willing as ever to insist that the first chapter of Genesis contains the beginning and the end of sound science; and to visit, with such petty thunderbolts as its half-paralyzed hands can hurl, those who refuse to degrade Nature to the levels of primitive Judaism.[203]

His next paragraph begins with this unforgettable sentence: "Philosophers, on the other hand, have no such aggressive tendencies." Why not?

> The majesty of Fact is on their side, and the elemental forces of Nature are working for them. Not a star comes to the meridian of their methods: their beliefs are 'one with the falling rain and with the growing corn.' By

---

202. Thomas Huxley, "The Origin of Species," (1859), in Frederick Barry (ed.), *Essays* (New York: Macmillan, 1929), pp. 105–6.
203. *Ibid.*, p. 106.

doubt they are established, and open inquiry is their bosom friend. Such men have no fear of traditions however venerable, and no respect for them when they become mischievous and obstructive;...[204]

He knew his contemporary enemies well. He realized clearly, as they did not, that their hypothesis of continuing special creations "owes its existence very largely to the supposed necessity of making science accord with the Hebrew cosmogony; but it is curious to observe that, as the doctrine is at present maintained by men of science, it is as hopelessly inconsistent with the Hebrew view as any other hypothesis."[205] Darwinian scientists from Huxley's day to the present have been able to make the same criticism of later attempts of Christian scholars to compromise the teachings of Genesis 1 and evolution. Sadly, Huxley's barb applies quite well to these professional academic compromisers: they are like the Bourbon kings. They never seem to learn that there can be no successful compromise between the rival cosmologies.

The six-day creation is not a narrow cosmology. It is as broad as the creation itself and the revelation of that creation given by its Creator. Evolution and uniformitarian geology (however modified the uniformitarianism may be) may appear very broad-minded, but only in the sense of Matthew 7:13: "Enter ye in at the strait [narrow, tight] gate: for wide is the gate, and broad is the way, that leadeth to destruction, and many there be which go in thereat."

---

204. *Ibid.*, pp. 106–7.
205. *Ibid.*, p. 108.

APPENDIX D

BASIC IMPLICATIONS OF THE SIX-DAY CREATION

Christian churches seldom lack an issue that can serve as a means of internal disruption and conflict: the mode of baptism, the age of one's first communion, the form of government, the role of the institutional church in non-church realms. The conflict between evolution and creation has not been one of these major and continuing sources of contention within the vast majority of Christian churches.

Prior to 1800, the concept of biological evolution had not been widely considered. A few secular philosophers—for example, Immanuel Kant—had argued for some form of cosmic evolution, but Christians were generally uninformed about, or unimpressed by, such speculation. Yet, after 1900, outside of a few so-called fundamentalist groups, the question of the time and mode of God's creation was no longer considered intellectually or ecclesiastically respectable as an important topic. People have been expected to "agree to disagree" as Christians; specifics concerning creation are officially relegated into the realm of *adiaphora*, that is, things indifferent to salvation or the life of the church. "Theistic evolution" or the "gap theory" or "progressive creation" or the "literary framework hypothesis" have served as alternatives to the six-day creation within those circles that still concern themselves with the question of biblical inerrancy.

Ever since 1900, we have witnessed a strange phenomenon inside the evangelical churches. Pastors have been dismissed by their congregations or their hierarchical superiors for mismanaging budgets, changing their minds about the mode of baptism, softening their views concerning the sabbath, or disrupting the autonomy of the choir director. But a heresy trial for a pastor who holds some variant of theistic evolution would be unthinkable in evangelical churches today. As a means of institutional confrontation, the choir is a far more

505

potent issue than the doctrine of creation. So powerful have been the forces of religious syncretism, philosophical pragmatism, and academic respectability inside the churches, that this crucial foundation of the faith has become operationally secondary—or less.

If pastors, clutching desperately at their advanced academic degrees from accredited colleges, have abandoned the defense of the faith, why should the layman think that he has any right to call the churches to repentance? How can a layman challenge the official expertise of certified scholarship and ordained respectability? This was Moses' question to God, basically, in Exodus 4:10. God's answer was straightforward: "Who hath made man's mouth? or who maketh the dumb, or deaf, or the seeing, or the blind? have not I, the LORD?" (Ex. 4:11). God is the source of all valid theories and all valid footnotes, not the geology department of Harvard University. His revelation of Himself in the Bible is the standard of accuracy, not the latest discovery (which will be refuted in five years by someone else) of hypothetically neutral science. If intelligent, devoted, and necessarily self-taught laymen do not make use of the services of the various creation research organizations in their efforts to call Christians back to the explicit revelation of the Bible and the historic faith of the orthodox churches, then a major battle will have been lost. The status quo in the churches today is our visible defeat; orthodoxy demands reconstruction. Assistance from the pastors in this struggle would be appreciated, but as it stands today, the laymen are necessarily the strategists and generals.

A. Here I Stand

Why take a stand here? Why should the doctrine of the six-day creation be a rallying issue? First, because it is the one issue that has established itself in the minds of many orthodox Christians as a necessary and legitimate area of confrontation between apostate science and Christianity. Men who would not be confident in challenging secular thought in the realms of psychology, politics, economics, or other academic disciplines, nevertheless do understand the false nature of the claim of scientific neutrality concerning evolution. As a result, the intellectual division of labor is greater in the areas of biology and geology than in any other Christian endeavor.

More people are already involved in the battle. Thus, it is tactically a solid place to take a stand. More important than tactics, however, is the centrality of the doctrine of creation to Christian faith. Langdon

Gilkey, a neo-orthodox theologian, nonetheless saw the issue more clearly than most supposedly evangelical theologians. He announced forthrightly:

> It is quite natural, of course, that Christian devotion and Christian thought should concern themselves most with God's redeeming activity in Jesus Christ, for upon this our knowledge of God as loving Father, and so of our hope for salvation, most directly depends. Nevertheless, the centrality of God's redeeming activity to our life and thought should not blind Christians to the divine work of creation, which, if not so close to our hearts, is just as significant for our existence and just as important if we are to think rightly about God. Through God's redeeming works we know that He is supremely righteous and supremely loving. But when we ask who is supremely righteous and loving, the answer comes in terms of God's original activity, creation: the Creator of heaven and earth, the Lord, is He who judges and redeems us. The transcendent "Godness" of God, what gives Him deity and so ultimate significance to our lives, is most directly manifested to us through His creative activity as the transcendent source of all being and of all existence. Without this transcendent aspect of "deity," the judgment and love of God would be ultimately unimportant to us, and the redemption promised by them impossible for God. The idea of creation, therefore, provides the most fundamental, if not the most characteristic, definition of God in the Christian faith. Among all the activities of God, creation is that activity or attribute which sets him apart as "God."[1]

The doctrine of the Trinity—the eternal, infinite, fully self-revealing and communing holy God who is three persons—has always been the starting point for Christian theology. But insofar as God has any relationship with men, the doctrine of creation is central. The fact that Gilkey, who is not orthodox, can see this, and evangelicals do not, testifies to the disastrous effects of syncretism. Christianity and antitheism cannot be successfully fused without destroying Christianity.

B. Creation Defined

The Bible testifies to the fact that a personal God created all things—matter and energy, structure and motion—out of nothing: *creatio ex nihilo*. The opening words of the Bible are concerned with the question of origins: "In the beginning God created the heaven and the earth" (Gen. 1:1). God repeats this fact to us again and again: "Yea, before the day was I am he; and there is none that can deliver out of

---

1. Langdon Gilkey, *Maker of Heaven and Earth: The Christian Doctrine of Creation in the Light of Modern Knowledge* (Garden City, New York: Doubleday Anchor, [1959] 1965), pp. 83–84.

my hand: I will work, and who shall let it?" (Isa. 43:13). We read in the New Testament concerning God the Son: "For by him were all things created, that are in heaven, and that are in earth, visible and invisible, whether they be thrones, or dominions, or principalities, or powers: all things were created by him, and for him: and he is before all things, and by him all things consist" (Col. 1:16–17). There is no more comprehensive statement in Scripture concerning the creation. Christ our savior is identified with God the Creator; were He not the Creator, He would not be the Savior. We would still be dead in our sins (Eph. 2:5). The Gospel of John, the most explicitly evangelistic of the gospels (John 20:30, 31), begins with the affirmation that Christ, the Word of God, is the Creator: "All things were made by him; and without him was not any thing made that was made" (1:3). God precedes all things: "Before the mountains were brought forth, or ever thou hadst formed the earth and the world, even from everlasting to everlasting, thou art God" (Ps. 90:2). He is therefore sovereign over all things: "Thou turnest man to destruction; and sayest, Return, ye children of men" (Ps. 90:3).

No knowledge of God as Creator could penetrate the minds of rebellious men sufficiently to bring them to repentance were it not for God's gracious self-revelation in the Bible, by means of the Holy Spirit. Men willfully hold back the knowledge they have of God as Creator (Rom. 1:18–23).[2] The saving knowledge of God comes only by means of His special revelation and special grace to His people. Therefore, all men are required to believe that God is the Creator, and not the creator devised by the rebellious human imagination, but the Creator as revealed in the Bible. Any old kind of creation will not do; we are not to adopt a doctrine of creation in the same way as we select salads in a cafeteria. The words of Genesis 1 inform us of the fact that God created all things in six days. This is repeated in the Decalogue (Ten Commandments): "...in six days the LORD made heaven and earth, the sea, and all that in them is, and rested the seventh day..." (Ex. 20:11). The creation was out of nothing, in response to the sovereign word of God: "By the word of the LORD were the heavens made; and all the host of them by the breath of his mouth...For he spake, and it was done; he commanded, and it stood fast" (Ps. 33:6, 9). Therefore, the Apostle Paul wrote: "For of him, and

---

2. Gary North, *Cooperation and Dominion: An Economic Commentary on Romans*, 2nd ed. (Dallas, Georgia: Point Five Press, [2000] 2012), ch. 2; Cf. John Murray, *The Epistle to the Romans* (Grand Rapids, Michigan: Eerdmans, 1959), I, p. 37.

through him, and to him, are all things: to whom be glory for ever. Amen" (Rom. 11:36).

Modern translators of the Bible have sometimes sought to revive the theology of the pagan ancient world, since a similar theology undergirds all modern apostate rationalism. They have translated Genesis 1:1–2 as follows: "When God began to create the heaven and the earth—the earth being unformed and void, with darkness over the surface of the earth. . . ."[3] The language, while grammatically possible, is theologically perverse. The translation is governed by the premises of apostate man rather than by the explicit teaching of the Bible. It is the Bible, not the presuppositions of rebellious men, which is to interpret the verbal revelation of God (II Tim. 3:16; II Pet. 1:20). Modern translators believe, far too often, in the co-existence of the material (or energetic) universe with the being of God. This assumption of the ancient cosmologies, contemporary "primitive" cosmologies, ancient philosophy (Aristotle, *Physics*, VIII), and modern evolutionism, is erroneous. When this pagan god began to mold the eternally existing "stuff" of the universe, he found that he was not sovereign over it, because he had not created it. He, like the "stuff" in front of him, behind him, above him, and beneath him, was governed by the independent laws of probability and chance. "Lots of luck there, God! We're pulling for you!"

In contrast to this is the Creator of the Bible. At best, the pagan god is Dr. God, while we humans are only Mr. But the Epistle to Hebrews testifies of another God altogether: "And, thou, Lord, in the beginning hast laid the foundation of the earth; and the heavens are the works of thine hands: They shall perish; but thou remainest; and they all shall wax old as doth a garment; And, as a vesture shalt thou fold them up, and they shall be changed: but thou art the same, and thy years shall not fail" (Heb. 1:10–12). God dwells in eternity (Isa. 57:15). He creates the new heaven and new earth (Isa. 65:17–18; II Pet. 3:9–13; Rev. 21:1). The Creator is the Savior: "Lift up your eyes to the heavens, and look upon the earth beneath: for the heavens shall vanish away like smoke, and the earth shall wax old like a garment, and they that dwell therein shall die in like manner: but my salvation

---

3. *The Torah* (Philadelphia: Jewish Publication Society of America, 1962). For a scholarly refutation of this approach to Genesis 1:1, see Edward J. Young, *Studies in Genesis One* (Philadelphia: Presbyterian and Reformed, 1964), pp. 1–7. Young's study also offers refutations of the so-called "gap theory"—eons of time between Genesis 1:1 and 1:2—and the literary or framework hypothesis, which argues against the chronological succession of the six days of creation.

shall be for ever, and my righteousness shall not be abolished" (Isa. 51:6). He who dares to tamper with the doctrine of creation compromises the revelation of the Creator concerning His own activity. If the latest finding of science—based, as it is, on the oldest antitheistic philosophy of creation—should be permitted to undermine the explicit revelation of God concerning one aspect of His relationship to His creation, there is no logical reason to draw back in horror when science also undermines the doctrine of salvation. Without the doctrine of creation there can be no doctrine of salvation—not, at least, an orthodox doctrine.

God is eternal and unchanging (Mal. 3:6). His words will not pass away (Matt. 24:35); His counsel is immutable (Heb. 6:17). "The Lord by wisdom hath founded the earth; by understanding hath he established the heavens" (Prov. 3:19). God's wisdom founded the world; the fallen world's wisdom cannot accept this. God's wisdom is foolishness to the world (I Cor. 1:20), and God warns His people not to be beguiled by the vanity of apostate philosophies (Col. 2:4–9). God is the standard of reference, the unchanging measure of all truth. Thus, the Bible rejects the pagan idea of creation through self-generated process, and it affirms the *fiat* creation by the word of God. Creation was a discontinuous event—*the* discontinuous event prior to Christ's incarnation. Process theology is the remnant of Adam's thought; by stressing the continuity between man's truth and God's truth, it relativizes God's truth. The shifting opinions of scientists replace the verbal revelation of God. Time, not God, becomes the framework of creation; chance, not God's eternal word, becomes the creative force in history. Evolution, the most consistent and most dangerous form of process theology, cannot be made to fit the categories of Christian faith.

C. Providence

The definition of creation goes beyond the concept of the original creation which ended on the sixth day. It simultaneously affirms the sustaining hand of God in time. It is Christ, "who being the brightness of his glory, and the express image of his person, and upholding all things by the word of his power" (Heb. 1:3), maintains the earth and the stars. "He hath made the earth by his power, he hath established the world by his wisdom, and hath stretched out the heaven by his understanding. When he uttereth his voice, there is a multitude of waters in the heavens; and he causeth the vapors to ascend from the ends of the earth: he maketh lightnings with rain, and bringeth forth the wind out of his treasures" (Jer. 51:15–16). Psalm 104 is a lengthy presentation of God's creative, sustaining providence in history. This applies equally to matters spiritual and physical: "Fear thou not; for I am with thee: be not dismayed; for I am thy God: I will strengthen thee; yea, I will help thee; yea, I will uphold thee with the right hand of my righteousness" (Isa. 41:10; cf. 42:5–6). The doctrine of providence reveals the total sovereignty of God.

D. Creator-Creature Distinction

Is God wholly removed from the world, as an eighteenth-century deist would have argued? Is God wholly identified with the world, as the pantheists have argued? As far back as we have written records, men have answered both ways. Sometimes, as in the case of the philosopher Plato and the neo-orthodox theologian Barth, secularists have held both positions simultaneously.[4] Aristotle's "thought thinking itself," deism's watchmaker god, and Plato's Forms or Ideas are all wholly transcendent, wholly aloof gods. Eastern religious monism and Western pantheism are examples of the god who reveals himself wholly in his creation. The first god has no point of contact with life and change; the second god cannot be distinguished from life and change. Neither is therefore cosmically personal.

The Bible affirms the existence of a *personal* Creator who is simultaneously transcendent and immanent. This is not held, as in the case of neo-orthodoxy, on the basis of modern philosophical dualism, but rather on the basis of a personal God's verbal and therefore understandable revelation of Himself to those creatures made in His image. God is not to be identified with His creation, yet the creation testifies to His existence. There is no uniform being that in some way links God and the creation—some ultra something that both God and creation participate in. There is no scale of being between the devil and God, with God as the possessor of more being than anyone else, and the devil drifting into non-being. The God of the Bible is personal and sovereign, unlike the secular transcendent God (who is too different or too removed to care about the world) or the secular immanent God (who is too similar and too close to the world to in-

---

4. On Plato's position, see Cornelius Van Til, *A Survey of Christian Epistemology*, vol. II of *In Defense of the Faith* (den Dulk Foundation, 1969), ch. 3. (This was published originally in 1932 as *The Metaphysics of Apologetics*.) On Barth's dualism between God as wholly revealed, yet wholly hidden, see Van Til, *Christianity and Barthianism* (Philadelphia: Presbyterian and Reformed, 1962), ch. 6.

fluence it). We are informed by Psalm 90:1–2 that God is our dwelling place (immanence), yet He existed before the foundation of the world (transcendence). The universe is therefore personal; in contrast to all forms of paganism, at bottom a personal God controls all His creation. Christianity affirms cosmic personalism.

1. Transcendence.

"For thou, LORD, art high above all the earth: thou art exalted far above all gods" (Ps. 97:9; cf. 135:5; Isa. 46:9). The Psalms are filled with the language of transcendence. "The LORD is great in Zion; and he is high above all the people" (Ps. 99:2). "Be thou exalted, O God, above the heavens: and thy glory above all the earth" (Ps. 108:5). While we do not need to accept the conclusions of the so-called higher criticism of the Bible, that is, the multiple authorship of many individual books of the Bible, there is no doubt that Isaiah 40–66 does stress the idea of the transcendence of God far more than Isaiah 1–39. Perhaps the crucial verses in the Bible dealing with God's transcendence are Isaiah 55:8–9: "For my thoughts are not your thoughts, neither are your ways my ways, saith the LORD. For as the heavens are higher than the earth, so are my ways higher than your ways, and my thoughts than your thoughts." Yet God's transcendence is not impersonal; He is on high, but He cares for His people: "For thus saith the high and lofty One that inhabiteth eternity, whose name is Holy; I dwell in the high and holy place, with him also that is of a contrite and humble spirit, to revive the spirit of the humble, and to revive the heart of the contrite ones" (Isa. 57:15). This same connection between God's transcendence and mercy is found in Jeremiah 32:17–18. But the most comprehensive statement of God's absolute transcendence is presented in Job, chapters 38–41.[5] No created being can challenge the creative hand of God.

It is therefore insufficient to argue merely for the separation of God and the creation. As Cornelius Van Til wrote: "The transcendence concept of theism is not clearly stated, if it is merely said that God is independent of the world. According to the ordinary use of the word, that would not exclude the possibility that the world would also be independent of God. And it is this dependence of the world upon God that a theist is interested in as much as the independence of God apart from the world. In fact God would not be truly inde-

---

5. Gary North, *Predictability and Dominion: An Economic Commentary on Job* (Dallas, Georgia: Point Five Press, 2012), ch. 6.

pendent of the world unless the world were dependent upon God. No one is absolutely independent unless he alone is independent."[6] The doctrine of creation prevents the appearance of a deistic view of transcendence, for the Bible's account of creation also teaches the doctrine of providence. God sustains the world. It is only in terms of His eternal decree that the world has existence or meaning.

2. Immanence

The transcendence of God the Creator implies His immanence. "But will God indeed dwell on the earth? behold, the heaven and heaven of heavens cannot contain thee; how much less this house that I have builded?" (I Kings 8:27). God is omnipresent; He cannot be contained in heaven alone. He dwells throughout His creation and far beyond infinity. Psalm 139:7–8 is the archetype passage: "Whither shall I go from thy Spirit? or whither shall I flee from thy presence? If I ascend up into heaven, thou art there: if I make my bed in hell, behold, thou art there." God asks Jeremiah: "Am I a God at hand ...and not a God afar off? Can any hide himself in secret places that I shall not see him? saith the LORD. Do not I fill heaven and earth? saith the LORD" (Jer. 23:23–24). *Near and far, God is present.* "For what nation is there so great, who hath God so nigh unto them, as the LORD our God is in all things that we call upon him for?" (Deut. 4:7). God's words are very clear in this regard. As Paul proclaimed before the pagans in Athens, "For in him we live, and move, and have our being...." (Acts 17:28a). Our physical bodies serve as the temple of the Holy Spirit (I Cor. 6:19; II Cor. 6:16).

Man is made in the image of God (Gen. 1:26–27). Man's inner being calls him to repentance and worship. Man's environment also calls him to worship the Creator: "The heavens declare the glory of God; and the firmament sheweth his handywork" (Ps. 19:1). Therefore, concluded Paul, every man is totally without excuse:

> For the invisible things of him from the creation of the world are clearly seen, being understood by the things that are made, even his eternal power and Godhead; so that they are without excuse: Because that, when they knew God, they glorified him not as God, neither were thankful; but became vain in their imaginations, and their foolish heart was darkened. Professing themselves to be wise, they became fools, And changed the glory of the uncorruptible God into an image made like to corruptible man, and to birds, and fourfooted beasts, and creeping things. Wherefore God

---

6. Van Til, *Survey of Christian Epistemology*, p. 16.

also gave them up to uncleanness through the lusts of their own hearts, to dishonour their own bodies between themselves: Who changed the truth of God into a lie, and worshipped and served the creature more than the Creator, who is blessed for ever. Amen (Rom. 1:20–25).

There is no escape from God's revelation of Himself; the whole creation proclaims His majesty. There is not sufficient natural revelation to save people from destruction, but there is natural revelation sufficient to condemn them for all eternity. The "work of the law" is written in every man's heart, "conscience also bearing witness" to his own evil nature (Rom. 2:15). Men seek desperately to escape this testimony. Again, quoting Van Til:

> The main point is that if man could look anywhere and not be confronted with the revelation of God then he could not sin in the Biblical sense of the term. Sin is the breaking of the law of God. God confronts man everywhere. He cannot in the nature of the case confront man anywhere if he does not confront him everywhere. God is one; the law is one. If man could press one button on the radio of his experience and not hear the voice of God then he would always press that button and not the others. But man cannot even press the button of his own self-consciousness without hearing the requirement of God.[7]

In short, "Psychologically there are no atheistic men; epistemologically [knowledgeably] every sinner is atheistic."[8] For this reason, the evil man in Jesus' parable of Lazarus asked to be allowed to return from hell to warn his lost brothers—not because he had a trace of goodness or compassion for the lost, but because if he could get God to admit that His revelation to the brothers was not sufficient to warn them, then God would have no cause to judge any man, including Dives. God, understandably, turned the request down flatly: though one rose from the dead (Jesus Christ), they would not be persuaded (Luke 16:27–31). Men's problem is not their lack of revelation; it is their willful rebellion against that revelation. God's creation reveals Him.

E. The Sovereignty of God

Job 38–41 is an important testimony to the sovereignty of God.[9] God, who created all things and sustains all things, rules all things. Nothing

---

7. Van Til, *Common Grace and the Gospel* (Philadelphia: Presbyterian and Reformed, 1973), pp. 176–77.

8. *Ibid.*, p. 54.

9. North, *Predictability and Dominion*, ch. 6.

happens outside the decrees of God; Satan had to ask permission in order to harass Job, and God set limits to everything he did (Job 1:12; 2:6). Everything is known to God beforehand, of course: "Known unto God are all his works from the beginning of the world" (Acts 15:18). In Isaiah 45 we learn of the extent of God's total direction of all events:

> I form the light, and create darkness: I make peace, and create evil: I the LORD do all these things. Drop down, ye heavens, from above, and let the skies pour down righteousness: let the earth open, and let them bring forth salvation, and let righteousness spring up together; I the LORD have created it. Woe unto him that striveth with his Maker! Let the potsherd strive with the potsherds of the earth. Shall the clay say to him that fashioneth it, What makest thou? or thy work, He hath no hands?...I have made the earth, and created man upon it: I, even my hands, have stretched out the heavens, and all their host have I commanded (Isa. 45:7–9, 12).

God is not the author of confusion (I Cor. 14:33), yet He controls and directs all things. There is no solution to this seeming intellectual dilemma in terms of the logic of autonomous man.

The image of the potter and his workmanship is a recurring one in the Bible. "But now, O LORD, thou art our Father; we are the clay, and thou our potter; and we all are the work of thy hand" (Isa. 64:8). Jeremiah 18, God's confrontation with Israel, is constructed upon this analogy: "O house of Israel, cannot I do with you as this potter? saith the LORD. Behold, as the clay is in the potter's hand, so are ye in mine hand, O house of Israel" (Jer. 18:6). But in Romans 9, the great chapter in the New Testament dealing with the total predestination of the world by God, Paul used the potter analogy to stifle the apostate and illegitimate conclusion of those who would argue that God's predestination is opposed to human responsibility. Paul's use of the potter analogy had no meaning except in terms of such an illegitimate use of human logic; he answered that issue, and only that issue, in these words:

> Therefore hath he mercy on whom he will have mercy, and whom he will he hardeneth. Thou wilt say then unto me, Why doth he yet find fault? For who hath resisted his will? Nay but, a man, who art thou that repliest against God? Shall the thing formed say to him that formed it, Why hast thou made me thus? Hath not the potter power over the clay, of the same lump to make one vessel unto honour, and another unto dishonour? (vv. 18–21).

God therefore has set explicit limits on the exercise of human logic. God is good, and He created all things good in the beginning, yet He uses evil and rebellion to fulfill His plan of history. Man is totally predestined by the Creator (Rom. 8:28–30; Eph. 1), yet man is wholly responsible for his actions. We are required to affirm both points. We are the vessels; God, the Creator, is the potter. Men are reminded that "The secret things belong unto the LORD our God: but those things which are revealed belong unto us and to our children for ever, that we may do all the words of this law" (Deut. 29:29). Creatures are not permitted knowledge as exhaustive as God's is, whether of outward affairs or of the heart (I Sam. 16:7). *Godly humility requires every Christian to submit to the sovereignty of God, acknowledging His total predestination as well as man's total responsibility.* Anything less than this affirmation—any quibbling concerning possible zones of human autonomy to make decisions respecting anything, including their salvation—involves men in outward rebellion. "The king's heart is in the hand of the LORD, as the rivers of water: he turneth it whithersoever he will" (Prov. 21:1). "A man's heart deviseth his way: but the LORD directeth his steps" (Prov. 16:9).[10]

F. Meekness and Dominion

Because God is sovereign over the creation, which exists only because of God's decree, and because man is made in the image of God, man therefore has a legitimate, though subordinate, *right of dominion* over the creation. This is man's *cultural mandate*: "And God said, Let us make man in our image, after our likeness: and let them have dominion over the fish of the sea, and over the fowl of the air, and over the cattle, and over all the earth, and over every creeping thing that creepeth upon the earth. So God created man in his own image, in the image of God created he him; male and female created he them. And God blessed them, and God said unto them, Be fruitful, and multiply, and replenish the earth, and subdue it: and have dominion over the fish of the sea, and over the fowl of the air, and over every living thing that moveth upon the earth" (Gen. 1:26–28).[11] This cultural mandate was reaffirmed with Noah and his sons (Gen. 9:1).[12] Man's meekness before a Creator God is the foundation of man's inheri-

---

10. For a more detailed introduction to these issues, see the chapter on God in my book, *Unconditional Surrender: God's Program for Victory*, 5th ed. (Powder Springs, Georgia: American Vision, [1980] 2010), ch. 1. This appendix is basically a summary of *Unconditional Surrender*.

11. Chaps. 3, 4.

12. Chapter 18.

tance of the earth, for the meek shall inherit the earth (Matt. 5:5).[13] Christ, who claimed to be meek (Matt. 11:29), was the one who drove the money-changers from the temple (Matt. 21:12)[14] and called the Pharisees sons of the devil (John 8:44). *Meekness before God gives man dominion over nature.*

> When I consider thy heavens, the work of thy fingers, the moon and the stars, which thou hast ordained; What is man, that thou art mindful of him? and the son of man, that thou visitest him? For thou hast made him a little lower than the angels, and hast crowned him with glory and honour. Thou madest him to have dominion over the works of thy hands; thou hast put all things under his feet: All sheep and oxen, yea, and the beasts of the field; the fowl of the air, and the fish of the sea, and whatsoever passeth through the paths of the seas. O LORD our LORD, how excellent is thy name in all the earth! (Ps. 8:3–9).[15]

Now we are made a little lower than the angels, but not forever. "Know ye not that we shall judge angels? how much more things that pertain to this life?" (I Cor. 6:3). Christians who retreat from the affairs of this world are, by their very actions, acknowledging the devil's view of God's sovereignty: Man does not have legitimate rule because God, in whose image man is made, does not have legitimate sovereignty. It should come as no surprise that as the doctrine of evolution has invaded the churches, the idea of meekness before God has departed. With it has departed the idea of man's legitimate rule over earthly affairs. Christians today are in full retreat almost everywhere.

I have noted that God is transcendent to, yet immanent to, His creation. Man, created in God's image, occupies an analogical position in the creation. He is under many of nature's laws, yet he is simultaneously above nature as God's subordinate sovereign. Gilkey, the neo-orthodox theologian, has called attention to this dual position of man.

> History takes on meaning, then, when man not only sees himself as a creature in a "good" nature, but, more importantly, has distinguished himself from nature. He must realize that he alone among God's creatures is not completely dominated by nature; he must become conscious of his own unique capacity for self-direction and meaning, and therefore of being in some sense transcendent to the repetitive natural order in which he partic-

---

13. Gary North, *Priorities and Dominion: An Economic Commentary on Matthew*, 2nd ed. (Dallas, Georgia: Point Five Press, [2000] 2012), ch. 4.

14. *Ibid.*, ch. 42.

15. Gary North, *Confidence and Dominion: An Economic Commentary on Psalms* (Dallas, Georgia: Point Five Press, 2012), ch. 3.

ipates.... If man is understood as totally out of relation to nature because
he is regarded as purely soul or mind, or if man is understood as totally
immersed in nature and so as purely creature, then no understanding of
history arises. Greek idealism lost a sense of history because it could not
understand the value of the natural world and of time [pure transcendence—G.N.]; Greek naturalism never achieved historical consciousness
because it understood existence only in terms of the cycles of natural life
[pure immanence—G.N.].[16]

Man's tool of dominion over nature is law. God has established patterns of regularity in the mind of man (logic) and in the creation
(natural law). He has also established ethical and social laws by His
revealed word. Rebellious man cannot acknowledge the fact that
God's sovereign word undergirds natural law, human logic, and ethical (revealed) law. The self-proclaimed autonomous man cannot even
explain the relationship between the logic of his own mind—especially mathematical logic—and the external universe he perceives,
although his science demands that such a relationship exist.[17] The
work of the law is in men's hearts (Rom. 2:15).[18] God established His
covenant with men, and His ordinances are continual (Jer. 33:25–26;
Heb. 8:10–12; 10:15–17). Our universe is orderly (Prov. 30:24–28).
It is orderly because God is its Creator (Ps. 136:6–9; Prov. 8:22–31).
Therefore, He calls us to repentance: "Now therefore hearken unto
me, O ye children: for blessed are they that keep my ways" (Prov.
8:32). "Let us hear the conclusion of the whole matter: Fear God, and
keep his commandments: for this is the whole duty of man" (Eccl.
12:13).

This is God's universe; He does as He pleases with it. Here is the
primary lesson from the book of Job. Nevertheless, men are to gain
power over earthly affairs through the godly exercise of biblical law
(Deut. 8). God covenants with men in terms of His law; though men
violate His statutes, yet He still shows mercy to many, as chapters 5–8
of the epistle to the Romans indicate. God's covenant, through grace,
is sure, for man can safely trust in God's word. Because of Christ's
sacrifice on the cross, God's wrath is placated (Rom. 5:8). Men can

---

16. Gilkey, *Maker of Heaven and Earth*, pp. 203–4. Cf. Stanley L. Jaki, *The Road of
Science and the Ways to God* (Chicago: University of Chicago Press, 1978), ch. 1.

17. Cf. Eugene Wigner, "The Unreasonable Effectiveness of Mathematics in the Nat-
ural Sciences," *Communications on Pure and Applied Mathematics*, XIII (1960), pp. 1–14.
Cf. Van Til, *Christian-Theistic Evidences*, Vol. VI of *In Defense of the Faith* (Den Dulk
Christian Foundation, 1975), chaps. 6, 7.

18. North, *Cooperation and Dominion*, ch. 3.

therefore subdue the earth in confidence through God's law (Gen. 9:1–7), for "the earth hath he given to the children of men" (Ps. 115:16).

G. Fall and Restoration

By breaking the law of God, Adam brought destruction to humanity (Rom. 5:12–21). Deny this historic event, and you deny the doctrine of original sin. Deny the doctrine of original sin, and man is left without an understanding of his desperate plight. He will think that his own efforts can bring him eternal life. Without a comprehension of the effects, both in time and eternity, of the ethical rebellion of man, it becomes impossible to appreciate the extent of Christ's atoning sacrifice on the cross. Theological modernism, so closely linked with an evolutionary cosmology, has produced precisely this state of disbelief.

Man's ethical rebellion took place in time and on earth. The death and resurrection of Christ also took place in time and on earth. The firstfruits of the new heaven and new earth are now manifested and will continue to manifest themselves in time and on earth. As men subdue their own hearts in terms of God's law, they work out their gift of salvation (Phil. 2:12).[19] God's gift of sanctification, personal and social, is added unto His great gift of personal justification. God gives the increase (I Cor. 3:7). Every good gift is from God (James 1:17).[20] The possibility of the restoration of the external world is set before God's people (Deut. 8; 28; Isa. 2; 65; 66).

The Fall of man involved a false claim of divinity on the part of man. Man, following the devil's lead, came to the conclusion that his own word, rather than God's, is ultimately creative. He made himself the judge of the reality of God's word. He would stand between God and the devil to test which one was telling the truth. He made his own hypothetical neutrality as the standard of judgment. He wanted to determine good and evil (Gen. 3:5), for knowledge is always preliminary to the exercise of power. This was the sin of pride (Isa. 14:12–15). Such a path leads to destruction (Isa. 14:16–23). Man is supposed to think God's thoughts after Him, not attempt to be an autonomous creature. When man becomes humble in all his ways before God, victory is within his grasp, in time and on earth: "And it shall come to pass, if thou shalt hearken diligently unto the voice of the LORD thy

---

19. Gary North, *Ethics and Dominion: An Economic Commentary on the Epistles* (Dallas, Georgia: Point Five Press, 2012), ch. 10.

20. *Ibid.*, ch. 35.

God, to observe and to do all his commandments which I command thee this day, that the LORD thy God will set thee on high above all nations of the earth: And all these blessings shall come on thee, and overtake thee, if thou shalt hearken unto the voice of the LORD thy God" (Deut. 28:1–2). Or, in other words, "But seek ye first the kingdom of God, and his righteousness; and all these things shall be added unto you" (Matt. 6:33).[21] Christ is given all power (Matt. 28:18).[22] He gives power to us.

H. Time and Development

"And as it is appointed unto men once to die, but after this the judgment: So Christ was once offered to bear the sins of many; and unto them that look for him shall he appear the second time without sin unto salvation" (Heb. 9:27–28). History has meaning; it determines the place of each man in eternity. "Every man's work shall be made manifest: for the day shall declare it, because it shall be revealed by fire; and the fire shall try every man's work of what sort it is. If any man's work abide which he hath built thereupon, he shall receive a reward. If any man's work shall be burned, he shall suffer loss: but he himself shall be saved; yet so as by fire" (I Cor. 3:13–15).[23] History had a beginning (Gen. 1:1), and the fallen earth shall have an end (I Cor. 15).[24] Therefore, in absolute opposition to ancient pagan philosophies, the Bible teaches that time is linear. It is also limited. Only after the final judgment shall the burden of time be removed from this world (Rev. 10:6). God is the ruler of time.

Sanctification in a personal sense is a progressive process, after God has imparted the perfect sanctification of Christ to us at the moment of regeneration. Paul spoke of running the good race (I Cor. 9:24) and fighting the good fight (II Tim. 4:7). As with the individual who strives against sin in his own life (Eph. 6:10–18), so it is with Christian institutions and nations. The earth is to be subdued to the glory of God, not just in eternity, but in time—not just after the final judgment, but before it, when sinners are still alive on earth (Isa. 65:20).[25] History has purpose, direction, and meaning, precisely be-

---

21. North, *Priorities and Dominion*, ch. 15.

22. *Ibid.*, ch. 48.

23. Gary North, *Judgment and Dominion: An Economic Commentary on First Corinthians*, 2nd ed. (Dallas, Georgia: Point Five Press, [2001] 2012), ch. 3.

24. *Ibid.*, ch. 16.

25. Gary North, *Restoration and Dominion: An Economic Commentary on the Prophets* (Dallas, Georgia: Point Five Press, 2012), ch. 20.

cause God's decree controls all events. Ours is a personal universe, not an impersonal, chance multiverse. Ours is a providential world. As Gilkey wrote: "Now in a world created by a transcendent and purposive God, such an ultimate coherence and significance is possible.... The belief that existence finds its ultimate origin in God sets each creaturely life in a context of coherence and significance impossible on any other terms.... And the sole basis for such a faith is the knowledge of the Creator. Without such knowledge, there is no basis for this context for coherence and significance, and without that context the meaning of life quickly evaporates."[26] If a neo-orthodox theologian can see this so clearly, why is the doctrine of creation so neglected in the pulpits of the supposedly evangelical churches? This optimism concerning God's decree in history made modern science possible.[27] Without faith in the possibility of progress, science loses meaning. By destroying the faith in creation, apostate science has almost entirely eroded the foundation of its own existence.[28]

Because God's eternal decree undergirds time, and because in His grace He assures His people that "all things work together for good to them that love God, to them who are the called according to his purpose" (Rom. 8:28),[29] Christians need not fear time. Time brings with it the curses imposed by God as punishment for the rebellion of man, and not until death is finally subdued and the new heavens and new earth appear will time lose all of its characteristic burdens, but Christians are not time's prisoners. Our citizenship is in heaven (Phil. 3:20). Unlike the pagans, whose chaos festivals like Mardi Gras and Carnival have symbolized a desperate attempt to escape time,[30] Christians are told to walk circumspectly, redeeming the time, that is, buying it back, prolonging it, conserving it, and using it diligently (Eph. 5:16). It is a tool for one's calling, a gift of God to His people. It is a resource to be used efficiently for the glory of God, and not a burden to be escaped by means of ritual debauchery or bloody revo-

---

26. Gilkey, *Maker of Heaven and Earth*, pp. 188–89.

27. *Ibid.*, pp. 65–66. See also Jaki, *Road of Science*, chaps. 1, 6, 19, 20.

28. Cf. Gunther Stent, *The Coming of the Golden Age: A View of the End of Progress* (Garden City, New York: Natural History Press, 1969).

29. North, *Cooperation and Dominion*, ch. 6.

30. For various examples of this attempted "escape from time," see the works of the comparative anthropologist, Mircea Eliade, such as *Patterns in Comparative Religion* (New York: Sheed & Ward, 1958), pp. 399–407; *Myth and Reality* (New York: Harper Torchbook, [1963] 1968), chaps. 3, 5; *Cosmos and History: The Myth of the Eternal Return* (New York: Harper Torchbook, [1954] 1959).

lution.[31] Time is therefore a means of production, not the justification for destruction.

I. Knowledge and Interpretation

I have already noted the scriptural instruction concerning God's wisdom as the foundation of the creation (Prov. 3:19–20). The revelation of God to man is the source of all human wisdom. Psalm 119, the longest chapter in the Bible, stands as the great passage dealing with the close relationship between wisdom and God's holy law: "Thy word is a lamp unto my feet, and a light unto my path" (Ps. 119:105). "Deal with thy servant according unto thy mercy, and teach me thy statutes. I am thy servant; give me understanding, that I may know thy testimonies" (Ps. 119:124–25). But it is in Job that we find most succinctly stated the basis of our knowledge: "But there is a spirit in man: and the inspiration of the Almighty giveth them understanding" (Job 32:8).

Elihu, the youthful fourth companion who came to visit Job, challenged Job and the other three "comforters" for their failure to consider the ways of a totally sovereign God.[32] Apart from God the sovereign Creator, no knowledge is possible. He has made all things, directed all events, and He comprehends all facts. We, as God's images, are to think God's thoughts after Him: "Behold, I am according to thy wish in God's stead: I also am formed out of the clay" (Job 33:6). It is only by God's grace, Elihu announced, that we are given knowledge: "Why dost thou strive against him? for he giveth not account of any of his matters. For God speaketh once, yea twice, yet man perceiveth it not. In a dream, in a vision of the night, when deep sleep falleth upon men, in slumberings upon the bed; Then he openeth the ears of men, and sealeth their instruction, That he may withdraw man from his [man's] purpose, and hide pride from man" (Job 33:13–17). God, through His gracious revelation, restrains the hands of evil men who are bent on destruction. He is not compelled to do so; His mercy is unearned by the recipients.

God finally replied to Job as Elihu had, announcing that He alone possesses original knowledge. He drove this point home by referring back to the creation; He is God the Creator![33]

---

31. Gary North, *Marx's Religion of Revolution: Regeneration Through Chaos* (Tyler, Texas: Institute for Christian Economics, [1968] 1989).

32. North, *Predictability and Dominion*, ch. 5.

33. *Ibid.*, ch. 6.

Where wast thou when I laid the foundations of the earth? declare, if thou hast understanding. Who hath laid the measures thereof, if thou knowest? or who hath stretched the line upon it? Whereupon are the foundations thereof fastened? or who laid the cornerstone thereof; When the morning stars sang together, and all the sons of God shouted for joy?...hast thou perceived the breadth of the earth? declare if thou knowest it all. Where is the way where light dwelleth? and as for darkness, where is the place thereof, That thou shouldst take it to the bound thereof, and that thou shouldest know the paths of the house thereof?...Knowest thou the ordinances of heaven? canst thou set the dominion thereof in the earth? Canst thou lift up thy voice to the clouds, that abundance of waters may cover thee? Canst thou send lightnings, that they may go, and say unto thee, Here we are? Who hath put wisdom in the inward parts? or who hath given understanding to the heart? (Job 38:4–7, 18–20, 33–36).

The lessons of these latter passages in the book of Job were repeated by Paul: "For who hath known the mind of the Lord? or who hath been his counselor? Or who hath first given to him, and it shall be recompensed unto him again? For of him, and through him, and to him, are all things: to whom be glory for ever. Amen" (Rom. 11:34–36). As the Creator, He *controls*; as the Redeemer, He *reveals*. All things are known to Him: A Psalmist wrote: "I will praise thee; for I am fearfully and wonderfully made: marvelous are thy works; and that my soul knoweth right well. My substance was not hid from thee, when I was made in secret, and curiously wrought in the lowest parts of the earth. Thine eyes did see my substance, yet being unperfect; and in thy book all my members were written, which in continuance were fashioned, when as yet there was none of them" (Ps. 139:14–16). God knows all things because He creates all things; His book sets forth what is or is not possible and actual. And in grace He redeems: "He that chastiseth the heathen, shall not he correct? he that teacheth man knowledge, shall not he know? The LORD knoweth the thoughts of man, that they are vanity. Blessed is the man whom thou chastenest, O LORD, and teachest him out of thy law; That thou mayest give him rest from the days of adversity, until the pit be digged for the wicked" (Ps. 94:10–13). God has revealed Himself preeminently through His Son (John 1). "Father, I will that they also, whom thou hast given me, be with me where I am; that they may behold my glory, which thou hast given me: for thou lovedst me before the foundation of the world" (John 17:24).

Men are not autonomous from God; they are *analogous* to God. Their knowledge should therefore be analogical to God's knowledge, that is, in conformity to His revelation concerning Himself, man, and the creation. Men are told that they are not the source of knowledge, because they are not the source of the creation. They have knowledge only to the extent that they think God's thoughts after Him. Even in their rebellious thought, sinners can be said to see the world only in terms of borrowed capital. To use Van Til's analogy, the child must sit on his father's lap in order to slap his face. He wrote, "Christianity is the only reasonable position to hold. It is not merely as reasonable as other positions, or a bit more reasonable than other positions; it alone is the natural and reasonable position for man to take."[34] Apart from God's revelation, all men are blind. God, in fact, deliberately blinds the minds of some men, so that they will not see the truth and be converted; Christ specifically said that this is why He spoke in parables (citing Isa. 6:9–10 in Matt. 13:10–15). Sinful men want to believe lies, so God sends them lies (Ezek. 14:9–11; II Thess. 2:11–12). "All scripture is given by inspiration of God, and is profitable for doctrine, for reproof, for correction, for instruction in righteousness: That the man of God may be perfect, thoroughly furnished unto all good works" (II Tim. 3:16–17). In all true knowledge there is grace. God the Redeemer is God the Creator. What He reveals is true because He created and sustains all things. Were He not the Creator, He could not be the Redeemer. His revelation could always be suspect—another possible interpretation in a random multiverse. In fact, His revelation of what He is and does would have to be false, since it is not compatible with a random multiverse. A God who is not the Creator is not the God of the Bible.

J. Ownership and Stewardship

God, as Creator, is owner of the universe. This is stated throughout the Bible, but especially in the Psalms. "The earth is the LORD's, and the fulness thereof; the world, and they that dwell therein. For he hath founded it upon the seas, and established it upon the floods. Who shall ascend into the hill of the LORD? or who shall stand in his holy place?" (Ps. 24:1–3).[35] "The heavens are thine, the earth also is thine: as for the world and the fulness thereof, thou hast founded them" (Ps. 89:11). Perhaps most famously: "For every beast of the forest is mine, and the cattle upon a thousand hills" (Ps. 50:10).[36] This

---

34. Van Til, *Common Grace and the Gospel*, p. 62.
35. North, *Confidence and Dominion*, ch. 6.
36. *Ibid.*, ch. 11.

being true, then man, as God's image-bearer, possesses subordinate ownership: "The heaven, even the heavens, are the LORD's: but the earth hath he given to the children of men" (Ps. 115:16). The foundation of ownership on earth is God's creation of the earth.

1. Limited Rights

God places limitations on the exercise of the rights of property. Secularists, whether Marxists, Keynesians, or anarchists, do not acknowledge these restrictions. God requires the tithe, and the whole book of Malachi is devoted to an exposition of the ethical and social impact of tithe-rejection.[37] In the Old Testament economy, God placed restrictions on the practice of lending money, prohibiting the taking of interest from a poverty-stricken fellow believer (Ex. 22:25–27).[38] There is no indication that this restriction is no longer binding.[39] During the time that Israel served God as His throne, containing the tabernacle and the Holy of Holies, it was also illegal to sell the family's land for a period longer than 49 years; in the jubilee year, all land was to revert to the original owner or his family (Lev. 25:23–28).[40] "The land shall not be sold for ever: for the land is mine; for ye are strangers and sojourners with me" (Lev. 25:23). With the rending of the veil of the temple, which had separated the Holy of Holies, at the point of Christ's death (Matt. 27:50–51), this unique position of the land of Israel departed from God's economy, but the general ownership of the whole earth by God still holds true. *Ownership is never autonomous. It is always covenantal.*

2. Personal Stewardship

Ownership thus involves personal stewardship. The use of property is bounded by the laws governing the various possessors: individuals, civil governments, private corporations, families, churches. Each has its own rules and regulations set by the Bible. None can ever be the exclusive owner, for no human or earthly sphere of life is ex-

---

37. Gary North, *The Covenantal Tithe* (Powder Springs, Georgia: American Vision, 2011).

38. Gary North, *Authority and Dominion: An Economic Commentary on Exodus* (Dallas, Georgia: Point Five Press, 2012), Part 3, *Tools of Dominion* (1990), ch. 53.

39. Gary North, "Stewardship, Investment, and Usury: Financing the Kingdom of God," in R. J. Rushdoony, *The Institutes of Biblical Law* (Nutley, New Jersey: Craig Press, 1973), Appendix 3. This is also reprinted in my book, *An Introduction to Christian Economics* (Nutley, New Jersey: Craig Press, 1973), ch. 31.

40. For an analysis of the Hebrew restrictions on the sale of land, see Gary North, *Boundaries and Dominion: An Economic Commentary on Leviticus*, 2nd ed. (Dallas, Georgia: Point Five Press, [1994] 2012), ch. 27.

clusively divine. As Proverbs 20 through 29 indicates, men are to be charitable, industrious, honest, just; in short, they are to be faithful stewards of the goods that God loans or leases to them. Each institution or individual has some legitimate rights of ownership that may not be infringed upon by another human sovereignty. Ahab was not acting legally when he killed Naboth to steal his vineyard (I Kings 21:18–19),[41] even though he was the king. God is the source of all wealth, not men, states, churches, or the devil (Deut. 8:18;[42] James 1:17[43]). Thus, when the devil offered Christ the world in return for Christ's worship of him, he was making an impossible offer (Matt. 4:9).[44] It was not his to give.

The cosmic personalism of the Bible's universe is obviously in total opposition to the autonomous multiverse of modern man. This is God's universe. He brings blessings and curses as He sees fit (Job 38–41),[45] but He has covenanted Himself to bring earthly blessings and troubles to communities (though not necessarily to individuals) in terms of their covenantal responses to Him. Deuteronomy 8 and 28 outline this relationship: blessings for obedience; curses for rebellion. All human sovereignties are derivative. All attempts to escape the limitations set by God on the exercise of property rights are therefore self-defeating.

K. The Good Creation

"And God saw every thing that he had made, and, behold, it was very good. And the evening and the morning were the sixth day" (Gen. 1:31).[46] The creation was originally good. This included even Satan himself. At a point in time he rebelled. He then led Adam and Eve into this same path of destruction (Gen. 3). As Van Til pointed out so well, our parents in Eden were tempted to think of themselves as determiners of reality. They would test God's word to see if it would hold true. They placed their own logic and interpretation of the universe above God's interpretation. Thus, they viewed the universe as problematical and therefore God's word as problematical. They denied the absolute

---

41. Gary North, *Disobedience and Defeat: An Economic Commentary on the Historical Books* (Dallas, Georgia: Point Five Press, 2012), ch. 22.

42. Gary North, *Inheritance and Dominion: An Economic Commentary on Deuteronomy*, (Dallas, Georgia: Point Five Press, [1999] 2012), ch. 22.

43. North, *Ethics and Dominion*, ch. 35.

44. North, *Priorities and Dominion*, ch. 3.

45. North, *Predictability and Dominion*, ch. 6.

46. Chapter 5.

sovereignty of God's word over history and nature. It was this that constituted the Fall—knowing (determining) not only good and evil, but also knowing (determining) the possible and impossible.[47]

1. Adam's Sin

Through Adam, sin entered the world (Rom. 5:12). Man's rebellion, like Satan's, was therefore ethical. It was not metaphysical, i.e., having to do with some abstract "being" or essential reality. It was not some flaw in man's being, but a willful rejection of God's sovereignty. It was an attempt to play God. It was a matter of purpose and will, not a defect in creation. Man did not slide into a lower realm of "Being in general"; he simply rebelled. Sin, therefore, is not a built-in eternal aspect of the creation. The fault was in the will of Satan and man: "Let no man say when he is tempted, I am tempted of God: for God cannot be tempted with evil, neither tempteth he any man: But every man is tempted, when he is drawn away of his own lust, and enticed. Then when lust hath conceived, it bringeth forth sin; and sin, when it is finished, bringeth forth death" (James 1:13–15).

Man's ethical rebellion led God to curse the world (Gen. 3:17–18).[48] Men are now ethically blind and willfully rebellious (Rom. 1). But this evil is restrained, as in the case of the Tower of Babel (Gen. 11:6).[49] It must not be regarded as a permanent phenomenon. The final end of rebellion is the lake of fire, into which hell, death, Satan, and all his followers will be dumped on the day of judgment (Matt. 25:41; Rev. 20:13–14). It is a place of true existence—the eternal reminder of the results of ethical rebellion, eternally glorifying God and His justice—but a place of utter impotence. But even as hell is only a temporary dwelling place of disembodied rebellious souls, so is heaven an equally temporary dwelling place for disembodied regenerate souls. Heaven is not a place of total bliss and perfection, just as hell is not a place of total desolation, for final bliss and final desolation come only after souls and bodies are reunited on the day of judgment (I Cor. 15:39–57). The souls of the slain saints of God are in heaven, John wrote, crying, "How long, O Lord, holy and true, dost thou not judge and avenge our blood on them that dwell on the earth?" (Rev. 6:10). Yet even this scene is temporary, for evil is limited in time, however strong it may appear prior to the final judgment.

---

47. Van Til, *Survey of Christian Epistemology*, pp. 19–20.
48. Chapter 12.
49. Chapter 19.

2. Restoration in History

God has promised a final restoration of edenic bliss for His elect
(Rev. 21; 22). Yet He graciously gives us a foretaste of this ultimate
internal and external victory as an "earnest"—down payment—on our
blessed hope. Isaiah 65 and 66 tell of a preliminary manifestation
of the new heavens and new earth, prior to the day of judgment, for
in these promised days of earthly peace, there shall be sinners still
alive (Isa. 65:20).[50] Similarly, Ezekiel 37 presents us with the famous
vision of the valley of dry bones. The dead shall be resurrected. But
this passage can be interpreted in terms of spiritual death as well as
physical death. In fact, it must be seen as applying to both forms of
death and both forms of resurrection. Ezekiel was called to "Proph-
esy upon these bones"; it was a preaching ministry to the spiritually
dead people of Israel. Men are spiritually dead (Luke 9:60); he who
believes in Christ "is passed from death unto life" (John 5:24). Ezekiel 37 therefore promises an age of spiritual rebirth as well as a day of
judgment and resurrection. "For this cause was the gospel preached
also to them that are dead, that they might be judged according to
men in the flesh, but live according to God in the spirit" (I Peter 4:6).
Spiritual death is the foretaste of physical and eternal death; spiritual
life is the foretaste of physical and eternal life. God promises to raise
up the dead bones of the valley, spiritually and physically. The image
loses its impact if either aspect is ignored.

Chapters 8–10[51] and 12–14 of the book of Zechariah are deeply
imbued with the spirit and language of external victory over evil. The
restoration of godly rule is prophesied in all of its force and clarity.
Restoration shall be in time and on earth; the rule of the saints on
earth is a preliminary of the day on which men shall judge the angels (I Cor. 6:3).[52] The nations and their false gods will be utterly de-
feated, wrote Jeremiah (Jer. 10:10–11). These false gods "shall perish
from the earth, and from under these heavens" (vs. 11). In Daniel's
explanation of King Nebuchadnezzar's dream, we learn of the great
kingdom stone of God: "...the stone that smote the image became a
great mountain, and filled the whole earth" (Dan. 2:35b). *Restoration
is the promise of the prophetic vision.*

How does God intend to bring this about? Not by some discontinuous political event, or some miraculous intervention into the daily

---

50. North, *Restoration and Dominion*, ch. 16.
51. *Ibid.*, ch. 33.
52. North, *Judgment and Dominion*, ch. 6.

processes of the world, but by steady spiritual progress. "For whatsoever is born of God overcometh the world: and this is the victory that overcometh the world, even our faith. Who is he that overcometh the world, but he that believeth that Jesus is the Son of God?" (I John 5:4–5). The day of judgment itself is not a discontinuous event in the midst of some steady, relentless spiritual decline, but rather a discontinuous event which will have been preceded by long ages of spiritual and social sanctification (I Cor. 15:25–28), and which will have been briefly interrupted at the end by a rebellion of a tiny minority ("remnant") of Satan's host (Rev. 19:19–21). Then the whole creation will be restored.

> For I reckon that the sufferings of this present time are not worthy to be compared with the glory which shall be revealed in us. For the earnest expectation of the creature waiteth for the manifestation of the sons of God. For the creature was made subject to vanity, not willingly, but by reason of him who hath subjected the same in hope: because the creature itself also shall be delivered from the bondage of corruption into the glorious liberty of the children of God. For we know that the whole creation groaneth and travaileth in pain together until now. And not only they, but ourselves also, which have the firstfruits of the Spirit, even we ourselves groan within ourselves, waiting for the adoption, to wit, the redemption of our body (Rom. 8:18–23).[53]

3. Blessings in History

Outward ethical conformity to God's Bible-revealed law brings God's covenantal blessings. The very blessings will tempt those who are only outwardly obedient to forget God and violate His statutes. But the regenerate community will use His blessings to further His glory and expand His kingdom into all areas of life. Thus, special grace is necessary to maintain common grace's blessings. (By common grace, theologians mean—or should mean—the unearned gifts of God to all men, including the unregenerate. All men deserve death as a result of Adam's sin [Rom. 5]; life itself is a sign of common grace, that is, an unearned gift.) We learn in Deuteronomy 8 and 28 that the external world of nature responds in terms of a community's outward conformity to or rejection of God's law. Thus, as always, ethical questions are primary, not metaphysical questions of being. The creation itself is closely liked to man's ethical response to God. It was cursed when man sinned, and it will be restored progressively as men are conformed once again to God's legal requirements.

---

53. North, *Cooperation and Dominion*, ch. 5.

God makes it plain that His requirements are ethical rather than metaphysical. Magic is therefore rejected as a means of pleasing God. Men do not manipulate God by manipulating some aspect of the creation. The magical formula, "as above, so below," which undergirds astrology, divination, and other forms of ritualistic manipulation, is a false formula. Man is only analogical to God, not a participant with God in some universal "being." God requires ritual, but not ritual devoid of spiritual content. "Will the LORD be pleased with thousands of rams, or with ten thousands of rivers of oil? shall I give my firstborn for my transgression, the fruit of my body for the sin of my soul? He hath showed thee, O man, what is good; and what doth the LORD require of thee, but to do justly, and to love mercy, and to walk humbly with thy God?" (Mic. 6:7–8). This is why God can promise external restoration; it will have been preceded by personal regeneration in the elect, and by outward conformity to the law of God by both the regenerate and the unregenerate.

L. Fatherhood and Adoption

As far as man is concerned, no more crucial distinction in the Bible exists: *created sonship* and *adopted sonship*. Men's eternal destinies rest upon this distinction. God has created all men. Paul, preaching to the Athenians, announced that God "hath made of one blood all nations of men for to dwell on all the face of the earth" (Acts 17:26a), and therefore all men are brothers in the flesh. This constitutes the equality of all men in Adam—absolute total depravity, regardless of race or color—and it serves as *the sole point of contact* in all men for the message of the gospel, since all men are created in God's image. There can be no other point of contact, certainly not in hypothetically "neutral" logical proofs of God.[54] Paul preached to the pagans of Athens, not using logical proofs of God, but using an appeal to their common, but sinful, humanity.

The Christian goal is not the universal brotherhood of man on earth and in time. We already have the brotherhood of man; we have had it since Cain and Abel walked on earth. What the Bible calls for is *the adoption of the elect into the family of God*. It is no accident that the

---

54. For a Christian refutation of the so-called "proofs of God," see Van Til, *The Defense of the Faith*, 4th ed. (Phillipsburg, New Jersey: P & R, [1955] 2008), pp. 332–44; cf. *Christian-Theistic Evidences*. Van Til asserted that the premise of all human thought must be the sovereign, trinitarian, Creator God of the Bible. Anything other than this as an operating presupposition is simply argumentation from a void to a void.

Gospel of John begins with a call to adopted sonship: "He came unto his own, and his own received him not. But as many as received him, to them gave he power to become the sons of God, even to them that believe on his name: Which were born, not of blood, nor of the will of the flesh, nor of the will of man, but of God" (John 1:11–13). The regenerate "have received the Spirit of adoption" (Rom. 8:15). This is God's greatest gift to individual men: ethical adoption by the imputation of Christ's righteousness into God's holy (set apart) family. "Even so we, when we were children, were in bondage under the elements of the world; But when the fulness of the time was come, God sent forth his Son, made of a woman, made under the law, To redeem them that were under the law, that we might receive the adoption of sons" (Gal. 4:3–5).

Adoption is exclusively in terms of God's total sovereignty and total predestination. "According as he hath chosen us in him before the foundation of the world, that we should be holy and without blame before him in love: Having predestinated us unto the adoption of children by Jesus Christ to himself, according to the good pleasure of his will" (Eph. 1:4-5). It could not be made any plainer than this. The children of God by adoption were chosen before the foundation of the world, even as God chose Jacob and hated Esau, before either was born or could do evil (Rom. 9:10-13). (The amazing fact, it should be noted, is that God loved Jacob, not that he hated the unregenerate, though unborn, Esau. Secularists and Arminians would paint the picture as a mirror image to the Bible's: it seems astounding to them that God could hate Esau.) In short, wrote Paul, "They which are the children of the flesh, these are not the children of God: but the children of the promise are counted for the seed" (Rom 9:8).

God imposes a basic division between men. There is no universal gift of peace on earth, good will toward men. Jesus' own account of His ministry could not be any plainer: "Think not that I am come to send peace on earth: I came not to send peace, but a sword. For I am come to set a man at variance against his father, and the daughter against her mother, and the daughter-in-law against her mother-in-law. And a man's foes shall be they of his own household" (Matt. 10:34–36).

There are therefore two distinct brotherhoods, for there are two fatherhoods: God the Father-Creator of all men and God the Father-Redeemer of some men. God disinherited the sons of the first Adam; He adopts sinners because of the work on the cross of His own Son, the

second Adam (I Cor. 15:45). All men are *brothers metaphysically*, a fact
which, were it not for God's saving grace (Eph. 2:8-9), would unite all
men in destruction. Not all men are *brothers ethically*; the brotherhood
of the promise of grace is limited to God's predestined elect.

M. Creation and Covenant

The Fall of man was ethical, not metaphysical. The creation therefore was originally good. The concern of the gospel of God's grace
through Jesus Christ is with adoption. This means that God's concern is exclusively covenantal. God covenants Himself with a chosen
and exclusive people. He will be their God; they will be His people.
He acts on their behalf as their sovereign monarch. He delivers them
from evil. He intervenes in a special way in the history of His people.
The so-called "two tables of the law" given by God to Moses were
not separated in terms of *two sets of five commandments each* (with the
second half—social laws—somehow less crucial than the first half, or
spiritual commandments). The two tables were almost certainly *two
sets of the same ten laws*, one serving as a copy for God the King, and
the other serving as a copy for His covenanted people. This was the
standard practice of kings in the second millennium, B.C.[55] God the
sovereign monarch sets forth the terms of His treaty with His people;
His people must respond in obedience, or else suffer the wrath of the
monarch's hand upon them. (This is the meaning of both circumci-
sion and baptism; an oath sign promising blessings to the faithful or
wrath to the unfaithful.)[56]

The prophets, time and again, confronted the people of Israel with
the claims of God. They recapitulated His dealings with them. The
God of Abraham, Isaac, and Jacob, who delivered the captive people
out of the bondage of Egypt, who led them into a promised land, now
calls His people to repentance. The focus is on the history and provi-
sions of the covenant. Stephen, in his testimony before his accusers,
began with God's call to Abraham to leave pagan Mesopotamia (Acts
7:2). In terms of the rituals of the chosen people, God is primarily
the God of the covenant. Ritually, He is only marginally the God
of Creation. In only one biblical passage, Psalm 136, is the creation

---

55. Meredith G. Kline, *Treaty of the Great King* (Grand Rapids, Michigan: Eerdmans,
1963), ch. 1.

56. Meredith G. Kline, *By Oath Consigned* (Grand Rapids: Eerdmans, 1969). Kline is
as superb in his studies of the meaning of covenant as he is appalling in his "framework
hypothesis" concerning the creation.

mentioned as part of the otherwise familiar recapitulation of God's covenant history.

This aspect of Bible history is in stark contrast to virtually all pagan and "primitive" (that is, degenerate) cultures. Pagans pay exclusive attention to the creation in their accounts of God's activities. The primary Christian and Hebrew festivals are associated with the Passover, that is, the exodus from Egypt. The first communion service held by the Christians was during the Passover (Matt. 26:17–35). Paul wrote, "Purge out therefore the old leaven, that ye may be a new lump, as ye are unleavened. For even Christ our passover is sacrificed for us: Therefore let us keep the feast, not with old leaven, neither with the leaven of malice and wickedness; but with the unleavened bread of sincerity and truth" (I Cor. 5:7–8). *The Passover feast was covenantal and ethical. The pagan creation festivals are exclusively metaphysical.* They assume a common bond between God and man—a common bond of pure being. The Passover assumed a covenantal and ethical bond between God and His people; in the communion service, this is symbolized by the eating of bread and the drinking of wine. Christ's body and blood are symbolized, and men participate in His perfect humanity. They hope for the day when they shall be recreated and dressed in perfection like His body (Phil. 3:21). But we can never participate in Christ's divinity. God is fundamentally different from man.

The pagan festivals have basic similarities. They all are based on the idea that the world was created by God in a massive struggle with chaos. Creation was not out of nothing; it was the triumph of order over chaos. God therefore is said to confront chaos. The implication is that God, no less than men, faces zones of pure chance and unpredictability. He faces a world that is only partially known to Him. In other words, we are like God, only less powerful and less knowledgeable, relatively speaking. By reenacting the original creation, men believe that they can participate in the original pre-time event. Men can share the act of creation, thereby escaping ritually (and, some cultures believe, actually) the bondage of time. Saturnalia, Mardi Gras, and Carnival are all chaos festivals. Laws are broken, mores are violated, masks are worn, and men are revitalized from below. They become co-creators, co-participants with God in the act of original creation.[57] The creation, since it was not an absolute creation out of nothing by the fiat word of a sovereign God, can therefore be thought of as just one more finite event, however important. Paradise is to be

---

57. See the references to the works of Mircea Eliade, footnote #30.

reestablished through ritual chaos—total moral discontinuity—which brings back the age of gold.

The biblical promise of the new creation is based upon the grace of a totally sovereign Creator. He restores men ethically. He puts His law in their hearts. This was the promise in Jeremiah 31:31–34; it was fulfilled by Christ (Heb. 8:9–13; 10:16–17). God's promises and His prophecies are being fulfilled or have been fulfilled in this age, the age of the church, the body of Christ. We can thus celebrate the covenant of God with the people of Israel, for we are called "the Israel of God" (Gal. 6:16).[58] Our celebrations are not disorderly, for they deny the existence of some metaphysical chaos confronting a limited God. Our rule is simple: "Let all things be done decently and in order" (I Cor. 14:40).

The celebrations of the church call us to acknowledge our total dependence, metaphysically and ethically, on the Creator God. He has covenanted with us out of mercy. We therefore do not celebrate the creation, for that act was exclusively God's as sovereign Creator. We had no part in it, due to the fact that we are the work of His hands. We do not participate in the acts of divinity, for there is an unbridgeable gulf between our being and God's being. The Son of God, through the incarnation, once walked on earth, perfectly human and perfectly divine, two natures in union but without intermixture. This is the foundation of our faith. Only through the greatest discontinuous event of all history—the incarnation of the Son of God—is man restored to wholeness. Christians therefore neglect the celebration of the creation, not because our God is not the Creator, but because He, and He alone, is the Creator. We do not attempt through ritual to participate in His divine acts or His divine being. We acknowledge the greatest of all distinctions, the Creator-creature distinction. And we announce, in confidence: "My help cometh from the LORD, which made heaven and earth" (Ps. 121:2).[59]

---

58. Roderick Campbell, *Israel and the New Covenant* (Tyler, Texas: Geneva Divinity School Press, [1954] 1982).

59. This essay first appeared in *The Journal of Christian Reconstruction*, I (Summer 1974), published by The Chalcedon Foundation. At the time that I wrote the original version of this essay, the crucially important works of the Benedictine scholar, Stanley Jaki, were not yet in print: *Science and Creation: From Eternal Cycles to an Oscillating Universe* (Edinburgh: Scottish Academic Press, [1974] 1980); *The Road of Science and the Ways to God*, op. cit., and *Cosmos and Creator* (Edinburgh: Scottish Academic Press, 1980). Jaki argued that without a concept of God, the Creator, and without faith in man's mind as competent to study the externally existent, orderly universe—faith in man as the image of God, in other words—there can be no scientific progress. Without

Conclusion

The doctrine of the six-day creation lies at the heart of biblical wisdom. God initially revealed Himself as the Creator who created all things in six days. Christians can accept this or not, but if they do not accept it, they lose access to a worldview that is provided only by God in His Bible. This worldview offers them unique insights into the way the social and economic world works. Without this worldview, Christians wind up baptizing this or that humanist outlook. They find themselves ensnared in the contradictions of humanism.

---

a concept of linear history, there can be no scientific progress. Jaki, as a Thomist, was a philosophical realist. He accepted as valid the proofs of God, something Van Til effectively refuted, at least insofar as such proofs begin with the assumption of the validity of neutral, autonomous reasoning. Nevertheless, Jaki's extraordinary scholarship makes plain one fact: that all modern science rests on presuppositions concerning nature's regularities and also on the interpretive ability of men's minds that are "borrowed premises." Only by assuming the validity of an essentially Christian view of man and the creation have Western scientists advanced their disciplines. And where these premises have not been accepted, there has been no scientific progress. Jaki's studies, along with those of the French scholar, Pierre Duhem, constitute some of the most remarkable works in historical revisionism that have ever been written. Anyone who is not thoroughly familiar with them cannot be taken seriously as an historian of science. This, it should be understood, in 2012 includes the vast majority of those who call themselves scientists. They are abysmally ignorant of the historical and philosophical roots of modern science.

APPENDIX E

WITNESSES AND JUDGES

And the LORD God commanded the man, saying, Of every tree of the garden thou mayest freely eat: But of the tree of the knowledge of good and evil, thou shalt not eat of it: for in the day that thou eatest thereof thou shalt surely die.

GENESIS 2:16–17

Good judgment. The Bible calls it wisdom. What is it worth to a godly man? This is what Solomon asked for (I Kings 3:9), and what the Book of Proverbs says is the most valuable asset that a person can seek (Prov. 1).

Adam was called upon by God to render good judgment. He was to exercise good judgment in three senses. The first sense was *economic or dominical judgment*, in the sense of technical and leadership skills, as a dominion man. Second, he was to exercise *judicial judgment*: to declare God's word in condemnation of God's enemies. Third, he was to exercise *moral judgment*. Most commentaries dwell exclusively on the moral aspect of Adam's Fall, but the dominical and judicial are equally important considerations.

The development of good *dominical judgment* as a godly subordinate was basic to Adam's calling before God. It is basic to humanity, for basic to humanity is the dominion assignment (Gen. 1:28).[1] Adam was placed in the garden temporarily in order to develop his dominion skills and judgment: managerial, agricultural, aesthetic, technological, etc. Later, he was to begin the conquest of the whole earth. *The garden of Eden was a training ground for him.* It was not to become a permanent residence. He could not stay there forever. He was to move out of the garden and into the world at large, bringing it under dominion. The garden was only a temporary residence.

---

1. Chapter 4.

The essence of good judgment in both the economic and judicial sense is the ability to "think God's thoughts after Him" as an ethically dependent subordinate. *Men are to exercise dominion over nature by remaining ethically subordinate to God.* Men are creatures. They are not to strive to attain exhaustive knowledge, which is an incommunicable attribute of God. They are to strive to organize the knowledge they possess in terms of the presuppositions and explicit revelations that God has given to man concerning the creation. God holds men responsible for such intellectual and moral subordination. He rewards them for obedience. *Thus, the starting-point of good judgment is man's affirmation of the reliability and ethically binding nature of God's word.* When men do not start with this presupposition, they cannot hope to exercise good judgment for very long.

A. Bearing False Witness

The serpent tempted mankind in a very specific way. He first raised doubts in Eve's mind concerning the reliability of her husband's testimony to her concerning God's word. "Hath God said, Ye shall not eat of every tree of the garden?" the serpent asked (Gen. 3:1). He quoted only part of God's word. Hadn't God opened up the entire garden to them?

Initially, she answered him properly. She told him of God's warning that they would die if they ate of one tree. So, the serpent escalated his attack: he denied that God's word is reliable. "Ye shall not surely die" (3:4). Then he made the accusation that God had a secret ulterior motive in establishing the prohibition: "For God doth know that in the day ye eat thereof, then your eyes shall be opened, and ye shall be as gods, knowing good and evil" (3:5). In other words, God is jealously monopolizing His position as the Lord of creation, a position that can and should be shared with others. Man, of course, should share in this lofty position, the serpent implied on behalf of Satan. He misled her, for Satan was the one with the ulterior motive: he believed that ultimately he should occupy God's position monopolistically.

Satan made a three-part claim: God's word is not what He says it is, God's position is not what He says it is, and the results of eating the forbidden fruit are not what God says they will be. In short, God is a liar. The heart of Satan's accusation against God was this: *God bears false witness concerning Himself and the creation.*

The phrase, "to know good and evil," implies power greater than mere intellectual comprehension. It implies the ability to *determine* good and evil, as Rushdoony has pointed out.[2] This is a God-like ability, and Adam and Eve desired it. So did Satan. Man hoped to make his own law, carrying out his will without interference from God or other men, and certainly without resistance from the creation. So did Satan. Neither man nor Satan achieved this goal.

Eve saw that the tree was good for food, for aesthetic pleasure ("pleasant to the eyes"), and for wisdom. She did not seek to confirm her new understanding of God's word with her husband. She sought autonomy of interpretation. She would test God's word for herself. She ate, and she gave her husband fruit to eat. The subordinate in the family took control of the situation. The results were predictable for those governed by God's word. Adam and Eve did not predict them.

Why did Satan begin by calling God's word into question? Because this was the essence of the temptation. The fruit was only the symbol; the reliability of God's word, and His authority to bring that word to pass, were the ultimate issues. Satan was challenging both. He was calling God a liar. He also was saying that God is not omnipotent: He cannot bring His word to pass. In short, Satan was saying that he was telling the truth, and that God was a false witness. Man had to decide. He had to make a judgment: Who was the false witness?

B. Two Witnesses

What modern commentators fail to emphasize, or even to recognize, is this: *The temptation in the garden was fundamentally a judicial proceeding.* Satan's agent was bringing a formal charge against God. The charge was bearing false witness. Yet this was more than bearing false witness; it was the charge of bearing false witness concerning God almighty. The serpent charged that God was not telling the truth about the "real" God. God later revealed to Moses that it is a capital crime to teach a family member to worship a false god (Deut. 13:6–11). Adam and Eve were the children of God and therefore deserving of death. But who would listen? To bring a charge of this magnitude against anyone, the accuser needs two witnesses (Num. 35:30). To begin his rebellion, Satan needed two witnesses to testify against God.[3]

Furthermore, who had the right to execute the death sentence? Not the accuser. The witnesses have this responsibility: "The hands

---

2. R. J. Rushdoony, *Genesis* (Vallecito, California: Ross House, 2002), p. 35.

3. This is why Satan's rebellion probably began in the garden, not in heaven days before or even before time began.

of the witnesses shall be first upon him to put him to death, and afterward the hands of all the people. So thou shalt put away evil from among you" (Deut. 17:7). Satan needed at least two witnesses who had knowledge of the actual words of God before he could see his goal achieved, namely, *the death of God*.

Adam had been given God's instructions concerning the forbidden tree. He was the witness whose word was fundamental to the trial. Eve knew of God's instructions, but only because Adam had told her. She had not been present when God had spoken these words to Adam. Her testimony would have been based on "hearsay evidence."

Judicially speaking, God's word could not be legally challenged in this court, for there were not two witnesses. But Satan proceeded as if he were in a position to bring charges. He appealed to Eve, who then acted autonomously, and who subsequently brought her husband into the court as an implicit witness against God, for she gave him fruit to eat, and he ate. Adam never verbally confirmed Satan's charge. He did not verbally lie. He simply acted out his rebellion. *But his act of rebellion constituted his testimony*, for implicit in his eating of the fruit was a denial of the binding authority of God's word.

The Christian view of God is Trinitarian. God is three Persons, yet also one Person. Each Person always has the corroborating testimony of the others. Therefore, God's word cannot be successfully challenged in a court. Two Witnesses testify eternally to the validity of what the other Person declares. Each has exhaustive knowledge of the others; each has exhaustive knowledge of the creation. The truth of God's word is established by Witnesses. As the supreme Witness, God casts the first stone on the day of final judgment, and then His people follow Him in executing judgment.

The doctrine of the two witnesses also throws light on the New Testament doctrine of the *rebellious third*. In Revelation 8, we are told that one-third of the trees are burned up (v. 7), one-third of the sea becomes blood (v. 8), and a third part of the creatures and ships in the sea are destroyed (v. 9). A third part of the rivers are hit by the star from heaven (v. 10), and a third part of the sun, moon, and stars are smitten (v. 12). In Revelation 9, we read that angels in judgment work for a time to slay a third part of rebellious mankind (v. 15), to testify to the other two-thirds of the coming judgment, yet they do not repent (v. 21). A third of the stars (angels) of heaven are pulled down by Satan's tail (Rev. 12:4).

Why these divisions into thirds? Because *for every transgressor, there are two righteous witnesses to condemn him.* God's final judgment is assured, for in God's court, there will always be a sufficient number of witnesses to condemn the ethical rebels.

C. Instant Judgment

What was the primary lure of this particular fruit? It would make men wise. But what kind of wisdom was this? It was the wisdom given to Solomon by God: *the ability to make wise judgments.* Satan's promise was that men would be able to determine good and evil and then act upon the information. On the other hand, God had told man that he was to avoid the tree, and by implication, to avoid the quest for instant illumination, meaning instant authority as a judge. But man did not obey. He did not want to wait.

How was man to achieve good judgment? By conforming himself to God's word. Man was and is required first and foremost *to obey God's word.* This requirement applied both to his role as a *judge*, declaring good and evil, and in his role as a *dominion man*, working out the implications of God's word, in time and on earth. In terms of his role as a subordinate sovereign over nature, he was to attain good judgment by bringing the whole world into subjection to God. When we are speaking of making economic judgments, we say that over time—possibly a lengthy period of time—man's skills in conforming his actions to God's standards would have progressively developed in him the judgment he needed.

In his role as a judge, on the other hand, man's field of testing was limited by God: to stay away from just one tree during a period of testing. Do this, the test implied, and you will eventually attain good judgment. Adam should have joined with Eve in trying and executing the serpent. That was his role as judge: to render judgment. Instead, they rendered judgment against God. They ate the forbidden fruit.

Adam could have achieved a position as a law-abiding, God-appointed judge by the end of the day, for he had another option: to eat of the tree of life. This would have served as a visible, public affirmation of man's belief in God's word. Eternal life is attainable only from that tree. *By eating of the tree of life, man would have declared ritually that he was subordinating himself wholly to God, relying wholly upon God's word concerning the true way of life.* Eating a meal from the tree of life would have meant communion with God—a ritual communion meal, eaten in faith while God was physically absent.

The moment that Adam and Eve had eaten from that tree, the ethical test—the test of Adam as a judge—would have been over. The possibility of death would have been removed. On the day that they ate of the tree of life, they could not have died. The penalty of eating from the forbidden tree would have been removed. *Without a penalty, there is no law.*

In all likelihood, God would have returned to judge Satan at this point. Adam's test would have been over. God would have declared the forbidden tree "on limits." Satan's trial would have been held on this day of judgment. There would have been no need for God to have retained His prohibition after His return to the garden and after the trial, for their ethical temptation would have been over. But as the final Judge, He would have had to declare His acceptance of their provisional judgment against Satan and Satan's interpretation of the tree of the knowledge of good and evil.

By conforming themselves ritually to God's word concerning eternal life, they would have attained man's assigned goal of rendering judgment against the serpent. But then they could not have attained their preferred goal: *autonomous judgment.* The issues were autonomy, the question of the reliability of God's word, and the authority to render final judgment concerning that word.

D. Witness: An Inescapable Office

The drama in the garden was a courtroom drama. We commonly speak of the garden as a "trial" for Adam, in the sense of a test; it was also a trial in a judicial sense. There was an intruder in the garden. He was tempting them to commit a capital crime—in fact, a crime doubly capital in its offensiveness: eating the forbidden fruit and perjuring themselves in a court of law regarding another person's commission of a capital crime. The penalty for committing perjury is the punishment that would have been imposed on the innocent victim (Deut. 19:16–19).[4]

Satan's charge, had he been able to prove it, would have required the death of God. This would have left Satan as the most powerful being in the universe, the one who renders final judgment. It was their responsibility to avoid all further contact with this intruder until they could bring formal charges against him when God returned. He had tempted them to deny the word of God and become false witnesses. He deserved death.

---

4. Gary North, *Inheritance and Dominion: An Economic Commentary on Deuteronomy*, 2nd ed. (Dallas, Georgia: Point Five Press, [1999] 2012), ch. 45.

Inevitably, they would have to testify. They were witnesses. Adam had witnessed God's word, and Eve had witnessed the serpent's. Eve should have gone to her husband and openly asked him what God had said. If she still had doubts, she should have waited for God to return to repeat His law. Had Eve remained faithful to her husband's word, she would have joined with him to try, condemn, and execute the serpent.

Had Adam served as a righteous witness, he would have asked the serpent to repeat the interpretation of God's word, which it had given to Eve (unless Adam had been silently present with her during the temptation). Then Adam would have issued judgment against the serpent and crushed his head.

They could testify against God or against Satan, but they could not escape testifying. God subpoenas all witnesses. From the moment of temptation, man became a witness. *This is the heart of the experience in the garden: man had to serve as a witness against Satan before he could serve as a judge of the angels (I Cor. 6:3).* This is also the experience of mankind throughout history, with some men testifying for Satan and against God, hoping to become *autonomous judges,* and others testifying against Satan and for God, hoping to become *subordinate judges.* Before becoming judges, men must first exercise judgment concerning which kind of witness they will be. They must also decide whose court it is, and who the prosecutor is. Most important of all, who is the presiding judge: God, Satan, or man?

If they testified against the serpent, and he was convicted, they would also have to execute justice against him. They would crush his head. It is clear why God established stoning as the normal mode of execution in a covenantal commonwealth. *Stoning is the symbolic equivalent of head-crushing.* To crush the convicted person's head is to destroy him. Also, the witnesses for the prosecution must take full responsibility for their testimony. This is the requirement of God for human courts, and it was the requirement in Eden. Bringing charges against Satan, they would have to execute the Judge's judgment.

There was no escape from the ethical obligation to witness against Satan and for God. There still isn't. There is also no escape from the ethical duty of crushing the head of the serpent (Gen. 3:15). It is done progressively, through cultural dominion. Man will eventually judge the angels.

Man is to crush the head of the serpent, and redeemed man does so as he witnesses against Satan, but now man is vulnerable to the bite of the serpent (Gen. 3:15). This would not have been true if Adam and Eve had executed the serpent. They should have then celebrated a communion meal at the tree of life. They should have awaited God's return, when they should have served as witnesses against Satan, telling God of the testimony of Satan's agent, the serpent.

Final judgment was delayed. They had to wait for God to return in order to obtain judgment. There had to be a trial. This delay was part of what repelled them. They wanted to declare instant judgment, and they believed that they could do this only by siding with Satan and eating from the forbidden tree immediately. They ate, thereby becoming *witnesses for Satan.* Their eyes were immediately opened, as promised by Satan—his partial word of truth—but they still had to wait on God. They wanted to become autonomous judges instantly, but they could not achieve their goal. They had to wait for God to return, for only God can declare final judgment.

E. Judicial Robes

Their immediate response to their new condition—at this point, an ethical condition, not yet a physical condition—was to sew fig leaves together to cover themselves. They needed a covering because of their shame. They could no longer work together without coverings. Their sin had interfered with the division of labor between them. I suspect that they worked separately, not as a team. This is an explanation which is most consistent with the nature of their rebellion: they hid from each other until their coverings were in place. Their sin alienated them ethically from God and from each other, as God's images. They sewed fig leaves together; they were probably not working together. Their ability to fulfill the terms of the dominion covenant in the God-designed division of labor was compromised by their perception of their nakedness.

It took time to sew these fig leaves together. They worked, not to subdue the earth, but to cover their shame. Rather than working together in their first joint project on their first day of independent labor, in all likelihood, they worked separately. It was each for his own glory—or at least lack of shame—that they worked. Man's imitation glory is simply a make-shift covering, a hoped-for lack of shame.

Why did they think they needed clothing? Shame is specifically mentioned in the text. But shame over what? Vulnerability? What kind of vulnerability? Was it their fear of God? If they were afraid of God, they needed protection. They still had access to protection: *the tree of life.* What seems astounding in retrospect is that they did not make a mad dash for the tree of life. God later closed the garden to them, and set a flaming sword in front of it, specifically to keep them from eating from the tree of life and gaining immortality (Gen. 3:22). The tree of life still retained its life-giving power. Why did they refuse to eat during God's physical absence?

We come to the heart of man's sin when we answer this question. *Man would have had to subordinate himself to God's word in order to receive eternal life.* They saw that they were naked. Their eyes had been opened. The serpent's word was partially fulfilled. God had not told them about this aspect of the tree of knowledge, and now the serpent was apparently vindicated. However, the second half of the serpent's word had yet to be fulfilled, namely, that on the day that they ate, they would *not* surely die. But God had said that they would die. So, the partial fulfillment of Satan's word—having their eyes opened— was insufficient to prove the case. This was merely the serpent's additional information vs. the silence of God. The crucial test was still undecided. What would be the outcome of the two antithetical words? Would the rebels die before the day was over?

The serpent had said that they would not die. Why would they believe such a thing? Because God is immortal. By implication, becoming as God would mean that they, too, were immortal. Would they not participate in the very being of God? Would not His attributes become theirs, including immortality? This temptation, James Jordan said, is the origin of the *chain of being* philosophy.

They were still clinging to their false witness. They would not admit that the serpent was lying, that God's word was sure. They did not go directly to the tree of life while there was still time remaining prior to the judgment of God. They refused to admit ritually that the day was not yet over, that God would surely come in judgment and slay them as He had promised. Instead, they spent their time making coverings for themselves. It was a question of *saving their skins* or *covering their hides.* They chose to cover their hides. Their pride condemned them.

Jordan argued that they sensed their need for coverings because they understood a judge's need for a robe. The robe in the Bible is *a robe of judicial office.* Joseph's long, sleeved robe (sometimes translated "coat of many colors") from Jacob was just this kind of robe (Gen. 37:3). It signified his authority over his brothers. When he told them of his dream that they would bow down to him (37:5–11), they stripped him of his robe (37:23) and tore it up (37:32). They refused to tolerate his authority over them. They cast him into a pit, and the pit was in the wilderness (37:22)—another familiar Bible theme.

Robes are given by God or those who are God's lawful subordinates. Adam and Eve wanted to manifest their self-appointed authority as judges, but without robes, they were visibly usurpers. They had judged God's word. By implication, they had to judge God and execute the sentence. Yet they were naked. A naked judge is not in a position to render judgment.

Adam and Eve were naked, not because they were sinless, but because they were children. As they matured, they would have been given clothing by God as a sign of their maturity, and as a sign of their authority as judges. Now that they had autonomously and *prematurely* grabbed judicial authority, they felt compelled to sew coverings for themselves. They were the image of God, and God wears clothing. He wears the glory cloud. In Daniel 8:9, the Ancient of Days is adorned in a white robe. In Revelation 1:13, the son of man has a robe that covers his feet. But God is not a sinner in need of covering. He is a judge who wears a robe. They, too, wanted to wear such robes.

It is significant that God in His mercy killed animals and made coverings for them. He simultaneously saved their skins (temporarily) and covered their hides, but only by sacrificing the life of an animal whose hide became man's covering. They were covered physically because of the shed blood of one or more animals. Their physical shame was temporarily removed from sight. (Ultimately, the shame of death can no longer be successfully hidden by clothing.) But this act of slaying the animal pointed to the necessity of the death of an innocent victim to cover man ethically.

Perhaps they were too ashamed to be seen running for the tree of life. They may have decided to clothe themselves before heading in the direction of the tree. They may have believed that, with their coverings, they would not be ashamed in front of each other or the serpent; they could eat of the tree of life after their coverings were in place. "First things first."

Prior to the judge's rendering of final judgment, witnesses can change their testimony. If they have perjured themselves, they must admit their guilt, but they can avoid the penalty by throwing themselves before the mercy of the court. *They incur shame, but they avoid the penalty for perjury.* But Adam and Eve would not accept shame. Rebellious man never does. They preferred to risk the penalty. Rebellious man always does.

They could have gone to the tree of life. They could have had a ritual communion meal with God. They could have attained eternal life. They refused. It was more important to cover their shame.

They had another option. When they heard God walking in the cool of the day, they could still have run to him and admitted their guilt. Instead, they hid from him, thereby abandoning their last opportunity to escape the penalty.

F. The Judicial Process

Immediately upon His return, God began His investigation. He looked at the evidence. They were wearing fig leaves. He concluded that their eyes were open. This meant that they had eaten from the forbidden tree (Gen. 3:11). Adam admitted that he had eaten, but first he blamed his wife. He refused to take the blame by himself. Misery loves company. He wanted the "bone of his bone" to suffer the penalty, too.

Then God asked Eve about what she had done. She blamed the serpent. In effect, both Adam and Eve blamed their environment, which God had made. They blamed God indirectly. But neither wanted to suffer the penalty alone.

This is the response of ethical rebels. It is not a godly response. What did Christ say? "Greater love hath no man than this, that a man lay down his life for his friends" (John 15:13). He accepted the full punishment. This is what Isaiah said the messiah would do for Israel: "Surely he hath borne our griefs, and carried our sorrows: yet we did esteem him stricken, smitten of God, and afflicted. But he was wounded for our transgressions, he was bruised for our iniquities: the chastisement of our peace was upon him; and with his stripes we are healed" (Isa. 53:4–5). What is rebellious men's response? Isaiah points to *shame*: "He is despised and rejected of men; a man of sorrows, and acquainted with grief: and we hid as it were our faces from him; he was despised, and we esteemed him not" (Isa. 52:3). Men hide their faces in shame, just as our parents did in the garden.

God judged the serpent without asking him to testify. No cross examination was necessary. Adam had admitted guilt; Eve had blamed the serpent. He had lured them into sin. The serpent had nothing to say in his defense. The serpent stood condemned. Soon he would crawl condemned. God had seen and heard. But God did not declare final judgment against the serpent. He declared *definitive judg-*

ment and announced a *provisional penalty*: the serpent would crawl on its belly and eat the dust of the ground. Eventually, its head will be crushed by the promised man (Gen. 3:15). There will be a final judgment. But Satan now has no response to give in God's court. He has been definitively condemned along with his covenantal agent.

What we see in the story of the garden is that God gives men time to repent and become faithful witnesses to the validity of God's word. But, once the final verdict is rendered, there is no escape. Men are cast out of the garden and away from the tree of life. They cannot attain eternal life through a return to the physical garden and a physical tree. Once God pronounces judgment, man's destiny is sealed.

The day in the garden is symbolic of each man's life on earth, as well as mankind's stay on earth prior to the final judgment. There is still time to repent of the act of bearing false witness against God. There is time to eat the tree of life. This is what the communion meal means: a ritual meal eaten in the spiritual presence of God, before He returns physically to render final judgment. When He returns physically, it is the time of final judgment, just as when He draws near spiritually (for example, in the glory cloud in Old Testament times), it is a time of provisional judgment. Ungodly men hide; godly men rejoice. God delays rendering final judgment for mercy's sake. He did so in the garden, and He does so today. But He will eventually return. The time of mercy will end.

G. Rendering Provisional Judgment

Man wanted to render autonomous judgment. He also wanted to render instant judgment. Eve had the authority to kill the serpent, who was an invader. She could have gone to Adam to tell him to render judgment. They had the authority to crush its head. They were to defend the garden's boundaries.[5] They chose not to do their duty as God's delegated agents. They refused to act as His agents. They instead chose to test His word.

Had they done their duty, God would have rendered judgment against Satan. They could have testified that the serpent told them to eat of the tree. They possessed lawful authority to crush its head.

---

5. In the 1987 edition of this book, I argued that they should have waited for God to return before rendering judgment against the serpent. But, as guardians of the garden, they had the authority to crush the serpent's head. They could lawfully render instant judgment against Satan's agent. They would have to wait until God's return in order to serve as witnesses against Satan by justifying their crushing of the serpent's head.

But they had neither the authority or the power to crush Satan's head. That was God's authority and power to execute. They were witnesses to what the serpent had said. They would have to wait on God to testify against Satan in God's court.

God spared the serpent's life. He spared Satan's life. He spared Adam's life and Eve's. The drama of the garden would be repeated again and again in history. More temptations would come. Men would serve as witnesses and judges, executing either God's judgment or their own.

The reason why man today can execute judgment provisionally is because he is made in God's image (Gen. 9:5–6). God has declared His judgment against sin in His word. This was a *definitive* declaration. He brings His judgment to pass in history. This is His *progressive* judgment. He will declare and execute judgment at the end of time. This is His *final* judgment. Men can therefore render provisional judgment because God has declared His judgment and His standards of enforcement in His law. He declared Himself definitively to Moses, as He had to Adam. Men are therefore called to render earthly, provisional judgment in God's name, as His lawful subordinates. But they must render honest judgment in terms of His law.

The temptation in the garden was in the form of a judicial proceeding. So is all of life. We are to render provisional, subordinate judgment in every area of life. We are to master God's Bible-revealed law so that we can render honest judgment, just as Adam and Eve should have rendered provisional judgment against the serpent in the garden by avoiding him and the forbidden tree before God returned physically to render final judgment.

Man wanted to be able to render autonomous, instant judgment. He ate of the forbidden tree. What he found was that final judgment is delayed. It is delayed against him, but it is also delayed against Satan. Satan remains man's enemy, bruising man's heel. God threw Adam and Eve out of the garden and banned their return to it physically, in time and on earth. But He offered them grace and a promise: Man will eventually crush the head of the serpent by steadily overcoming Satan's kingdom in time and on earth. Redeemed men will witness against him formally, in the court of life, and then execute judgment against him. But now the delay in God's physical return is more than one afternoon. Rebellious man declared instant judgment against God and for Satan; redeemed man must now struggle against Satan and the works of Satan's people, developing his good judgment over time.

Man must serve as a judge in history. He must declare judgment *progressively* in terms of God's *definitive* judgment and the promised *final* judgment. Man is now outside the garden, which was to have served as his training ground before he entered the world at large. Now the garden is closed to him, and the earth is cursed. This cursing of the ground also delays man's judgment, under God. It takes longer to render judgment as he works under God to build up the kingdom of God, in time and on earth. He struggles ethically against Satan and physically against the thorns. Adam had hoped to be an instant judge, but only Satan was willing to promise him that option, and then only if he testified against God.

So, man's dream has been turned against him. Hoping to *render judgment autonomously and instantaneously*, he has had to *render judgment subordinately and progressively*. His dream of autonomy has also been thwarted. He can declare judgment against God under Satan, or he can declare against Satan under God. But he is a provisional judge, not a final judge. He is always under the overall sovereignty of God, but ethically he places himself under the judicial sovereignty of either God or Satan.

H. Standards of Judgment

What God has declared *definitively* must serve as man's standards *provisionally*, for man will be judged in terms of these standards *finally*. This points inescapably to the continuing validity of biblical law. Rebellious man will attempt to adhere to the dominion covenant by rendering judgment, but as he grows more consistent with his condition as a covenant-breaker, he will seek to declare his own standards, and to render final judgment.

There are two humanistic standards that covenant-breakers substitute in place of biblical law: *natural law* and *positive law*. Natural law theorists declare that man, as judge, has access to universal standards of righteousness that are binding on all men in all periods of time. These standards are therefore available to all men through the use of a universal faculty of judgment, either reason or intuition. In fact, to declare judgment in terms of such a law-order, the judge must exercise both reason and intuition, in order to "fit" the morally binding universal standard to the particular circumstances of the case. What is therefore *logically binding* becomes *morally binding* in natural law theories. What is logical is therefore right.

Positive law does not appeal to universal standards of logic in order to discover righteousness. It appeals to the particular case. Circumstances determine what is correct. In the United States, the legislature (Congress) declares definitively what the law is, and this becomes the morally binding code of justice. But the legislature has a rival: the judiciary. The judge interprets the law in terms of a written Constitution and also previous judicial declarations. In other societies, there is no such authority of the courts. Judgment *finally* becomes the true law, if "the people" (or the executive) are willing and able to enforce what the judge declares. In short, *what the state can enforce is therefore right.*

Neither the legislature nor the courts can escape the need to declare some sort of coherent (logical) standard, and neither branch of civil government can avoid the use of some non-logical human facility (intuition) to apply the law to specific cases. "Circumstances" do not speak with a universally clear voice, nor does "reason." Both must get an answer to this question: By what standard? Autonomous positive law and autonomous natural law rely on each other. As Cornelius Van Til has said, each side makes its living by taking in the other side's laundry. Both natural law theory and positive law theory are apostate. Both cry out together against the universally binding nature of God's Bible-revealed law. Both sides define justice in terms of what man can discover and enforce, not in terms of what God has declared, has enforced, and will bring to final judgment.

It is more common for self-styled Christian social, political, and legal theorists to declare the doctrines of natural law. Natural law seems at first glance to be closer to a concept of eternal law made by God. Natural law theorists can also appeal to the fatherhood of God (Acts 17:26) as the foundation of their universal valid categories of law. But the fatherhood of God is a doctrine that condemns man, for it points to fallen man's position as *a disinherited covenant-breaker*, not an ethical son. How can a disinherited son agree with an adopted son about the nature of their mutual responsibilities to themselves and to the Father, let alone agree about the final distribution of the inheritance? Did Isaac and Ishmael agree? Did Jacob and Esau agree? Did Cain and Abel?

What was the "natural law" aspect of God's prohibition against eating of the tree of the knowledge of good and evil? The serpent at first tried to lure Eve into eating by an appeal to what appeared to be a universal law. Hadn't God said that they could eat of every tree in the garden? In other words, why not eat of this one tree? Eve replied appropriately: God has forbidden us to eat of this particular tree. This was a specific revelation to her husband. If she had stuck with her initial resistance, Satan would have thwarted his plans. If man had relied on natural law theory to guide his actions, he would not have offered even this token resistance to the temptation. The general law—eat from every tree—would have prevailed. It took God's verbal revelation to warn them about the prohibited tree.

It is not surprising to find that those Christian scholars who have been most open in their denial of the continuing applicability of re- vealed Old Testament law have also been vociferous promoters of some version of natural law theory. Natural law theory offers them a time-honored, man-made covering for their shame, for they fear be- ing exposed as unfashionably dressed in the eyes of their humanist colleagues. *Natural law theory is the conservative antinomian Christian's fashion preference in the world of fig leaf coverings.* The "bloody skins of God-slaughtered animals"—the forthrightly biblical morality of Bi- ble-revealed law—are just not adequate for him.

There was also an element of positive law in the temptation. The serpent denied that God's sanction would come true. So, he was ask- ing them to test the reliability of God's word with respect to the sanc- tions. "Go ahead and test this. You're in charge. See if I'm correct about the outcome." Adam and Eve attempted to establish an alterna- tive legal order by eating. They sought to impose a different outcome in history from the one God had declared.

Conclusion

The development of a godly sense of judgment takes many years. The emphasis of the Bible on the importance of training in the law is central to the question of godly judgment. "And these words, which I command thee this day, shall be in thine heart: And thou shalt teach them unto thy children, and shalt talk of them when thou sittest in thine house, and when thou walkest by the way, and when thou liest down, and when thou risest up" (Deut. 6:6–7). *The mastery of God's Bible-revealed law is fundamental for rendering righteous, provisional, sub- ordinate judgment, just as it was on that first working day in Eden.*

One of the main reasons why Christians are culturally impotent today is that, for well over three centuries, they have been taught alternative theories of law. They have been told that Christianity can survive under any system of law. The accent is on mere survival. There is supposedly no prospect of Christians' exercising godly rule in every area of life. Of course, we are told, Christianity cannot be expected to flourish under any system of law, not because of specific kinds of flaws in humanistic law systems, but because the church is supposedly impotent by nature in history. For many of those who believe that Christianity is doomed to historical impotence, there seems to be no reason to call forth ridicule, let alone persecution, on themselves by declaring that all humanists are wearing fig leaves, and that Bible-revealed law is the only way that God wants us to cover our nakedness, through grace. Meanwhile, they can buy an "off the rack" fig leaf wardrobe from the latest humanist collection—well, maybe not the latest, but a discount version that is only ten years out of date. "Better to be trendy ten years late than never to be trendy at all!"

Fig leaves do not stand up to the howling winters of a cursed world. When Christians finally learn this lesson, they will be ready to begin to exercise godly judgment.

BIBLIOGRAPHY
(1982)

Economics

It is difficult to recommend a list of books on Christian economics, since the thesis lying behind my writing of this book is that the Christian world has neglected the whole question for three centuries. There is nothing on a par with Adam Smith's *Wealth of the Nations* or Ludwig von Mises' *Human Action*. The best we have available are collections of essays, monographs on certain topics, and one very introductory textbook.

The textbook is Tom Rose's *Economics: Principles and Policy from a Christian Perspective* (Mott Media). He co-authored (with Robert Metcalf) *The Coming Victory* (Memphis, TN: Christian Studies Center).

I compiled a collection of 31 essays, *An Introduction to Christian Economics*, published by Craig Press in 1973. It is presently out of print. It is scheduled to be reprinted by the Institute for Christian Economics. I wrote these essays for several magazines and newspapers from the late 1960s through the early 1970s.

For those interested in Marxism, my out-of-print book, *Marx's Religion of Revolution: The Doctrine of Creative Destruction* (1968) might be useful. No one who makes a detailed study of socialism can afford to miss Ludwig von Mises' classic refutation, *Socialism: An Economic and Sociological Analysis* (1922), which is available from Liberty Classics (Indianapolis, IN). It was published in the United States by Yale University Press in 1951.

I offer a critique of the epistemology of modern schools of economic thought in my essay, "Economics: From Reason to Intuition," in North (ed.), *Foundations of Christian Scholarship* (Vallecito, CA: Ross House Books). Two humanist books criticize the assumption of value-free economics: Walter E. Weisskopf, *Alienation and Economics*

(E. P. Dutton, 1971) and Mark A. Lutz and Kenneth Lux, *The Challenge of Humanistic Economics* (Benjamin/Cummings), published in 1979.

Two issues of *The Journal of Christian Reconstruction* are devoted to the topic: "Christian Economics" (Summer, 1975) and "Inflation" (Summer, 1980).

Books on economic development by the British economist, P. T. Bauer, are important: *Dissent on Development* (1972) and *Equality, The Third World and Economic Delusion* (1981), *Reality and Rhetoric* (1984), all published by Harvard University Press. He is the co-author (with Basil Yamey) of *The Economics of Under-Developed Countries* (Cambridge University Press, 1957). Bauer stresses the importance of freedom, the attitudes of citizens, people's willingness to sacrifice for the long run, and similar issues. He says that without the proper attitudes toward economic success and the freedom to pursue personal goals, long-term economic growth is unlikely.

Complementary to Bauer's books are Helmut Schoeck's *Envy: A Theory of Social Behavior* (Harcourt, Brace, 1970) and Edward Banfield, *The Unheavenly City Revisited* (Little, Brown, 1974). Both books point to the importance of the future-orientation of economic actors for the success of the economy. Banfield argues that economic classes should be defined in terms of future-orientation, not income or capital. My book, *Successful Investing in an Age of Envy* (1981), applies the insights of Schoeck and Banfield to the economy and politics.

The works of Wilhelm Röpke are very important, not simply because he was a fine economist (greatly influenced as a young man by Mises), but because his perspective was far more broad than virtually all other free markets economists. He asked the tough questions about the effects of market freedom on social institutions. He was interested in the moral foundations of freedom, not just in questions of economic efficiency. Most important are his books, *A Humane Economy* (1957), distributed by the Intercollegiate Studies Institute; *Economics of the Free Society* (1963), published originally by Henry Regnery Co., Chicago; *Against the Tide* (1969), a posthumously published collection of his essays, distributed by I.S.I.; *Civitas Humana* (1948); *The Social Crisis of Our Time* (1950); and *International Economic Disintegration* (1942); all published in London by William Hodge & Co. (British books are most easily ordered through Blackwell's, Broad Street, Oxford, England.)

The books written by Murray Rothbard, the anarcho-capitalist, are all very clear, well documented, and powerfully argued. They include *Man, Economy and State* (1962), *America's Great Depression* (1963), and *What Has Government Done to Our Money?* (1964), available from the Foundation for Economic Education. His book denying the legitimacy of all civil government is very good on the economic effects of various kinds of government regulation and taxation: *Power and Market: Government and the Economy* (1970).

F. A. Hayek's books are basic to any understanding of the free market. The most important are: *The Road to Serfdom* (1944), *The Constitution of Liberty* (1960); *Individualism and Economic Order* (1948); *Studies in Philosophy, Politics and Economics* (1967); and the trilogy, *Law, Legislation and Liberty* (1973–80), all published by the University of Chicago Press. Also important is his study of the rise of socialist thought, *The Counter-Revolution of Science* (1952), which has been reprinted by Liberty Press.

By far the best book on the economics of information is ex-Marxist economist, Thomas Sowell: *Knowledge and Decisions* (Basic Books, 1980), which provides more unique insights, page for page, than any economics book I have ever read. His *Race and Economics* (David McKay Co., 1975) is also very good, as are *Markets and Minorities* (1981) and *Ethnic America* (1981), both published by Basic Books.

Two books by Bettina Greaves are suitable for an introduction to free market thought: *Free Market Economics: A Syllabus* and *Free Market Economics: A Basic Reader*, published by the Foundation for Economic Education. FEE also publishes the monthly magazine, *The Freeman* (subscription by request, free).

Very important are the works of R. J. Rushdoony, which are related to questions of economics: *The Institutes of Biblical Law*, Vol. I (Craig Press, 1973), and Vol. II (Vallecito, CA: Ross House Books); *Politics of Guilt and Pity* (1970) and *The One and the Many* (1971), both published by Thoburn Press. Also important for political and social theory is *The Foundations of Social Order: Studies in the Creeds and Councils of the Early Church* (1969), also published by Thoburn Press.

The sociologist Robert Nisbet has written many books that are important for social theory, including *The Quest for Community* (Oxford University Press, 1952), *The Sociological Tradition* (Basic Books, 1966), *Tradition and Revolt* (Vintage, 1969), *Social Change and History: Aspects of the Western Theory of Development* (Oxford University Press, 1969), *The Social Philosophers: Community and Conflict in Western Thought* (Crowell, 1973), *Twilight of Authority* (Oxford University Press, 1975), and *History of the Idea of Progress* (Basic Books, 1980). Nisbet is a pluralist and decentralist, in marked contrast to so many sociologists. His essay, "The Year 2000 and All That," *Commentary* (June, 1968), is important for its investigation of the fascination of the coming of the third millennium, a.d., in Enlightenment thought.

Evolution

Gertrude Himmelfarb's book, *Darwin and the Darwinian Revolution* (1959) created a kind of revolution itself. It is very good on mid-nineteenth-century British thought, and why Darwin appealed to that culture. Reprinted by Peter Smith, Gloucester, MA.

Philip Appleman's *Darwin: A Norton Critical Edition* (Norton, 1970), is very important because of its extracts from Darwin's major works, as well as contemporary criticisms and evaluations of Darwin. It also includes modern evaluations. Conclusion: man must now take control over the evolutionary process.

Henry Morris' book, *The Troubled Waters of Evolution* (San Diego, CA: C. L. P. Publishers), ch. 2, has many citations from modern evolutionists who have adopted the "man, the animal, becomes man, the predestinator" paradigm. It becomes obvious, after reading pages of these citations, that evolutionism is a religion.

On the coming of Darwinism, see the biography of William Irvine, *Apes, Angels, and Victorians* (McGraw-Hill, 1955); Charles Coulston Gillispie, *Genesis and Geology: The Impact of Scientific Discoveries Upon Religious Beliefs in the Decades Before Darwin* (Harper Torchbook, [1951], 1959); Francis C. Haber, *The Age of the World: Moses to Darwin* (Johns Hopkins University Press, 1959); and Stephen Toulmin and June Goodfield, *The Discovery of Time* (Harper Torchbook, 1965). Also useful is Robert Nisbet's book, *Social Change and History* (Oxford University Press, 1969). He deals with "development" as an idea and an ideal in Western thought. Loren Eiseley's *Darwin's Century: Evolution and the Men who Discovered It* (Anchor, [1958] 1961) is important, especially for the chapter on Alfred R. Wallace, the co-discoverer of natural selection, who concluded that man's mind could not have evolved by slow, steady steps.

On the humanistic implications of evolution, see George Gaylord Simpson, *The Meaning of Evolution* (Yale University Press, [1949] 1967) and *This View of Life* (Harcourt, Brace, 1964). Simpson gives us most of the clichés of modern humanism. Any he may have neglected are provided by Sir Julian Huxley, in *Knowledge, Morality, and Destiny* (Mentor, 1957), and his essay, "Evolutionary Ethics," in *Touchstone for*

Ethics, 1893–1943 (Harper & Bros., 1947). Theodosius Dobzhansky's *The Biology of Ultimate Concern* (New American Library, 1967) offers a clear introduction to man, the new divinity.

Indispensable, of course, is anything written by Lester Frank Ward, especially his 1883 classic, *Dynamic Sociology* (Greenwood Press). He used the idea that man has transcended animalistic evolution to promote the idea of a planned society. The new evolution will be a man-directed evolution.

On the importance of the doctrine of creation in the development of modern science, the works of Stanley Jaki are indispensable. Jaki argues that it was only in the Christian West, where men believe in linear time, that science ever developed. Cyclical time, which is the almost universally shared view in pagan societies, never has been conducive to scientific progress. Jaki's erudition and documentation are extraordinary. His works have been neglected by all but a handful of specialists in the historiography of science. His more easily available books include *The Road of Science and the Ways to God* (University of Chicago Press, 1978), a book that is slow reading but overwhelming in its impact; *The Origin of Science and the Science of Origins* (South Bend, IN: Gateway Editions); and *The Milky Way: An Elusive Road for Science* (New York: Natural History Press, 1975). Extremely important is *Science and Creation: From Eternal Cycles to an Oscillating Universe* (Edinburgh, Scotland: Scottish Academic Press) and the small book, *Cosmos and Creator* (Scottish Academic Press).

Also important are the works by the French scholar, Pierre Duhem. His 10-volume *Système du monde*, published from 1913 through the 1950s, presents a similar thesis to Jaki's books. English-language readers can read translations of two books by Duhem, *The Aim and Structure of Physical Theory* (Atheneum, 1962) and *To Save The Phenomena: An Essay on the Idea of Physical Theory from Plato to Galileo* (University of Chicago Press, 1969).

Made in the USA
Thornton, CO
07/22/23 09:16:56

291002ca-d87f-446a-b7d9-9136a7c2122cR01